To Our Children: Memoirs of Displacement

Jews of Poland

Series Editor

Antony Polonsky (Brandeis University)

ACADEMIC
STUDIES
PRESS

To Our Children: Memoirs of Displacement

A Jewish Journey of Hope and Survival in Twentieth-Century Poland and Beyond

Włodzimierz Szer

Translated from the Polish by **Bronisława Karst**

Boston
2016

Library of Congress Cataloging-in-Publication Data:
A catalog record for this book is available from the Library of Congress.

Copyright © 2016 Academic Studies Press

ISBN 978-1-61811-478-5 (hardback)
ISBN 978-1-61811-479-2 (electronic)

Book design by Kryon Publishing
http://www.kryonpublishing.com/

Published by Academic Studies Press in 2016
28 Montfern Avenue
Brighton, MA 02135, USA
press@academicstudiespress.com
www.academicstudiespress.com

In memory of Felusia

—Włodek

Contents

List of Illustrations

Acknowledgments

We owe a great deal of gratitude to our life-long friend, Bronia Karst, who translated this memoir with love and care. She interpreted our dad's book keeping his voice alive and stayed true to his own words. He would have been thrilled with this English version of his writing. We also want to thank Fred Rothzeid for his help in the editing of the final manuscript and Meghan Vicks for her guidance during this process. We are indebted to Drs. Halina Sierakowska and Kazimierz Wierzchowski for their beautiful tribute to our father.

Foreword

For a very long time our father had been a man without a past. When we were growing up he almost never spoke about his childhood, his relatives, or how he had survived the war. We were aware of some facts: that he grew up in Warsaw, that his mother was a seamstress and his father worked as an accountant. We knew about his maternal grandmother and that his grandfather had once lived somewhere in the US. That was all. There were no details, no stories. Our parents' wonderful and loving friends became our surrogate uncles, aunts, and grandmother. We knew our paternal grandfather lived somewhere in a remote village in a Siberian forest against his will. He would eventually come to live with us for a brief time in Warsaw in 1956. What we did not know was that our father's silence and his refusal to speak about the past was typical of many Holocaust survivors. We did not fully appreciate that recalling his personal history and speaking of his mother, whom he loved so much, would bring to mind her terrible death in the Treblinka death camp. He felt great appreciation toward her for forcing him at a young age to join his father in the Soviet Union shortly after the war broke out, thus saving him from an almost certain death. In his book he declares that she gave him life for the second time. But he also felt guilt for leaving her behind, although he would certainly not have been able to protect her. He was equally unable to share stories about his grandmother and other relatives because the fate they had suffered was so terrible.

But Dad's past came alive in his memoir. He began writing it in 2006 in his beloved Polish and continued over a period of several years, referencing letters and notes on postcards and photographs he had kept meticulously for decades. Mostly he wrote from memory, using his profound intellect to bring to life the people and places of his youth. As we read his memoir we were moved to find answers to the many questions we had concerning those years. Initially he did not intend to have this memoir published; he simply wanted to share his life with us, his daughters, before he passed away because he had found it so difficult to tell us about it. But as family members and friends and especially our mother read excerpts, we encouraged him to publish it, to tell the story of a world that no longer exists and about which virtually no eyewitnesses remain. He did not live to see his book published as a historical document by the Jewish Historical Institute in Warsaw in November of 2013, but he was involved in every aspect of the process, including selection of the book cover and photos, many of which we had never before seen. Despite a number of controversial issues, the memoir was well received. He died three months before its publication.

The book opened a new vista for us. We had always known that our father was a polymath with outstanding accomplishments as a scientist and teacher. Yet we knew next to nothing of his childhood and his education, first in a Bund-run school where he developed a love affair with Yiddish literature and music, and later in a Polish high school, which gave him a life-long passion for learning. Here we learned the story of his escape from Nazi-occupied Warsaw, details of his life in Siberia, and how he came back to Poland as an officer of the Polish regiment of the Russian army, getting badly wounded along the way. The first two chapters of the book were a true revelation for us. They not only revealed our father as a young man, but they allowed us to understand the man he had become and grasp the reasons for his reluctance to share this part of his life with us. Through his words we were also able to "meet" our relatives: our grandparents, and our many aunts, uncles, and cousins, and catch a glimpse into their lives. We learned a great deal about the Bund's influence on our father's political views and about the rich Jewish life in pre-war Poland. The third chapter provided us with previously unknown details of our parents' life immediately after the war. It described how other Holocaust survivors tried, with greater or lesser success, to rebuild their shattered lives after years of horror and death. The many interludes that a family's history is made of were now in our grasp, for us and for our children and their children to build upon, continue the legacy, and never forget.

Dad concluded his memoirs with our family's immigration to the United States in 1967. It was a relatively peaceful and happy time in his life, no longer defined by struggle and adversity, but it was far from ordinary. In New York he continued his work at the Biochemistry Department of the NYU School of Medicine. Within six years he became a full professor and acting chairman of the Department of Biochemistry, securing NIH[1] funding for his work,

---

[1]   Tr: National Institutes of Health (NIH).

PhD and MD/PhD candidates and postdocs. He saw his research published in prestigious journals and enjoyed invitations to chair sessions at national and international symposia. In short, he became a rock star in biochemical circles, publishing over 170 scientific papers. When he "retired" to San Diego, California, he continued attending seminars and enjoyed mentoring well into his eighties at Scripps Institute in La Jolla.

Perhaps his happiest years came with his grandchildren. Although an avowed agnostic, he used to say that his grandchildren had the ray of God in them. He adored them all and kissed them on their heads while tenderly holding their necks in his special "Dziadziuś (Polish for Grandfather) grip." He felt that they were the most beautiful children in the world and he eagerly conversed with them about the weightier matters in life, always with a pack of minty flavored Trident gum in his pocket to share. He called them on birthdays and if no one answered, he would leave a message singing birthday wishes. Our father was instrumental in instilling in our children the importance of education and in making the most of every opportunity. Each of the five had a unique relationship with him and each loved him a great deal.

Dad was a Renaissance man in the truest sense of the word. He spoke multiple languages and was a stickler for proper pronunciation and for never "throwing in" English words. For everyday interactions it was the language of the person he was speaking with—English, Russian, Yiddish, or Polish, with a preference for Polish. For counting he preferred Polish. And for his research, "symbols," of course.

He read literary works in the original and multiple newspapers in four languages. He was an expert on European art, music, and history and could regale audiences with factual treatises on any number of subjects. Even on his deathbed he recited poetry by Pushkin and famous Polish poets, which he had memorized more than 70 years earlier. He loved the Polish language most and taught us to use it precisely. He traveled tirelessly and he and our mother enjoyed touring European and American museums. He loved good food, good drink, and good company: wine with his evening meals and a dry Martini during symphony concert intermissions. Ever the congenial host, his bar at home was always well stocked for visitors who came by and there were many. Our parents, who lived in the heart of Manhattan for 26 years, frequently hosted guests, especially from Poland, often inviting them to stay over in their spare bedroom.

Our father's memoir provides a vivid tapestry of Jewish life in Poland in the past century, of its traditions, changes, and upheavals, and of the great turmoil that dominated that era. He was honored to have his memoirs published as a historical document, making them available to readers other than us. We feel that the title "To Our Children" has a double meaning: it is addressed not only to us, but to our children, their children, and to children of generations to come. It is a record of a time and place about which so little is known, fascinating and colorful, full of horrors, heroes, and human frailty. It is a personal account of a war that must never again be allowed to happen. It is a story of hope and optimism in the face of crushing adversity and in no small measure it is, ultimately, a story of the triumph of the human spirit. We also hope that it conveys the remarkable man who was our father.

Karina Rothzeid and Ilona Szer

PART I

Before the War

It was the beginning of December 1939, the fourth month of the war. Posters glued to the building walls for several days now had been ordering us to wear armbands with the Star of David on the right sleeve. The armband's width, the star's size and colors—all were specified with German precision. It was then that Mom told me to flee Warsaw; to go and to stay with Dad. For some months Dad had been living in Baranowicze in eastern Poland, which had been taken over by Russia. Mail delivery was working so we knew Dad's address. We wrote open messages: postcards which were easier for the censors to read. I didn't want to go away and leave Mom and Grandma, but Mom insisted. I wanted us to escape together, but Grandma replied that sneaking across the border wasn't for her. Mom could go with me and she would move in with her beloved younger sister, Aunt Ewcia, who lived nearby with her husband, Uncle Isidor. But Mom wouldn't agree. She didn't want to leave Grandma Helenka. Besides, she said, there's war, lawlessness, and if we left an empty apartment we would lose it. It wasn't actually our own apartment, but a rented one. If we wanted to move out we would have to pay a so called withdrawal fee (in other cities called a key fee) and the amount was enormous, well beyond our means. Mom had other arguments as well. "I have seen it all during the last war. At first Germany wins and later—since England and France are mighty and also because Roosevelt will not allow Hitler's victory either—they will lose. It's just a matter of time and we cannot afford to forfeit the apartment. I remember them well from the Great War (as the First World War was then called). They wouldn't harm a woman. After all it is Beethoven's nation (Mom worshiped him). They took leave of their senses with that Hitler, but it is temporary. Calm down. This is the best educated country in Europe. And you are tall, too tall for your age. They could sign you up for forced labor and take you away."

Such were the deliberations in those days and they couldn't have been any more wrong. No one is clairvoyant. This lasted for several more days, and finally Mom said that a neighbor of ours was going to travel east, beyond the Bug River, and that I had to go with him. This is how Mom gave me life for the second time.

It was completely dark that dawn when we said our goodbyes. I was fifteen, and I never saw her again. Now she exists only in my thoughts. She lives in my memory and in my dreams. The dreams come in cycles. I only see Mom's face, but I feel that she is in a crowd of naked people, forced with whips into a gas chamber. Mom walks, then runs and walks again for couple of steps. They are constantly hitting her. I can sense it, but I am helpless. Only Mom's face changes in these dreams. Sometimes it is beautiful and young—she was only thirty-nine when we parted, but sometimes it is older and wrinkled with strands of gray hair. I don't know where this image comes from since I have never seen her like that. Years after her death I would wake up my wife Felusia with my screams, tell her my dreams, and she would calm me down. The rest of the night would be sleepless.

I have been wondering: if I could push a button, launch a bomb and murder 95 percent of Germans as they had murdered us, would I do it? It is the nonsense of helpless rage of course. Years later these are different generations, innocent people. But was my mother guilty? What of collective responsibility? Didn't our forefather Abraham ask Yahweh (God) not to destroy a city if it had only a few (10) righteous among the people? Just so, but where were those righteous ones in Hitler's Germany?

Before the war, each movie was preceded by the Polish Press Agency's newsreel illustrating the previous week's most important events. So many times I watched enormous crowds cheering him. I remember most vividly Hitler's triumphant entry into Austria in 1938 after the Anschluss. He was standing in an open car, paw in the air with a sea of people on both sides of the road, their expressionless eyes glued to him, incredible screams. This was the truest, the most sincere kind of enthusiasm. It continued like this all the way to Vienna.

So what about that button? Let's leave it. These are idle thoughts. The whole thing is pointless.

My wartime wanderings started at the beginning of December 1939.

In my earliest childhood memories I see a beautiful woman wearing a coat with a fur collar. As I watch she enters a room full of people: Dad, Grandma, relatives, and friends. This woman is my mom, who came back home after a lengthy stay in the United States. I was nearly four then and I didn't have sequential memories. This came later when I was about five. Perhaps I remember that moment with all the details because when Mom entered, Michał, Lutka's[1] husband (Ilonka hadn't been born yet), who was shaving, put his straight razor on the table under which I sat, almost invisible, and upon which I had put my right hand. Blood gushed, a commotion erupted, and possibly this is what I remember. I still have the scar. There was no bathroom in the apartment (among our family and friends very few had a bathroom in those days). Men shaved in their room. Since razor blades weren't widely used, they used straight razors with big, long blades.

From my parents and grandma's stories I know that Mom brought enough money from America for the withdrawal fee and from that time until the war we had an independent apartment: number 23 on 6 Karmelicka Street in the back part of the main structure, on the second floor. It was the third building from Leszno Street. The most expensive apartments were the ones in the front part of the building. They had rooms with windows overlooking the street. The further you lived from the front, the lower the rent. Until Mom's arrival we lived in a rented room with some family. Still, this independent apartment we moved into was far from beautiful. The front door faced the toilet door and the hallway was so narrow that both doors couldn't be opened at the same time. The toilet was tiny, somewhat triangular and very uncomfortable. It was cold in the winter because of the lack of heating. But at least we had a toilet. Among our friends many families had to use communal toilets, something every Warsaw apartment building had to have.

Our building was constructed in the nineteenth century, or perhaps earlier, without central plumbing. An alcove in a rather long hallway leading from the front door was separated from the hallway by a curtain. This alcove was very important because behind the curtain stood a little iron stove with a pipe going into the wall to the chimney conduit. That was our "bathroom." We heated the water in a big pan on the stove. A sort of small tin tub was suspended on the wall behind the curtain. It was placed on the floor so one could wash oneself in it with warm water in a standing or kneeling position. Bathing was a weekly ritual. Otherwise every day we washed with cold water at the kitchen sink, since that was the only running water in our apartment. The faucet and the sink—small and made of metal—were located in the kitchen's corner.

---

[1] Tr: The author's mother's best friend.

The whole process was neither comfortable nor pleasant. It was done in two stages; first from the top to the waist with a towel fastened around the waist; then from the waist down.

Dad often went to a public bath, sometimes taking me along, but I didn't enjoy it. In the late 1930s some of my parents' friends, for example Lutka Flutsztejn and Ruta, had bathrooms in their apartments. Mom liked to take a bath while we were visiting them. In her entire life, my mom never had an apartment with a real bathroom.

In the middle of the hallway across from the stove was a door that led to a room and the kitchen door was at the hallway's end. The room one entered from the hallway was square and a big window overlooking the back courtyard brought light into the room. It was the nicest room in the entire apartment. It was furnished with colorful, varnished pieces: a table, stools, and a big, glazed bookshelf. There was also a sofa where I slept. Plants were placed under the window and on window sills: a big rhododendron, rubber plants, and cacti. When the crisis[2] began and Dad lost his job, after 1930, and Mom started sewing dresses for girls, she received customers in this room.

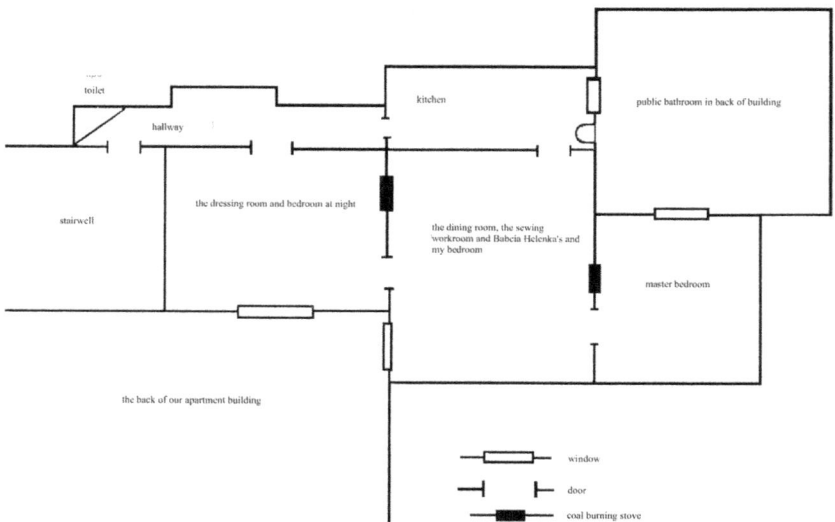

Figure 1 The layout of my parents' apartment on 6 Karmelicka Street, number 23, second story, back of the building.

---

[2] Tr: "The crisis" refers to the Great Depression.

Our kitchen was small and long with windows overlooking a "blind" small courtyard between buildings. In it we had a coal stove and an oven for baking. A gas plate with two burners stood on the stove. From the kitchen and from the first room one entered the largest room. It was long and dark with a single window in the corner. The room had a big table, chairs, a wardrobe, and Grandma's metal folding bed. That served as our dining room. During the day Grandma's bed was folded and looked like a small table. It was covered with a throw and had decorative trinkets, some figurines and such placed on top of it. The metal coils, mattress, and sheets were all hidden inside this "small table." It was also Mom's sewing room.

A door from the dining room led to my parents' small room, which contained a bed and a wardrobe. The room's window overlooked the same blind courtyard as the kitchen window. From this courtyard one entered a common toilet on the ground floor. In the summer, when it was hot we couldn't open windows either in the kitchen or in our parents' room because of the foul stench. For several years during the crisis after 1930 when we didn't have enough money to pay the rent, a tenant, Mr. F. (I don't remember his name) lived in this room. He paid almost half of the entire rent. For my parents this income was a great relief. They slept in the first, nice room. I slept on the folding bed in the dining room, which I shared with Grandma.

Figure 2 My parents and me, 1925.

Essentially no one had their own space. Mr. F. had to enter his room through the kitchen and the dining room. He was an elderly man, very nice. He tried not to be in the way. Usually he would leave in the morning and come back in the evening. He worked in some capacity at the reformed synagogue, The Great Synagogue on Tłomackie Street.

There were two tiled coal-fired furnaces in the apartment. Each furnace heated two rooms. One had a hearth in the first, pretty room with one of its tiled sides in the dining room. The second one had the hearth in the dining room and it also heated the small, last room. During cold weather the small metal stove in the hallway was used as well. In general the furnaces held the warmth for at least two days. Mom liked to stand with her back to the furnace with her hands touching the tiles when she was cold. I liked that too. The apartment's electric wiring was placed on the outer side of the wall. Apparently the electricity was connected to the building after it had been built. In some places on the walls one could see small metal gas pipes. At one time, before electricity, gas was used for lighting. I learned that from Grandma.

When I was five, a year before starting school, Mom's cousin Tuśka taught me to read. She used a simple and effective method. She would take me for a walk and read the letterings on shops' signboards aloud and I would repeat them to her. Tuśka was a good ten years older than I. She was very pretty and extremely nice. I liked her a lot. At the same time, before I began school, Dad taught me how to play chess. This was very important, because at the school I attended many boys played chess, and I wasn't any worse than they were. Chess playing has stayed with me for my entire life. It was also then that I had my first contact with music, when Mom took me to a concert at the philharmonic. Radio didn't exist yet, only screeching records and gramophones with a bizarre, huge tube instead of a speaker (You may have seen it on old ads and logos for RCA Records, "His Master's Voice," which featured a dog listening to music coming out of such a tube). For the record to turn, one had to wind the spring mechanism by hand. We didn't have such a gramophone, so concerts were the only source of music. Although Dad accompanied Mom to concerts, she was the real music enthusiast in our household. Beethoven alone occupied the apex, with Tchaikovsky and Chopin on the tier below. In my hierarchy, Tchaikovsky, whose music—especially ballets, but not exclusively—I liked a lot, would have figured less prominently. I am more partial to Bach, Mozart, and Haydn. My wartime generation seems to favor baroque's calm and classicism's restraint more than romantic exultation. Zeitgeist? Probably, but such lists and classifications make little sense. There is enough room in the pantheon for all great composers.

Figure 3 Karola Fajnsztein, 1919. That year my mother earned her High School diploma.

After the war, I liked Friday concerts at the Warsaw Philharmonic on Jasna Street. Until our departure I had a subscription and a seat in the fourteenth row on the left. In New York I had a subscription to Carnegie Hall, which I attended more often than Fisher Hall, where the New York Philharmonic Orchestra performs. Fisher Hall is gigantic, too overwhelming, but Carnegie Hall reminds me a little of the Warsaw Philharmonic. Even Carnegie Hall's bartender, a likable Irishman, knew me and during intermission, he would hand me my drink, a Martini, over the heads of the crowd besieging the bar. I would send him the money by the "return mail." During the last years before leaving New York I had a subscription to chamber music concerts at Carnegie Hall, where soloists or small ensembles performed in a smaller space. Somehow it suited me better than huge symphonic orchestras playing in the main concert hall, although it did lack a bar in the hall. Tastes change with time and not because I love great virtuosos so much. To tell the truth, with some notable exceptions (Yo-Yo Ma!), I cannot distinguish between a great virtuoso and a competent performer. But my mom was very enthusiastic about great soloists' performances. Her favorites included the violinist Bronisław Huberman, pianists Artur Rubinstein and Witold Małcużyński, and the blind Hungarian, Imre Ungar.

Does great music inspire great work? Looking back it seems to me that good ideas for my lab work (if I ever had such at all) came to me after concerts at the Warsaw Philharmonic and later Carnegie Hall, so perhaps there is some truth to that. I had a similar feeling when vacationing in the mountains, but never at the seashore. I liked to write scientific papers at home, not at the institute or at the university, always at night when everybody was asleep and always quietly while listening to music, usually baroque, especially Pachelbel, Bach, or Corelli.

In the 1980s, I was able to organize at "my" New York University's medical school popular lectures on the theory and history of music. A professor at our university's School of Music, a musicologist and expert of harpsichord music, visited us once a week for four years at the start of the fall semester. He explained each work's interior structure and its origin. Everything he discussed was synchronized with excellent musical illustrations. He talked about the Renaissance and the Baroque periods, classicism and romanticism and, separately, operatic music. He also showed the correlation between the music, fine arts, and literature of each historical period. I found it all extremely interesting. I had been listening to classical music since childhood, but those lectures gave me a specific satisfaction that comes only with a basic understanding of theory. After several years, my music expert began to produce CDs with a similar theme. He was so successful that he no longer had time for lectures, which weren't nearly as lucrative. Too bad, he was very good and witty. He said that Bach and Handel were geniuses, but while Bach composed music for himself and for God, Handel did it for people and money and Bach won! He was about to discuss modern music, which would have been particularly useful for me, when all the fun ended. For many years I had to tolerate the unavoidable short conductor's inserts, known to every listener of classical concerts. Those inserts, say Sandor Ligeti, Carl Maria von Webern, or Arnold Schoenberg, were shoved between "real" music like Brahms, Mozart, etc. The first time I began to take such "inserts" seriously was in Warsaw. I had arrived at the last moment, straight from the lab to a Friday concert. I managed to enter the concert hall, but had no time to get the program. Of course I tried to guess what was being played—we all do it and now I do it too when listening to the radio. It wasn't difficult: Bach. I looked at the program during the intermission and it turned out that yes, it was Bach, but, surprisingly, Bach's choral work arranged by Schoenberg. Well, so Arnold Schoenberg knew his craft and had he wanted to . . . But in that case could Jackson Pollock and Mark Rothko also have painted a "lifelike" flower bouquet or a female nude instead of their doodles and colorful rectangles superposed on each other, if they wanted to? I later discovered that acceptance of contemporary music is largely a matter of familiarization and that acceptance of fine arts is dependent on some experience and understanding. We have to let a great artist lead us by the hand, remembering that Igor Stravinsky's "The Rite of Spring" was booed in Paris (in Paris? yes, in Paris) in 1913. But how does one know whether one sees a future Amadeo Modigliani or junk because so many seek appreciation and . . . money. It's not easy, especially because vulgar snobbery and passing fads impede our judgment. Competence and experience help, and the divine spark that is so difficult to define is useful as well. And yet . . . and yet I'm not sure if 500 years from now people will visit an exhibit of, let's say Warhol, to see cans of Campbell's tomato soup in the same way they go to see Michelangelo's frescos in the Sistine Chapel. The Russians have a saying for such a dilemma: "pozhiviom, uvidim."[3] But speaking about contemporary music: I was unable to convince myself that "I should like a particular piece of music because it was by a prominent composer" when I was listening to, for instance, Philip Glass' minimalist music. Only later when I watched a ballet based on his music did I realize how beautiful it was. And yet that is not how I reacted to Léo Delibes, Georges Bizet, Stravinsky, and other ballet music. It's all so strange.

There was a lot to see during my 30-year-long stay in New York. In the 1980s the Guggenheim Museum exhibited Wassily Kandinsky's retrospective. The building by Frank Lloyd Wright was already a true work of art; it would be difficult to imagine a more ideal fusion of beauty and functional solutions. Inside, the young Kandinsky occupied the top part: nothing special, good, post-impressionist art. But descending on perhaps the best-known spiral staircase in the world—and the paintings were shown chronologically—one could distinctly follow his break with representational art. Finally there were enormous canvases of "pure" abstracts placed on the lower levels in a multitude of colors and shapes. It is remarkable that many of that period's greats, such as Picasso and Georges Braque, who knew how to deform reality in various incredible ways, didn't cross the border between representational art and abstraction.

---

[3] Tr: Poshiviom uvidim (Russian): Time will tell (literally: we will live and we shall see).

There was a fascinating exhibit at the old Lexington Armory on Lexington Avenue that in fact was a repeat of a famous exhibit that had taken place 50 years earlier. It was at this same place in 1913 that American audiences for the first time were able to see European paintings from post-impressionists through pointillism, Van Gogh, fauvism all the way to Matisse, Picasso, and abstractionism. This was a time when American art was no longer in its infancy, but Europe still represented the authority in the art world. In the annals of American art, the Armory exhibit is considered a turning point that had shocked the public and even many art communities. Photos of several paintings destroyed in Europe in two world wars were now shown in their place; nothing was missing. New York press reviews from the original exhibit were gathered in the next room. It was incredible! People read them and laughed out loud as most of the reviews and opinions were decidedly negative. Some said that it was the end of painting and of art in general, that these were some indecent jokes of nincompoops and people devoid of talent who didn't know and didn't understand Art with a capital A. It would be difficult to imagine a more enlightening event. It was 1963. I was working at the NYU medical school at the time and hardly ever left the lab, but I couldn't say no to such an exhibit. The Armory on Lexington Ave is within short walking distance of the school. I was in New York for a year without my family. Felusia and the girls had stayed in Warsaw as hostages—literally. I had to leave them since that was the accepted norm in that hopeless "socialism"—downright barbarism. Permission to go abroad was a favor accorded by the rulers, that is, by the owners of the Polish People's Republic. And yet Poland had been considered, and perhaps rightly so, as the best part of the entire Gulag (from Russian: Glavnoye upravleniye lagerey i koloniy; Main Administration of Corrective Labor Camps and Labor Settlements). It was much harder to leave other socialist countries for scientific training in the west. Indeed in Russia it was almost impossible. Some years later, in 1967, after the Six-Day War in Israel and after the anti-Semitic campaign started by Gomułka[4] and other dimwits—Poland's owners ("ciemniak"/"dimwit," a term made up probably by Stefan Kisielewski[5] to describe the sham communist elite that was ruling Poland; I don't know of a better one). Later, when it was time to leave Poland, my year-long work at NYU medical school's biochemistry department proved to be very important to our entire family.

---

[4]   Tr: Władysław Gomułka (1905–1982): Polish communist leader, head of the communist party and of the Polish government from 1945 to 1948 and from 1956 to 1970.

[5]   Tr: Stefan Kisielewski (1911–1991): Polish writer, composer, publicist, and politician.

When I was six I began attending a secular primary school taught in Yiddish. There were a few such schools in Warsaw and some other regions of Poland as well. The schools were run by an organization called CYSHO[6] (Centrale Yiddishe Shul Organizatsye—Central Jewish School Organization), set up and dominated by the Bund.[7] Dad was a Bund member and wanted his son to know Yiddish. Bund programs stipulated, among other things, the teaching of Jewish national and cultural autonomy. The Bund promoted Yiddish language and culture, which made sense, since the Jewish population in Poland totaled more than three million people. Math, literature, history, natural sciences—all these subjects were taught in Yiddish in my school. We also had daily Polish lessons—just as Latin or French is taught in high school—just more frequently. In hindsight I'm not certain that this setup was a good idea. There is some data, I don't know how accurate, that shows that before the war only about 20 percent of Polish Jews knew Polish well. Probably the majority of Jews didn't strive to be assimilated. But did Polish society attempt to accept us? How many of Orzeszkowa's[8] followers where there? No doubt there were some, but not many.

Shortly before his death Jacek Kuroń[9] wrote that if it weren't for Piłsudski,[10] Poland would have been ruled by the NDK[11] during the period between the two world wars. He knew about what he was writing. And if all the Jews in

---

6 Tr: Centrale Yidishe Shul-Organizatsye (Central Yiddish School Organization), known by its acronyms TSYSHO or CYSHO, established in Warsaw in 1921 and led mainly by Bund members, was the creator and administrator of secular Jewish schools with a rich curriculum. Main subjects were taught in Yiddish, and Polish history and literature—in Polish.

7 Tr: Bund: a secular Jewish socialist workers' party active between 1897 and 1920 in the Russian Empire (Poland, Lithuania, Latvia, Belarus and Ukraine). Its Polish chapter separated itself from the rest in 1914 and operated until 1948, while most other groups were absorbed by the Soviet communist party. The Bund's ideology considered Jewish culture to be the crucial element and the uniting force of Jewish identity and, advocating Jewish life in the Diaspora, opposed Zionism and separatism. Its members were Jewish artisans, craftsmen, and workers, as well as Jewish intelligentsia. The Bund led its own trade union movement and a self-defense organization that protected Jewish communities from pogroms.

8 Tr: Eliza Orzeszkowa (1841–1910): Polish novelist who urged Poles to reject anti-Semitism.

9 Tr: Jacek Kuroń (1934–2004): one of the main leaders of democratic opposition in Poland during communist rule.

10 Tr: Józef Piłsudski (1867–1935): Polish statesman; Chief of State (1918–1922), First Marshall (from 1920), and leader (1926–1935) of the Second Polish Republic.

11 Tr: Narodowa Demokracja or NDK: National Democracy, a fascist anti-Semitic party of Poland established in 1886 and dissolved in 1947.

Poland had spoken Polish perfectly, without any foreign accent, then frankly what would have been different? German Jews perished in the Holocaust despite being totally assimilated. Jews in Germany numbered 1 percent—in Poland 10 percent—and they admired German culture. It didn't help them at all. The situation of Jews in the United States is completely different from that of European countries, not because Jews are different, but because America is different—it does not strive to be nor sees itself as a single ethnicity. (Creation of the country of Israel after the war makes a difference as well.) There is no question of assimilation here. In the US there is total integration. For example, my grandson is serving as an officer in the US Air Force. A New York saying from the 1960s illustrates the point rather well. "If you want to become New York's mayor, in order to receive enough votes you have to kiss the (pardon my language) shit covered behinds of babies from the three 'I's'": Ireland, Italy, and Israel, to demonstrate your love for those three nations, which represent a great number of voters. So, first of all, the Jews are as well integrated as Americans as, say, those of Italian or Irish origin. And second, we also have our "second" fatherland—and it was our actual country of origin. I don't believe I have exhausted the topic; the Weimar Republic's unresolved problem of the upside-down Jewish social pyramid remains. Perhaps some other issues also remain, among them "melting" of Jews in the American sea. I will come back to this later.

Grandma Helenka wasn't at all happy about the school chosen for me. She was afraid that her only grandson—my mom was also an only child—would speak Polish with a bad, "Jewish" accent. Poles had contemptuous names for this way of speaking. Grandma belonged to our family's first assimilated generation. She spoke Polish correctly and loved Polish literature. She spoke excellent Yiddish of course. But the school was exceptional, despite classes that sometimes numbered forty children. This is because a school is as good as its teachers (universities as well!) and the teachers were, without exception, outstanding pedagogues. The school was located at 36 Krochmalna Street, in the middle of the poorest section of the almost entirely Jewish northern Warsaw district. Krochmalna Street began near a huge market called Hale Mirowskie (two identical shopping areas) and continued west. The part of the street adjacent to the market was known for dives frequented by thieves and fences as well as for brothels. Ballads about Krochmalna Street, some of them really neat, are still part of the Warsaw folklore. As a child I was afraid to be on that street and often went out of my way to avoid it. School was a bit further, eighteen houses away from the market, and the area there was calmer. No matter how close or far from the Hale Mirowskie, the borough was one of poverty and the gutters stank.

Figure 4 My parents with Grandma Helenka, July 25, 1922, Warsaw, Poland.

From the very beginning I had a serious problem at school. I was placed in a lower grade because of my poor knowledge of Yiddish. We spoke Polish at home. (Later I had two other language problems—Russian and English.) At home my parents spoke Yiddish when they didn't want me to understand. I listened trying to catch separate words, but it wasn't much. I may have been the only child in my class who didn't know Yiddish, and that wasn't good. I became the laughing stock of the entire class and children can be cruel. Time and again I was saved by our teacher, Lererin Zonszajn (in Yiddish we say lerer, lererin, that is "teacher," before adding the last name. And so I will call my teachers from Krochmalna Street). She was not only a great teacher, but a marvelous person. She understood the situation and always defended me. It was thanks to her that

I quickly learned to speak, read, and write in Yiddish. She taught all subjects to our class for the first three years. She was short, wore glasses, and always had a kind smile on her face. She was modest, not someone who attracts attention when they enter a room, but I absolutely adored her. My good lererin didn't survive the war. She perished in the Holocaust.

A very popular teacher in our school was Lerer Tropiański. Tall and slim with a head of unruly, black hair, he was always laughing. Unusually expert in many fields, he taught math, physical education, singing, and crafts and he directed the school's choir (from which he had me removed since I couldn't carry a tune—no hard feelings). He also could play a small accordion called a concertina beautifully. Lerer Tropiański had some concerns about my math because, surprisingly, at first I couldn't for the life of me grasp fractions. My talented Lerer Tropiański didn't survive the war either. He perished in the Holocaust. His young wife and a baby born a few years before the war perished as well.

In fourth grade our class counselor was Lererin Gutgestalt, the mother of my then best friend Gabryś. The family lived on 43 Dzielna Street in the second courtyard opposite the Pawiak prison. (During the Nazi occupation, Pawiak was a place of torture and executions.) On his way to school Gabryś passed my house on Karmelicka Street. I would often wait for him at the gate and we would continue together. It was a long walk: Leszno, Solna, Ogrodowa to Chłodna Street and further by Walicόw to Krochmalna. We never went to school by streetcar. I don't know why. Perhaps it was too expensive. And in any case the connection wasn't good: one had to transfer several times. Our conversations revolved around two subjects. The first was Mirka P., with whom both of us—as well as other boys—were in love. Mirka was very pretty, but one grade higher. She didn't pay attention to little kids like us and I doubt she was aware of our existence or our juvenile yearnings. She was only interested in boys a couple of years older, like for example Izio R., an excellent pingpong player, which was actually a serious plus.

Politics was the second subject of interest. This was perhaps odd for children our age, but that's how it was. We had both been interested in politics from an early age because we both came from Bundist families and those subjects were discussed at home. In fact the entire community was into politics. Every day we read the same Bund newspaper, Folks-Zeitung (People's Paper), which was published in Yiddish. Sometimes my dad even liked to check whether I had read it. After school we preferred to meet in Gabryś' apartment because in those years we had a dressmaker's atelier at home and there was no room to play. We conducted wars on the floor where paper soldiers fought and died (tin soldiers were too expensive). We also had cannons, horses, and all that was needed for combat cut from sheets of cardboard. We both worshiped Napoleon and his reign. We knew by heart all his wars, battles, and marshals' names. I lost my interest after reading, still in Poland, Żeromski's[12] *Ashes*, and later Tolstoy's *War and Peace* in Russia during the war. Years later when I was in America I came to despise Napoleon after reading Metternich's memoirs (he too, was a despicable scoundrel).[13] I came to realize that Napoleon's pride was unparalleled, as was his contempt for human life.

Although I was not a bad chess player, Gabryś was better. My very first friend and his entire family: his mother Lererin Gutgestalt and his father, an office employee by day and a writer in Yiddish by night, perished in the Holocaust. Beautiful Mirka and her family didn't survive the war, either.

I attended the Krochmalna Street school for six years. In fifth and sixth grade our class counselor and Jewish literature teacher was Leib Olicki, a known poet. He survived the war in Russia. I saw him from time to time in the 1950s in Warsaw. Thanks to him I got to know the great writers of Yiddish literature. Mendele Mocher Sforim (a pen name, literally "Mendele, the book peddler") was recognized as the father of Yiddish literature. Isaack Leib Perez was the most versatile talent of the three classical writers. Sholem Aleichem (a pen name meaning "peace be with you"), was a great, exceptional talent, a bit like Chekhov, a bit like Maupassant, but with a uniquely Jewish humor (when you don't know whether to laugh or to cry). At that time I belonged to the Grosser Library on Leszno Street—it was also a Bund institution that not only lent books, but published, together with CYSHO, thin volumes in soft covers for children. I liked to buy and collect them.

Back to Olicki: besides literature he paid special attention to the correct Yiddish pronunciation. The most correct, proper pronunciation was, according to him, the one spoken by Jews in the Volyn region (Woliner Yiddish), but all the others, especially the colloquial Warsaw speech and the one from Lodz (even worse) were in his opinion almost vulgar. He was right. There are no longer any Jews in the Volyn region, but the tradition of elegant pronunciation has perhaps remained here and there. The course of my life was such that there was little room for Yiddish. Although my Yiddish is far from perfect, I still can speak it using both the low-class Warsaw pronunciations and the proper one. Until recently I subscribed to and read the Bund monthly *Unzer tsayt*

---

12 Tr: Stefan Żeromski (1864–1925): Polish novelist and dramatist.
13 Tr: Klemens Wenzel von Metternich (1773-1859): Austrian polititian and statesman.

(Our Times), published for decades in New York by Dad's old comrades. One can find interesting things in it, like pearls from Jewish history, reprints of old Bund masters from years ago and, what's very important, death notices so we know who is still alive and who is not. In general, Bund members were friends and knew each other well and, when necessary, helped each other—like a sort of team-spirited mafia, only very respectable. There were no ID cards. I was a member simply because I was the son of Misha, that is, of the old Szer, who served time in a Bolshevik prison for his Bund, and of his wife Karola. Some months ago *Unzer tsayt* ceased to be published—not enough readers and writers. It ended because the world of Polish Jews ended and the Bund had been deeply rooted in that world for decades, since the end of the nineteenth century. It was this world's truly organic component. This last sentence may sound artificial, even pompous, but it is accurate. I admit that the older I become the stronger my affection for the Bund gets—it's odd but true. Yes, just affection and not much more than that, because everything happened completely differently from what the Bund could have predicted. Szmul "Artur" Zygelbojm, the only person who consciously sacrificed his life—he killed himself—to protest the world's indifference to the Holocaust, was a prominent Bund leader. During the war he was the representative to the Polish government in exile in London. And? He could do nothing to stir the Allies' conscience, not even to at least bomb the rails leading to Auschwitz. No wonder Jews are "supersensitive" when it comes to anti-Semitism.

While attending school on Krochmalna Street I was very tempted to play with children in the courtyard behind our house. It wasn't at all simple. Grandma believed that a boy from a "good family" had no business in the courtyard. To get Dad's permission was the simplest way to get around Grandma's dictate, but he was rarely at home at the appropriate time. And Mom, caught between Dad and her mom, could not always be counted on. Sometimes she would say "yes" and sometimes "no." And when it was a "no" I sat at the window watching the other children play in the yard. The courtyard was not big, almost square, covered with asphalt and bordered by cobblestone, without a single blade of grass or any green vegetation whatsoever. A wooden rack for dusting carpets stood in the middle; one could beat bedding, rugs, etc. until eleven in the morning. After eleven the frame would turn into a gymnastic contraption, much to the annoyance of our building's caretaker Józef. The children, mostly boys, practiced all kinds of exercises, some of them rather reckless. The girls preferred games of hopscotch. There was always something going on in the courtyard. Tradesmen and peddlers who came there called with singing voices, stretching out the words: "knives, I sharpen kniiiiiives" or "I buy rags, raaaaaaags." In the summer, hawkers brought ice in a white crate on a manual cart to sell in chunks to housewives—there were no refrigerators. Also in the summer, they would carry pieces of watermelons kept on ice in a box on their back or hanging in front from around their neck. They called, in Yiddish: *a trink's a khmal far a finever,* which meant that for 5 grosz you could appease your thirst and hunger with a watermelon! One cannot translate it literally, but if you think about a piece of cold watermelon on a scorching summer day on our courtyard's asphalt, there was more truth to that than in many of today's American advertisements.

From time to time street musicians appeared in our courtyard, sometimes several of them, a small band. Mostly they played so-called hits, popular dance music, or sang tear-jerking gobbledygook about broken hearts and unrequited love. People from the entire building stood by open windows, listened and threw the musicians change wrapped in pieces of newspaper. Sometimes a circus came, that is, performers. They did all kind of acrobatics on a rug spread on the asphalt. They knew how to "swallow fire," could throw five or more balls in the air and juggle them so that none would fall down, and other such tricks. Kids would surround the rug with their eyes glued to the performers. My courtyard longings went away sometime between fourth and fifth grade when a new fascination began, this time with books and reading. This one proved permanent.

From time to time shouting emanated from Józef's apartment, which was located on the first floor (actually the first floor above the lobby, which would typically be called the second floor in most Western countries) diagonally across from ours. Grandma would shake her head then, saying with a grave voice: Józef is beating Mrs. Józef again. The voice that Grandma used and her head shaking contained everything: contempt and anger at Józef, pity for his wife, and helplessness. Józef was taciturn, a big guy, squat with huge arms. He wore high boots with pants tucked inside and a uniform cap with a small visor. Mrs. Józef was slight and usually with a kerchief on her head. They had no children. Grandma couldn't stand Józef and turned her head every time she went by him, but she liked to chat with his wife. Yes, Józef was different, primitive. Józef's family were the only Catholics in our building. It was the same in almost every tenement house in Warsaw's northern Jewish district. Józef's duties included opening the gate after eleven at night. For him this was a source of extra income. The gates of buildings in the entire city were locked at eleven and whoever came home late would give the caretaker the generally accepted rate of at least 20 grosz "for his troubles." Of course this caused arguments and quarrels because people hurried to get back before the gates closed, but the caretakers set their watches early and closed gates ahead of time. Those few minutes gave them more money than an entire night. For 20 grosz one could buy four small "Kaiser" rolls.

The crisis that began in the States at the end of October 1929 reached Poland in the years 1930–1931. Dad lost his job. The business where he worked as a bookkeeper (now we call it accountant) went bankrupt. A tragedy unfolded. Our family found itself on the brink of disaster, facing complete financial ruin. I was old enough to understand the situation or perhaps to feel it intuitively and I have no doubt that those times shaped me to a great extent. I think that experiencing something like that when one is a kid has a greater influence on one's personality than all adult rules and admonitions combined: do this, don't do that, be nice, etc. The first step undertaken by my parents was renting the last, small room, that is, their bedroom, to Mr. F. who paid 50 zloty for it (the entire rent was 90 zloty). In fact, as I later learned from Mom, it was not he who paid, but his rather wealthy children who didn't want to have their old father in their house. Mom was outraged. She would never think of acting this way with Grandma Helenka. Grandma was a family member, period. Three generations in one apartment was normal then, at least among the people we knew. Perhaps it was different among the rich.

The next, extremely important step was Mom's decision to establish in our apartment a dressmaker's shop solely for children, mainly for girls. Readymade clothes for adults and children were much less common than they are today. Having such clothing made to order by a seamstress or by a tailor was a normal practice. Mom worked by herself at first. Grandma helped a bit by sewing buttons, basting, and hemming. Later the atelier grew and Mom hired a "senior assistant" and a "junior assistant," the lowest level in the dressmaking hierarchy. Mom never had more than two employees. The senior assistant was a disagreeable older (senior) woman who stayed with Mom until the end, that is, until the war. Mom valued her a great deal, but I didn't like her. I don't know why, or perhaps I do. It was different with the junior girls. Generally they were young women who never stayed long. They either got married or found a better job; I don't know. They often sang while working and Mom sang as well. Mom was cheerful, perhaps not as merry as Dad, but cheerful. Their repertory consisted mostly of Jewish folk songs and Chopin. Only the senior assistant didn't sing.

I liked one of the junior girls, Tobcia G., a beautiful, attractive girl, always joyful and singing. She had typically Jewish looks, even a slightly crooked nose, but nice and small, not like mine. She was five or six years older than I and much more experienced in every respect. She worked for Mom for a short time. Later on I would meet her at the "Morning Star" sports club ("Morgenstern" in Yiddish, another Bund institution) where I was taking gymnastics. We were good friends; too good. Tobcia got married just before the war.

There were two sewing machines in the atelier, both of them Singers, and a table where Mom cut the fabrics generally provided by customers. In the afternoons, when children were back from school, Mom received girls for fittings in our nicest and best room, the one with the entrance from the hallway. During the hours when customers were expected I tried to hide in the farthest corner of the apartment so that someone else would have to answer the doorbell and open the door to the hallway. I was afraid to encounter a girl I might know and be discovered as a seamstress' son. My marvelous Mom, brave and hard working, did her best to support the family and I, stupid pipsqueak, was ashamed of her profession. I still cannot forgive myself. I think Mom understood the situation, but never said anything critical. I sometimes think that in the United States a boy in a similar situation would never even imagine such false shame. No doubt some unwritten but deeply rooted democratic tradition exists here and distinguishes this country from the Old Continent. Europe, Poland: was it a different mentality, dissimilar traditions, perhaps an unconscious influence of class differences, of bourgeois prejudices and of aristocratic culture? I don't know. Regardless of these reflections—or perhaps excuses—all I know is that I behaved like a scoundrel.

Before the crisis, Dad worked for a business called RoLis (short for the owner's name Rosenbaum, and for slats).[14] They produced wallpaper (since very few people painted their apartments) and all kinds of slats for picture frames and for curtains. After bankruptcy they distributed lots of slats and frames among employees—possibly the owners had no money or perhaps they just wanted to keep it for themselves. Some of the slats were gilded with complicated, as if sculpted, designs, very ornate and yet machine made. We had lots of this stuff in every corner piled almost to the ceiling. I doubt that my parents had any use for them. Who needs frames when there is no money for the most basic needs like food, rent, or clothing? The frames disappeared slowly as my parents gave them to their friends and acquaintances. Just before the war there were none left.

After losing his post, Dad tried everything. For almost four years the jobs were only temporary. For a time he worked as a night watchman on a construction site where he guarded building materials. Mom worried and was very afraid. She said that not only would thieves steal whatever they wanted, but they would also beat Dad up. Fortunately that didn't happen.

---

[14] Tr: Slat- in Polish: listwa.

In the winter, the Municipal Administration hired people on a day to day basis to clear snow. Dad would leave at dawn—first come first served—to get that job and earn some money. The best job he had in those years was his participation in organizing an exhibit about the beginnings and history of the Bund. Money for that exhibit was given by Jewish labor unions in America. Dad guided visitors. Although he didn't earn much, it helped significantly. When the exhibit closed several months later the situation became desperate again. Dad suffered greatly despite being a generally happy and amusing person. Many years later, after his death in New York in 1962, his Bund friends said in a death notice published in the book *Bund's Generations* (New York: Doyers bundistn, *Unzer tsayt*, 1968) that he was well liked and that "a friendly smile never left his face." That is the honest truth.

Grandma Helenka also did whatever she could to help with finances. For as long as I can remember Grandma worked every year in the summer until the war. Grandma worked at the camp for Jewish children in Ciechocinek.[15] Her close friend from before the World War I, Mrs. Celina G. was the camp's director and Grandma was the manager. She always left for Ciechocinek in the middle of May, two to three weeks before the camp started, hired cooks, cleaners, and the rest of the crew for the summer season, and prepared accommodations for children. She worked hard from morning till night because everything, from finances to staff and supplies, was her responsibility. Once when I was twelve, I went there and I saw Grandma in circumstances very different from those in Warsaw—she was in her element, very happy. The camp was nicely located across from Forest Park, a few kilometers from the town center with its Spa Park, more elegant than the Forest Park and famous for its beautiful flowerbeds. We often went there for walks with our counselors. Only Polish was spoken at the camp—it wasn't a Bund venture. When the holidays were over at the end of August, but before the start of the school year, Grandma would stay for some time in Ciechocinek to wrap everything up and to safeguard the buildings owned by the camp for the winter. There was one more reason why Grandma stayed awhile in Ciechocinek. Food in Warsaw was much more expensive than in the countryside and Grandma would prepare copious amounts of delicious food that could be preserved and secured in hermetically sealed glass or earthenware jars. These were not just fruit preserves or pickles. Grandma also brought dry meats and all kinds of fruit, for example the varieties of apples that could be kept for a long time in a cellar. Usually Grandma came back by train, laden

---

[15] Tr: Ciechocinek: a spa-town in northern Poland known for its saline springs.

with chickens and sometimes with geese, already cleaned, and with other foods that could spoil quickly and had to be cooked or baked or somehow taken care of right away.

We waited for Grandma at the station and went back home by a horse cab (there were taxis, but more expensive and besides, a taxi ride was bordering on extravagance). A day later a horse cart from Ciechocinek would arrive filled with canned goods, fruit, dry meats, and all kinds of things, everything that Grandma had bought or made! Józef had to open not only a door in the gate, but the entire gate for the cart to get through to the yard. That was more expensive than 20 grosz. We would immediately bring everything down to the basement. Each family had a little cubicle in the basement, secured with a lock. All of the cubicles belonging to our building's tenants were under our staircase. People mostly kept coal, potatoes, and apples in there. I didn't like the basement. It had one long, narrow passage with entrances to the cubicles on both sides. At the end of the passage a solitary small light bulb sometimes gave light, but sometimes it didn't, so the basement was either dark or completely dark. I was afraid of mice and rats. But even though I was often sent to the basement to fetch various things I never saw a rodent of any kind.

Although my grandma was not generally a cheery person, she would be bursting with pride after returning from Ciechocinek. She was proud not to be a burden for her beloved daughter and to be able to contribute to the family's livelihood. Grandma hardly earned any money at the camp, but she received free room and board. She wanted to save what little she earned and use it for the family's needs. Mom wouldn't allow it, saying that Grandma already had spent too much for the food she had brought. Grandma's answer was that one couldn't miss such opportunity since food in Ciechocinek was very cheap and she was buying everything wholesale from the same suppliers who brought food for the camp throughout the entire summer. Such were their conversations, but Mom was inflexible.

In 1935, Poland was slowly coming out of the crisis. I was eleven, in fifth grade at school, when Dad got a job in his profession at a big vegetable and fruit wholesaler. It looked like a permanent job and so it was. Suddenly everything at home changed. It was as if a loud sigh of relief could be heard: I would be able to go to high school, and this was most important. Until that moment my parents weren't sleeping at night, worried about not being able to educate me after elementary school (we then called it "general school"). I was well aware of it. It was now also possible to have Mr. F. leave and to reclaim my parents' bedroom.

Before the war a seven-year-long elementary school was mandatory. Generally at fourteen (one typically went to school at seven years old, but I began at six—Jews are always in a hurry), young people either started working or went to a trade school. High school had two levels: four years of comprehensive education (earning a "lower diploma") or an additional two year long education with three specialties (comprehensive, classical, or math and science). After this, one took final exams to obtain a diploma that provided access to university studies. Children who were going to continue their education in a high school didn't go to the seventh grade at the elementary school, but began high school after sixth grade. In this way one got a high school diploma after twelve years of studies. I was in fifth grade, one year before high school, when it became clear that I would be able to continue. At first Dad didn't earn much, only fifty zloty a week (with time he got several raises), but Mom didn't have the slightest intention of giving up her business. She liked that work and was much sought after because she had good taste and was very conscientious. She treated her job seriously. In addition, she provided work for two assistants.

Choosing a high school was a problem. There were private schools, generally good and expensive, but also state and city schools that were free and also good. To get into the latter, one had to pass a competitive exam. My cousin, Bernard F., four or five years older than I, had passed such an exam in 1931 and was accepted at a state high school. I wasn't a great student, especially not in math and there was talk at home about hiring a tutor. It didn't happen for a simple reason; times in 1936 were different than in 1931. Hitler had already been in power for several years, and scary things were happening in Germany and indeed throughout Europe. Also, anti-Semitism was rising in Poland, though it was less blatant, but oddly very fashionable among people. It was even more prevalent among intellectuals, or rather pseudo-intellectuals; the latter always being more numerous than the former. In 1936, after Józef Piłsudski's death it took a miracle, like the one with the proverbial camel and the eye of a needle, for a Jew to be accepted at a state high school. So hiring a tutor made no sense. I mentioned Piłsudski because as long as he was alive and respected even by his adversaries, anti-Semitism was restrained. Only two great twentieth-century Polish statesmen—Józef Piłsudski in the first half of our unhappy century and Karol Wojtyła[16] in the second half—were not anti-Semites.

Back to the subject of high school: it was rather important to know why my parents had a negative attitude toward both private and public high school other

---

[16] Tr: Karol Wojtyła (1920–2005) was Pope John Paul II from 1978 until his death.

than simply financial considerations. Poland had a concordat (agreement) with the Vatican: religion was taught in schools and a high school diploma required a religion exam grade. My parents, especially Dad, preferred a school with no religion, like my elementary school. When he was a child, Dad went to a cheder (orthodox elementary school for boys, which at the beginning of the twentieth century wasn't much different from such schools in the Middle Ages, except that only religion was taught there) and for the rest of his life he retained a strong dislike for all religion, especially in schools. And my parents found a school that was coed and secular! What's more, it had an additional advantage and not a small one. It was considerably less expensive than other private schools. It was the Bolesław Limanowski[17] high school of the Workers' Society of Children's Friends in Wilson Square in Żoliborz. The school was located at the Warsaw Housing Cooperative's residential colony number 1. In short, the school was run under the auspices of the Polish Socialist Party and of the cooperative movement, that is, the Polish non-communist left, the most noble-minded people under the sun. Too bad there aren't more of them.

Figure 5 In Cracow on a school trip to Wawel in 1937 or 1938. Standing first from left is Heniek Kwaśniewski, second Zdzisiek Polak, last the author. Sitting, on left is Gienek Pietroszkiewicz, on right Jarek Ładosz.

---

[17] Tr: Bolesław Limanowski (1835–1935): Polish politician, historian, and journalist, one of primary advocates of socialist ideas in Poland.

Bolesław Limanowski, a historian, was, at the end of the nineteenth century, one of the creators and most prominent activists of the PPS.[18] At that time in Poland there were two active Zionist workers' parties: Poale Zion Right (Ben Gurion's party, its continuation is the present Labor Party in Israel) and the smaller one, Poale Zion Left (later Mapam party in Israel) which belonged to the Second International. Before the war, the left had a standpoint similar to that of the Bund in the matters of Yiddish culture and education. For example, its members were active in CYSHO and supported Yiddish literature. The right was against Yiddish because, in its opinion, it was necessary to break with all of the Diaspora's remnants, thus with the everyday language, and to replace it with Hebrew. The right won. What I'm going to say now is neither an opinion nor an evaluation, but an attempt to consider, in retrospection, the problem of Hebrew. The metamorphosis of a dead language used for about two thousand years almost exclusively in liturgy and in religious books into a live, everyday language of the Israeli people is a unique phenomenon (just like the society itself!). It is as though—although on a smaller scale—Latin were made the everyday language of the Catholic population, or old Slavic used in orthodox liturgy became the everyday language of Russia! It's true that being a country comprised entirely of immigrants helped Israel adapt to a new (old?) language. And perhaps there is a grain of truth in the presumption of Jews that their ability to adjust to new situations was supposedly acquired in the Diaspora.

And so in the fall of 1936 I began my high school studies. Most of the children from my class remained at the Krochmalna Street school for the last year. The seventh year of elementary school was to be the last year of their education. Ahead lay manual work, often tailoring (Jews made clothes for half of Poland) or other types of trade. Only my friend Gabryś and two or three girls went to high school, but not Limanowski. I felt deeply embarrassed by my privilege. Such were the times.

Directly after the war I tried to find pupils from my elementary school class. I found one girl in Israel and another one in Canada. My search was aided by the Committee for Polish Jews, formed after the war and by the Red Cross. Those who had survived immediately registered with these organizations. Perhaps some others stayed alive; I don't know. Certainly the majority perished in the Holocaust. I remember high school with great satisfaction and deep emotion.

---

[18] Tr: Polska Partia Socjalistyczna (or PPS): Polish Socialist Party, one of the most important Polish political parties from its creation in 1920 until its merger with the Communist Polish Workers' Party in 1948. It was re-established in 1987.

It was excellent in all aspects because, just like at the Krochmalna Street school, the teachers there were outstanding. Before getting my diploma in 1942 I attended three different schools in Russia; two were totally abysmal and the third—that was my last year—was not that bad. Still, it couldn't begin to compare to the Limanowski School. What a shame that this period of my life was only three years long. Then came 1939 and war arrived. I went to school in Wilson Square by streetcar, since the distance was too great for a morning stroll, the way I used to do it. By some miracle, my pre-war school ID allowing for a reduced price for streetcar rides survived. I would get to Żoliborz either directly from Leszno by streetcar number 15 without transfer or by number 9 to Bielańska Street and then by number 17. Just before the war, an embankment and viaduct over the Gdańsk Railroad Station had been built. Earlier the streetcar turned right and drove down in front of the rails (later trains from the Umschlagplatz[19] traveled on those tracks to Treblinka),[20] passed under the rails toward Żoliborz, then up, left and along Mickiewicza Street and across the Inwalidów Square to Wilson Square. No self-respecting boy would get off at Wilson Square. They jumped off before the stop from a moving tram. I did the same. The stop was across from the school where one of the girls might have seen me and, God forbid, think that I was a ninny. You had to jump back onto the right foot. But I was cautious enough to jump from the last door of the last car! At most I could hurt myself, but I wouldn't lose an arm or a leg. And such accidents happened.

The dominant person of my high school recollections is Jerzy Kreczmar, the schools' principal[21] (or "dyr" in student lingo), a Polish philology scholar and, for a time, my class counselor. Exceptionally erudite, he was a Polish literature expert and much more. He was able to awaken in all of us love for literature, fine arts, theater and culture; and not only Polish. I admired his knowledge of poetry. He knew many poems by heart and often, when it was appropriate, recited them in class. Nor was he lacking in imagination. For example I remember a test: free choice of a topic with a use of expressions of foreign origins! He was able to keep a tight reign over the boys, which was necessary. Otherwise we would have destroyed the school. Girls, being girls, were better behaved. I was tall, perhaps the tallest in my class, so they called

---

[19] Tr: Umschlagplatz (German: collection point or reloading point): the square in Warsaw under German occupation, where Jews were forced to gather for deportation from the Warsaw Ghetto to the Treblinka extermination camp.

[20] Tr: Treblinka: a Nazi extermination camp established in 1942 in Poland. Nearly a million Jews were killed in Treblinka, mainly in gas chambers, during its fifteen months of operation.

[21] Tr: Principal: in Polish, "dyrector."

me Longinus. The story was that when I stretched my legs—and I always sat in the back—they reached the teacher's desk.

Often the entire class went to the theater. We had other excursions as well. This is how I visited Cracow, Vilnius, Lvov, Poznań, and other cities. After the war, Kreczmar became a professor at the State Theater Academy in Warsaw and also directed plays. It would be difficult to overestimate what I had learned from him—what I owe him. He came from a family steeped in Polish culture. His brother Jan was an extraordinary actor and a professor at the Academy as well. During the tsar's rule, the previous generation of Kreczmars had established a famous high school commonly called "kreczmarówka." Another teacher, Jan Wesołowski, was the founder and first director of the famous Baj Theater.[22] After the war I sometimes met the math teacher, Mr. Poprożenko, at Lodz University, where he was an algebra professor. The Latin teacher Dora Kaganówna—a tough but excellent teacher (these two things go together)—in three years succeeded in hammering Latin into my thick skull so well that some remains even now. And a conviction also remains: that Latin is a very important component, even the basis of a comprehensive education. Perhaps this is why I made sure not to let our two daughters enter life without Latin. They in turn did the same with their children and so Latin passed on to the grandchildren! And that's how the world turns.

Right after the war I tried to look for my high school classmates. It wasn't easy because, unlike in the case of Jews, a detailed list of those who survived didn't exist. Following leads step by step I figured out that many of them died in the Warsaw Uprising[23] and in the Resistance. My closest friend from that period, Lolek Ankerman, perished in the Holocaust. Quiet, thoughtful beyond his years and excellent student, he was a year ahead of me. His father was a tailor. They lived on Chłodna Street. Lolek slept in a windowless atelier behind the tiny shop. At the rear there was also a room (miniscule) with a window overlooking a little back yard. The windowsill was precisely at the level of the yard's tarmac; it was a sort of half-basement. This room also contained a kitchen.

---

[22] Tr: Baj Theater, whose name means "fairy tale," is the oldest Polish puppet theater. Established in 1928, it exists to this day.

[23] Tr: The Warsaw Uprising (August 1944): a major World War II operation was organized by the Polish resistance Home Army (*Armia Krajowa*) in an attempt to liberate Warsaw from Nazi Germany. It was timed to coincide with the approach of the Soviet Army. The Russians, who planned to eliminate the Polish non-communist leadership, fearing its potential opposition to a Soviet-backed government in Poland, stopped their offensive in order to enable the Germans to regroup, destroy the city, and defeat the rebellion.

One had to go few steps down to enter the shop from the street; hence the shop's window was on the same level as the sidewalk. A sign was placed above the window and men's clothing hung inside in two rows, coats, etc. Everything was sort of diminutive, but extraordinarily neat and clean. I went to the area frequently because there were cheap movie theaters on Chłodna (a ticket cost 25 grosz, while the regular price in Warsaw was at least 55 grosz) that showed old cowboy films, our favorites. We would meet at Lolek's and go together to the movies. I liked his parents. They were gentle, very warm and hospitable toward me. His dad, short, always busy, would raise his eyes from the sewing machine and then would get up to greet me although I was just a kid. No one from that family survived the Holocaust.

We used to walk in the city a lot, especially along nice, bustling streets outside our district. Krakowskie Przedmieście, Nowy Świat, Piłsudski Square with the Saski Palace (destroyed and still not reconstructed) with the Tomb of the Unknown Soldier and the monument of Prince Poniatowski, Aleje Jerozolimskie, Marszałkowka Street—these were our routes. Sometimes we ventured as far as Łazienki.[24] This was a great expedition, all the way per pedes.[25] I like this place to this day and visit when I'm in town.

A game that boys often played was trying to recognize the make of a car as it approached from far away; was it a Skoda, a Tatra, a Buick, or a Ford. The first one to identify it correctly won. Although there were many private cars and taxis in Warsaw in those times, horse carriages or jalopies were predominant. There were few trucks. Merchandise was transported mainly in huge platform carts hitched to a couple of large Belgian draft horses. When I was at home and feeling sad, Grandma used to say: "Don't worry, little Włodek.[26] Belgian horses have huge heads. Let them worry."

A few years before the war, sinister inscriptions like "Jews not welcome" or "Aryan establishment" began to appear on the windows and doors of some coffee shops on Nowy Świat and Aleje Jerozolimskie between Nowy Świat and Marszałkowska Street, where Lolek and I often took our walks. The Constitution didn't allow open discrimination, but these kinds of anti-Semitic occurrences were becoming ever more common. This was mainly the work of NDK and its even more fascist offshoots, such as the National Radical Camp, All-Polish Youth, and others. Moreover some of Piłsudski's (then no longer alive) associates

---

[24] Tr: Łazienki Park, designed in the seventeenth century, is the largest park in Warsaw, occupying 188 acres.
[25] Tr: Per pedes (Latin): on foot.
[26] Tr: Włodek: diminutive of Włodzimierz. In Russian: Vladimir or Volodia.

competed with NDK and also permitted themselves to carry out anti-Semitic acts, hoping to increase their popularity (thus creating an unfavorable image of their nation or perhaps just displaying their own opinion concerning that nation). For example, a year or two before the war Józef Beck, the Foreign Affairs minister, declared in the Parliament that Poland had room for at most half a million Jews. This gentleman neglected a small detail—that of the other 2.5 million, many of whom had lived in this country for hundreds of years or more, perhaps even longer than Mr. Beck's family (Beck is not a typically Polish name). The minister had idiotic dreams about resettling Jews in Madagascar. Hitler saved him the trouble.

Another scoundrel was General Kordian Zamorski. As the chief of State Police, that is, of the Blue Police,[27] he traveled every year to Nuremberg for the Nazi party's congresses, the so called Parteitag, to admire (as it was said) Aryan strength. That didn't last long and the General experienced firsthand that strength. At home we said that had he been so eager to go to Nuremberg during Piłsudski's life, he would have lost his job. This police general didn't enjoy a good reputation among people in my parents' circles.

One day, a year or two before the war, on a rainy fall day I was coming home from downtown. In front of our building an old Jewish woman was selling bagels from a basket, loudly extolling their quality. The poor woman didn't see the policeman who came from behind and kicked the basket so that all her pitiful merchandise landed in the mud. The woman burst into tears. I'm sure that this policeman would never have dared to behave this way in a "good" Polish neighborhood. Jews, especially those who were poor and shabbily dressed and didn't speak Polish well, were afraid of the police. Priests also went to Nuremberg, for example Stanislaw Trzeciak, famous for his anti-Semitic views, although those congresses were, in fact, pagan revelries. This was not a surprise since the prelate's highest superior, Cardinal August Hlond, Poland's primate shortly before the war, declared that "the Jewish problem" will exist as long as the Jews. No, I don't allege that the cardinal had clairvoyant powers to foretell this so called problem's "final solution." Rather, it was a matter of the eternal striving to convert Jews and bring them to the bosom of the Church, a dream abandoned, it seems, only in the times of the last few pontificates, starting with John XXIII. Still, in retrospect the cardinal's words sound horrifying.

---

[27] Tr: The author seems to be mistaken in calling the police "blue," as it did not exist in the days described here. The Blue Police, called by this name because of the color of its uniforms, which operated from 1939 to 1944, was the Polish police formed by Nazi Germany in the occupied areas of Poland.

Yes, those several years before the war were the bad times. Anti-Semitism was rampant and assumed more sinister forms. A frightening thing happened to me as well. I was coming back from a solitary walk and was at that point on Krakowskie Przedmieście, on the opposite side from the University's gate, when I noticed a few students selling the ONR rag "Prosto z Mostu," meaning straight from the bridge (Straight Talk). Standing by a table with this poisonous paper they chanted:

Warsaw and Cracow are Polish cities,
And you, Bedouins, scram to Palestine! Beat it!

They didn't posses much poetic creativity, so we became—what an irony—"Bedouins" to rhyme with "Palestine" (In Polish, Beduiny and Palestyny). Awful. But worst than their pathetic chanting, they "smelled" a Jew, which was not difficult because I looked very Semitic. I was about fourteen, tall, and could appear much older. A few of them, armed with bats, started to run after me. It was known that these hooligans often had razor blades fastened to the bats and that they hit hard. I found speed I never knew I possessed. I believe I would have broken the record of a medium distance run. I ran by the Europejski Hotel, then across the Piłsudski Square to Wierzbowa Street, the beginning of the Jewish district. I was safe. They were afraid to pursue me farther.

Wierzbowa and Bielańska streets constituted a promenade. Young Jews flocked there in the afternoons and evenings. The University area was full of NDK trash. Lots of students were members of various NDK affiliates. Of course this incident is a totally nonessential detail compared to the Jewish war experiences, but I cannot discard from my memory the terror I felt at that moment. Mom forbade solitary walks in "dangerous neighborhoods" and that was that. And yet it was the same city where, at the Żoliborz High School, I never experienced the slightest apprehension or felt different even though the majority of my colleagues and teachers were not Jewish. I felt at home there and in fact I was in my city and among friends. This feeling has never left me.

The years 1935–1939 were relatively good for my family. The crisis was over. Dad was working and the threat of financial ruin ceased to hang over our heads. My parents had many friends, led a rich social life, and liked to receive guests. They even talked about going to Paris for a few days, but then the war broke out and like so many plans it never materialized.

Grandma's circle was narrower. Her social life mainly came down to family gatherings of the older generation, typically traditional Friday dinners at the home of her sister, Aunt Ewcia. It was a ritual for which Grandma would get ready with a lot of care. She dressed in her best, usually a dark-colored skirt and a light-colored blouse with a ruffle. She arranged her hair in big waves— Grandma had beautiful hair—and baked a cake, which she took with her to the dinner. Aunt Ewcia and Uncle Isidor lived close by on 32 Nowolipki Street. They had a studio apartment with a kitchen on the first floor, with an entrance from the front gate. From a small hall one turned left to the kitchen, which had a window overlooking the yard, and right to a rather large room crammed with furniture probably dating from when they had a bigger apartment. My uncle made cherry brandy, which he kept in huge glass jars on the outside windowsills. Signs placed diagonally from top to bottom on the outside of the windows said, "Artistic Darning" (each window was made of two framed oblong glass panels and there was one word on each panel). Artistic darning was Aunt Ewcia's profession. Clothes were expensive. It wasn't possible to throw them out as carelessly as we do today. If a hole appeared it had to be darned. And Aunt Ewcia did it beautifully so perhaps her darning was indeed "artistic."

In addition my aunt "turned" clothes. For example, when pants were worn and started to look shiny, yet the fabric was still strong, Aunt Ewcia turned the fabric to the other side and the pants looked "like new." If the fabric had a hole somewhere else, she would darn that too. I don't know why clothes turning was not advertised on the window. Possibly it was understood to be part of "Artistic Darning." My aunt was not tall, rather corpulent with a round face, blue eyes, straight nose, and a beautiful crown of silver-white hair. She didn't "look" Jewish. She must have been very pretty when she was young. I said "when she was young," yet Aunt Ewcia couldn't have been more than sixty-something. At that time it was considered old age because people didn't live as long as they do now. Her husband, Uncle Isidor, also worked at home when he was employed, but his work was done in the kitchen. I don't know what his profession was called, but I will try to describe what he did. My uncle received skins from his employer for making small leather goods, mostly gloves, wallets, etc. They were processed, that is, tanned, typically black or brown. The skins were thick with something like gray pulp on the inner, untreated side; this had to be removed. He would stretch the skins on a big board placed on the sill of the kitchen window. It was the same type of board as used for rolling dough, only bigger. He would fasten a skin to the board with nails with the pulp side facing up. Then the main work began. Uncle Isidor removed the pulp with steady movements of a tool that resembled a cleaver. This instrument's blade came straight from the handle, rather than from its side as with a cleaver. This cleaver-not-a-cleaver had to be held with both hands and constantly sharpened on a special whetstone.

After sharpening, the whetstone was usually dipped in water although sometimes my uncle simply spat on it. Uncle Isidor wore a leather apron with a big front pocket in which he kept the whetstone. This work was difficult and exacting because the skins needed to be thin and delicate and one false move with the cleaver could easily cut and destroy them. Uncle Isidor would be accountable for this. He was a homeworker, paid by the piece, that's it. Vacations, insurance, and eight hour work days weren't for him. He just wanted to have some work. I read that the Bund had tried to organize a union for homeworkers, but without much success.

My uncle looked a bit like his wife, short, rather portly and with a belly. He also had blue eyes, a small nose, and salt and pepper hair. I liked this couple and I liked to watch my uncle work. Their professions—darning, turning clothes, treating skins—didn't bring them much; they barely made ends meet. And they had no children. Grandma said that it was a pity there were no children because Ewcia and Isidor were such good people. God didn't give them any, she would say, although a belief in God really wasn't part of her philosophy of life. Years before, when she was young, sometime near the end of the nineteenth century, she married an anarchist.

Aunt Malcia, Grandma's eldest sister, was a widow and often came to the Friday dinners on Nowolipki Street. In the middle of the 1930s, Aunt Malcia left for Argentina, where her sons had been living since World War I. Grandma's youngest brother, Uncle Wowcio, was a regular guest. Born around 1880, he served ten years in the tsar's army (yes, yes, in the nineteenth century the tsar drafted men for 25 years and only the rich could buy their way out) and participated in the disastrous Japanese War of 1904–1905. He was tall, slim, and perhaps the only one in our family with a mustache (black, shaped like those of almost all the men in the Middle East). His hair was black, thick, cut short, and barely touched by gray. He held himself straight and right away one could recognize him as an old soldier. Uncle Wowcio had the same profession as Uncle Isidor—his brother-in-law had taught him.

Uncle Wowcio married after returning from serving in the tsarist army. He and Aunt Polcia had one son, much older than I and with whom I never became friends. Aunt Polcia was a midwife. In those days women gave birth mostly at home. Midwives were at a premium and my aunt was paid well. When family members were sick, Aunt Polcia took care of them. She had authority equivalent to a doctor's assistant, that is to say she could treat simple illnesses, make injections, for example vaccinations, do cupping, etc. This profession was rather popular, since a doctor's visit was expensive. People saw doctors only in serious cases, often as the last resort. I liked Aunt Polcia. She and Uncle Wowcio lived in the same building as we did, in the front part, on the fifth floor. There was no elevator. Aunt Polcia died of cancer in 1933 or 1934 and for the first time I encountered the death of someone close. A funeral procession formed in our yard. I went to the funeral and to the cemetery and it affected me profoundly. For a while I was afraid of death and of darkness. After some time it stopped.

After my aunt's death, Uncle Wowcio was not able to afford the apartment and had to take in several lodgers. Cardboard walls were placed in the hallway and strangers hovered everywhere. I stopped going there. One day in the summer, possibly before Aunt Polcia's death, I saw Uncle Wowcio sitting at a table in a coffee shop on Leszno, very close to Karmelicka Street. A green railing placed on the sidewalk in front of the café separated the tables from passersby, as it is commonly done. I saw that my uncle was playing chess in the company of a stranger. Later I found out that he played splendidly. At the café he generally played for money, one zloty a game. Mostly he won and that's probably how he made extra money. People liked to play against him and even to lose precisely because he was so good. He told me that he had played a lot during his longtime military service. Dad thought that Uncle Wowcio had a great deal of natural talent, but that he didn't know chess theory and didn't treat the game seriously enough. He seldom played with me and won whenever he wanted to. In the summer when he played outside in the "garden" I could observe him. Uncle Wowcio wasn't grim, but serious and taciturn. Unlike Uncle Isidor, he seldom smiled and was not easily likeable.

Of Mom's generation, her cousin Rudek Grycendler visited Aunt Ewcia from time to time on Friday evenings. Rudek was the nephew of Wowcio and of the three sisters. His father hadn't been alive for a long time. I never knew him. Rudek was perhaps the most prosperous of the entire family. I'm not sure what he did. Occasionally he would give me very good penknives. It was said in the family that Rudek represented foreign businesses producing metal accessories, including, of course, penknives. Rudek was always well dressed, wore three-piece suits with waistcoats and elegant shirts with stiff collars. He was always calm and somewhat stand-offish. He would never fail to bring good things to the Friday dinners: chocolates, etc.

Rudek lived with his wife Irena and daughter Krysia on Elektoralna Street in a nice, front-side apartment on the second floor. It was there that for the first time I saw a telephone. My parents, Grandma, and I visited them on New Year's Day, but seldom otherwise. My family said that Irena wore a pound of powder, rouge, and lipstick on her face. Moreover, she was a melodramatic snob who wanted so badly to show how assimilated she was that she pretended not to know Yiddish at all. This certainly was not true and the family didn't like it. Krysia was a few years younger than I, slight, pretty, with big black eyes and dark complexion. She was almost pathologically shy and seldom lifted her gaze higher than the tips of her shoes. She blushed constantly. In my parents' opinion Irena was silly and didn't know how to raise Krysia. Rudek was spending Fridays at Aunt Ewcia's because it was an opportunity to be as far away as possible from his wife. Irena was scared to death that by accident Krysia might hear something about sex. When she thought a conversation might be heading in an "improper" direction, she immediately delivered a bilingual expression: *Attention, das kind!*

Krysia was learning French. In Irena's view it was an elegant language of high society, *de rigueur* for her daughter. But Krysia knew no German and not a word of Yiddish was allowed in her presence. Hence Krysia was meant to understand the first part of the expression, but wasn't supposed to be able to guess that it was all about her. The others were expected to comprehend the hint and interrupt the dangerous conversation. For years the entire family laughed to tears at this nonsense.

Food at Aunt Ewcia's Friday dinners was always the same: stuffed carp in aspic with challah, followed by country-style cottage cheese (fresh and very tasty), various jams, breads, and butter. The dessert, often brought by my grandma, was served with tea. It was usually a pound cake or a honey cake, less often an apple cake. The sisters drank cherry brandy and Uncle Isidor and Rudek—cherry infusion. Uncle Isidor added alcohol to the residue left after straining the brandy and that's how he made the infusion. Wowcio didn't drink it. Instead a quarter of a liter of pure alcohol was placed next to his plate, a habit left from his time in the tsarist army. Wowcio poured the alcohol into a tiny glass, drank it in one gulp and usually said, "Why should I drink two glasses of vodka when I can drink one glass of pure alcohol." This is a literal translation which doesn't even begin to recreate Wowcio's melodious, Yiddish chant: *far vus zol ich trinken zvey gleyzelach bronfn, az ich ken trinken ayn gleyzele spirt.* The table was covered with a white tablecloth and two candles were lit. Hence it seemed that the tradition was being fulfilled, though neither a prayer nor a blessing was said. The uncles frequented a synagogue quite haphazardly. They didn't take the reform "German" synagogue on Daniłowiczowska Street seriously because women sat there together with men and who had seen such a thing? Moreover, it was a place for the rich, not for *pushet Isroel* (ordinary Jews). They claimed that many people didn't walk to this synagogue, but came by horse carriage or by taxi and that they got off of their carriage out of view to hide their sin since it was forbidden to ride on the Sabbath. For years they went to a small synagogue they called shtibl (literally: tiny room). This one wasn't ideal either and they complained about the rabbi, an orthodox one of course, who in their opinion was an ignoramus. The two brothers-in-law looked funny coming back together from the synagogue, the tall, slim Wowcio with a rather stern face and next to him the rotund Isidor, reaching to his shoulder, always with a smile. They wore their dark suits and black hats for special occasions and carried prayer books and a tallit (a white ceremonial prayer shawl) under their arms. That's how they remain in my memory. Women didn't go to a synagogue, except perhaps during high holidays.

After the Friday dinner, the women cleared the table and the whole group would sit to play "Red king," a totally non-hazardous card game. Stakes were minimal and we had a tradition that the winner would give the money to me and my cousin Janek, four years my senior, for "movie tickets." Janek came there on Fridays less often than I, but Krysia never went at all. Perhaps her mother forbade it, but how could she? They were just ordinary Jews who, although they spoke Polish well, often switched to Yiddish when they weren't paying attention. My grandma, her siblings and brother-in-law didn't have many pleasant activities and amusements except for Friday dinners.

After the war, I didn't find my beloved grandma Helenka or the beautiful and nice Aunt Ewcia, nor the serene Isidor, nor the tsarist soldier and chess player Wowcio. They had all perished. Solid Rudek, his crazy wife Irena, and shy Krysia, about whom we used to say that her enormous black eyes were filled with the sadness of two thousand years of galut (exile) perished as well. The Holocaust spared none of them.

At the beginning of the 1930s I spent a lot of time with Janek. His parents, Łucja (my mom's cousin) and her husband Bernard, were extraordinarily popular and widely liked Bund activists. They were my parents' close friends and neither Janek nor I had siblings. I was impressed by Janek because he was older, but he would brazenly use our age difference to his advantage. For example, when we played horses at Aunt Ewcia's on Friday evenings he would invariably be the driver while I was the horse. I was prodded around the table where the adults played cards. Another example: Uncle Isidor had a big, gold, round watch on a chain (perhaps it was gold-plated, I don't know) in his waistcoat. Such a watch was called an onion—one pushed a little spring in the onion's lid and the watch face became visible. While now it's a rarity, at that time a gold onion fastened to a gold chain was a sign of a certain social standing, or at least a desire for it. Janek bragged to me that he would inherit our uncle's onion because he was older and Uncle Isidor had no children. As boys we would sometimes spend summers outside of Warsaw. In our games I was generally the "pale face" while he was an Indian who would shoot me with a bow and arrow or scalp me. That's how it went. Mom checked on us from time to time and the games drove her crazy. We were close friends and during the last two to three years before the war, Janek treated me mostly, but not entirely, as an equal.

In the second half of the 1930s, Janek's parents got divorced and his mom left for Argentina, where her brothers were living. Janek stayed in Poland with his dad. Through Janek I met a group of his colleagues and friends; many of them, including Janek, later became accomplished adults.

Janek's fate during the war was extraordinary. After escaping from Warsaw in September 1939, he found himself in Vilnius, which became part of the quasi-independent Lithuanian Republic under the Soviet protectorate. In 1941, he obtained a USA visa and traveled by train across Russia to China, where he was supposed to board a ship for the States. But the Japanese attacked Pearl Harbor and Janek sat out the entire war in China. He learned the language and by the end of the war was working as a translator at the Polish consulate. Because of that the Americans decided that he was a communist "diplomat" and retracted the visa. So Janek spent his entire life in the Far East. After the communist takeover of China, he moved to Tokyo and later to Hong Kong. Upon retiring he settled in Israel, where his daughter and her family were living. As a young man in China he started working at the lowest clerical level in a big Anglo-American business. With time he became its president and a wealthy man. We got together in the 1970s and 1980s when he came to New York on business. He visited us at home and me at the University. I think that we both tried to become closer. It should have been easy. We could reminisce about our childhood and our families; we both subscribed to the same papers (and of course to the Bund's *Unzer tsayt*) and also Jerzy Giedroyc's leftist *Kultura* from Paris (the best Polish publication in exile advocating the country's sovereignty). He did this from Tokyo and I from New York. Yet despite all this we really weren't able to reconnect in a meaningful way. We had lived too long in totally different environments without any personal contact with each other, and friendships need to be nurtured. Janek died in 1997 in Israel. His dad Bernard had died in 1959 in New York and his mom Łucja in Buenos Aires in the 1960s. They are buried on three continents. That is the lot of the Jewish people.

There was an eye-catching, enormous sign: "Production and Sales of Umbrellas" on the second floor level of the building at the corner of Nalewki and Świętojerska streets, right across from the Krasińskich Garden. Two of my

Mom's cousins, Mela and Henia, had inherited that business from their parents and managed it before the war. Mom was good friends with the younger one, Mela. After a long engagement, Mela got married a few years before the war and moved out of the big family apartment that she had shared with her sister. This multi–room, privately owned apartment, together with the workshop, the store, and the office, occupied the building's entire second floor. When I was young I really liked that place. It was very different from our apartment. I could run back and forth between the residential part to the workshop, watch the workers and observe the very busy street from the balcony. Nalewki was the Jewish district's main commercial street. Stores and workshops were everywhere: on buildings' front sides and in courtyards on first, second, and even third floors. One could buy all kinds of things, but perhaps the majority were shops selling fabrics and off the rack clothing. Many years ago, little streets of New York's "Lower East Side" reminded me of Nalewki. Maybe this is why I had a fondness for them, a nostalgia that in fact is not entirely justified.

Mela's husband Adaś was an optometric technician and worked in a store in the city's very good Polish district, far on Marszałkowska Street. This man had an unparalleled ability to whistle beautifully, particularly classical music. He used only his lips and sometimes modulated with his hand. He had chestnut hair, a pug nose, blue eyes, and didn't look at all Jewish. This turned out to be very useful in the last years preceding the war because even during the time of "Jews not welcome" signs, he didn't lose his job. But his Aryan looks didn't help him during the war. Adaś, Mela, and their little baby perished in the Holocaust.

At the time when Mela moved out, or perhaps a little earlier, the umbrella business ceased to prosper. I noticed this by the apartment's shrinking size. In addition to the store and the workshop only two rooms were left, one with an alcove, and a kitchen. The spot where a door to other rooms used to be was walled up; apparently they were let to other tenants. And then Henia, the older sister who was managing the business, got married. The marriage was arranged; Henia was neither young nor particularly pretty. The wedding was traditional, the reception sumptuous with many guests, a band, a rabbi, and a chupa, that is, a canopy under which the couple stood during the ceremony. This was the first and the last time that I saw such a celebration before the war. It took place in a private party hall on Bielańska Street. The newlyweds' happiness didn't last because it soon turned out that Miron, the groom, who was no longer a young man, was also not a decent person. He pretended to be wealthy and wore a bowler hat and a white silk scarf with an elegant dark coat. But he was lazy and didn't apply himself at all to his work at the firm. It was said among family members that things were even worse then they appeared. He played cards and was losing the rest of Henia's money. He was originally from Kowno, a small city in eastern Poland (now known as Kaunas in Lithuania), so the Nowolipki crowd, who for generations had been Warsaw inhabitants, looked down at him. Moreover, he feigned his non-existent affluence when he frequented the reformed synagogue on Tłomackie Street. Wowcio and Isidor held it against him that he and Henia, who had become devout under his influence, lit candles on Friday, but served ham. The problem was not so much the ham, since the in-laws weren't very strict about keeping kosher, but they minded the hypocrisy of having lit candles and ham. Miron once took me to synagogue with him. I think that was the only time that I attended a service before the war.

A year, perhaps a year and a half after her wedding, Henia was diagnosed with cancer. Grandma said that Henia got sick from worrying. She had wanted so much to have a husband that she finally married a loser. In a bed in the alcove behind a curtain, Henia suffered and slowly faded away. The business ceased to exist. Nobody was making umbrellas any more and they sold the rest of the stock. Mela with her baby often visited her sister. I went there together with Grandma and Mom as well. Henia's funeral was exceptionally depressing and sad. After her death, Nalewki Street ceased to exist. That's how the wealthier part of my impoverished family came to an end. I know nothing about Miron. I don't think I looked for him after the war.

When I was eight or nine I got scarlet fever. I couldn't stay at home because Mom was receiving customers, young girls, and scarlet fever is especially contagious. I spent six weeks in Aunt Justynka Kerner's (née Fajnsztein) apartment on 49 Królewska Street. Justynka was Mom's father's sister. From the time of my illness I remember her as the personification of kindness. My parents and Grandma visited me often. One day they gave me a radio. This rather primitive device brought great joy to my monotonous existence and I fiddled with it endlessly. Justynka and her husband Jakub had two children: Tuśka, who was much older than I and taught me to read, and Semek, with whom I often played. He was four or five years older. Uncle Jakub, Justynka's husband, worked in hat production. We called him an "expert" because it was not respectable to have a manual worker in our family. Financially they fared very poorly.

Jakub and Semek immigrated to Argentina in 1934 while my aunt and Tuśka stayed in Warsaw, since they didn't have enough money for ship fare (it was then called "shifscarta") for all four of them. Also, beginning in a new country is usually very difficult for women. They got rid of their apartment on Królewska Street and moved in with us. Therefore one more folding metal bed was placed in the room where Grandma and I slept and where Mom's workshop functioned in the daytime. After nearly a year, my uncle and Semek brought them both to Argentina. This is how this part of the family found itself outside the reach of the Holocaust and survived. Was it a coincidence? Of course I corresponded with them immediately after the war, but none of them are still alive and I have nothing in common with Semek's children. Tuśka got married in Argentina and had no children.

Adam Fajnsztein, Mom's uncle, his wife Mania, and son Mietek lived on 5 Żabia Street across from the entrance to the Saski Garden. Adam was Justynka's brother and Mania was Jakub Kerner's sister: two sets of siblings who married among themselves. Mietek was Semek's age and also a good friend of mine. This family fared badly as well. They had a canteen on Solna Street called "Home Cooking." The food was very good and much less expensive than at a restaurant. They served neither wine nor vodka. There were many such places in Warsaw at the time. Aunt Mania, a rather portly woman, stood at the stove cooking while Uncle Adam, in a waiter's white coat and with a white towel on his left arm, seated the diners and served. Sometimes (but very seldom) I had dinner there and was always cordially received. Apparently "Home Cooking" didn't do well in the city during the summer. So to make ends meet, my uncle and aunt were forced to manage a guesthouse, usually in Kazimierz Dolny, a picturesque and popular summer spot on the Vistula River near Puławy. And this family, my uncle, aunt, and Mietek, also perished in the Holocaust.

Mietek, Semek, and a third cousin, Bernard, were big, strong boys. They were called the "kings" of Saski Garden or at least of the part near Żabna Street. Being younger I was under their protection and no one was allowed to pick on me or to beat me up. This provided a strong sense of security, especially on the soccer field, where it was easy to be walloped by the older boys. Bernard Fiszer, a cousin many times removed whose war experience was similar to mine, became one of my closest friends ever. His mother, Aunt Andzia, was Jakub Kerner's and Aunt Mania's sister. Aunt Andzia and Uncle Natan were exceptionally fine, kindhearted and lovely people. They were among those few in our family whom the Holocaust didn't claim. They spent the war years in Russia and lived until old age in Lodz.

My parents had a large circle of friends and acquaintances in pre-war Poland, much bigger than my wife and I had in Warsaw after the war. Most of their friends were Jewish and typically associated with the Bund, but not all. Lutka, my Mom's closest friend, had a unique place compared to other friends. This was an extraordinary friendship, a friendship that lasted more than years because it continued for generations. I suddenly realized that about a hundred years ago from this moment—this being 2006—the two girls, Karola and Lutka, sat down at the same school desk in tsarist Warsaw. And they continued sitting at this desk for two (in Poland, school desks were always for two) until 1919, when they both graduated. I have Mom's photo from that year: she is wearing a black high school uniform with an ankle-length skirt, a white lace collar and cuffs, with her hair in a bun and low-heeled shoes hardly showing from underneath the skirt. She is lovely and delicate. She is sitting at a bamboo desk that was then fashionable and is writing, or rather pretending to be writing, since the photo certainly was posed.

My family from Argentina sent me this, along with some other old photos, right after the war. In some, taken some years before my birth, one can see quite a few family members whom I have described: Grandma Helenka, Wowcio and Polcia with their son, Łucja and Bernard, Henia and Mela, and some others. And in each of them, the only non-family member: Lutka, either alone or later, after getting married, with Michał. The pictures were taken at a photographer's studio. I think that it was an expensive and complicated undertaking, since a good number of people had to be assembled at the same time in one studio. Such photos demonstrate close ties between people. I am touched when I see,

Figure 6 The family, 1922. Sitting, second from left Grandma Helenka Feinstein (maiden name Grycendler), fourth my mother. Standing, second from left Uncle Wowcio Grycendler, officer to the tsar (mustache!) and a fine chess player, third Lutka Flutsztejn, my mother's best friend, fourth her husband Michał, fifth my father Michał (Misha) Szer, seventh Uncle Bernard Goldsztajn, a well known Bund activist.

in our two daughters' homes, Lutka's face among the framed pictures of Felusia and of my family. Indeed she was their true grandmother in post-war Warsaw. That's what they called her when they were little. She was a wonderful grandmother for them and they had no other. She replaced Karola, and I believe that her friendship with Lutka was one of my mother's most beautiful chapters in her short life.

Among our friends, only Lutka and her family did not live in Warsaw. Both she and Michał lived in Miedzeszyn and commuted to work in Warsaw by electric train. Their house was small and modern; Michał's sister and her family lived with them as well. It stood on a large, nicely wooded plot. Many friends and acquaintances visited Michał and Lutka in Miedzeszyn because their house was welcoming and open and so totally different from all Warsaw apartments. We also visited often, especially on Sundays in the summer. We went on beautiful walks in the direction of the Vistula. Sometimes I played chess with Michał, and I always lost. It was only after the war that I was able to win against him for the first time. I was somewhat more successful playing my dad and he was always proud of me when I won—that's how it is. Mom liked and valued Michał. She considered him to be smart and straightforward—she used this precise word "straightforward"—often holding him up as a role model for me. These were very pleasant gatherings that sometimes turned hilarious—Michał was a witty man, as was Dad. To this Adam would add by whistling Beethoven symphonies. Still, the shadow of Nazi Germany hung above all this. There were ceaseless discussions about what was happening to Jews in Germany and speculation on how this would influence attitudes in Poland, in Europe, etc., and on how it would end. I listened and absorbed it all. Yet, in hindsight these conversations seem not really serious. The true magnitude of the threat was never grasped. But who could have known how it would develop?

Hitler wasn't the only danger hanging over us. There were other, closer ones. NDK gangs were rampant at universities. The year after Piłsudski's death a pogrom occurred in the tiny town of Przytyk, near Radom. Later, in 1937, there was a pogrom in Mińsk Mazowiecki near Warsaw and another in Brześć on the Bug River in 1939, among others. These are known facts. It's true that the perpetrators were prosecuted, but for us it was small comfort. Not everyone was anti-Semitic, of course. Vast sections of the Polish population opposed these anti-Semitic actions. For example, PPS and the entire left, numerous Piłsudski supporters, liberal intellectual elites, and interestingly, many members of the Polish aristocratic families like the Radziwiłłs opposed anti-Semitism.

Was a majority of the population opposed? I can't say for certain, but I do not think so.

While German fascism threatened from the west, a different threat, not as easy to recognize in the 1930s, lay to the east. A year or two before the war, Dad gave me a small Yiddish book by Victor Alter to read called *Proletariat's Dictatorship*. It's hard to imagine a more devastating critique of Soviet Russia under the communist party's rule. Victor Alter and Henryk Erlich, two legendary Bund leaders of that time, were not just respected and popular, but also extremely well liked. They were also known outside Poland, since they were both members of the second Socialist International's executive committee together with the heads of all European socialist and social-democratic parties and the British Labor Party. After the beginning of the war, they found themselves in eastern Poland under Soviet occupation and were immediately arrested by the NKVD (Narodnyi Komissariat Vnutriennikh Diel; People's Commissariat for Internal Affairs). Since the Bolshevik revolution of 1917, this secret soviet political police had changed its name several times and at the end was known as the KGB. No matter what they were called, they were always criminals and murderers.

After the German invasion of Russia in June 1941, the Soviet government, for propaganda purposes, created the Jewish Anti-Fascist Committee. It included many well known people from the west of Jewish origins: artists, writers, and scientists (almost all of the Committee members were murdered shortly after the war). The idea was to improve the opinion about the Soviet Union in the USA and in England. Erlich and Alter were offered the opportunity to participate in the Committee and they decided they could not refuse. They reasoned that any action that supported the war against fascism should be pursued. They were suddenly arrested in December 1941, six months after Hitler's invasion of Russia, when the Germans were on the outskirts of Moscow and the situation was dire. Even with the very existence of the Soviet Union in question, its leaders nonetheless found the time and resources to murder[28] two old Jews. "Socialists fascists" is what the communists contemptuously and hatefully called Bund members, as well as all socialists and social democrats, that is, people linked to the Second International. But the Soviets didn't just hate the Bund. Immediately after the war ended, almost all of the Anti-Fascist Committee's members were also murdered. Some years later, shortly after the

---

[28] Tr: The most recent reseach has revealed that Erlich committed suicide in prison and that the Soviets, not sure how to reveal this, subsequently executed Alter.

United Nations was founded, Eleanor Roosevelt demanded an accounting of why Erlich and Alter were shot. Andrei Gromyko, the Soviet representative at the United Nations answered that such punishment was justified because, objectively speaking, they had acted to the detriment of Soviet Russia's war efforts. It was incredible that the Soviets would reiterate such false charges.

I was in New York in 1991 at a fiftieth anniversary memorial of the murders. Some Bund members were still around, living in the city. Erlich's younger son Viktor, a retired professor of Slavic literature at Yale, was in attendance. The Russian ambassador had announced his presence, but had seemingly other, more important things to do because he sent some pen pusher from the embassy to read an excerpt from a decree that Erlich and Alter had been "rehabilitated." And that was that. I wanted to throw up. The term "rehabilitation" reminds me of a macabre joke my dad once told me. Felix Edmundovich Dzerzhinsky, the creator of Bolshevik secret police in 1918, who was admiringly referred to by communists as "Iron Felix, the revolution's sword and shield," was supervising construction of orphanages for homeless children and youth who flocked to Russian cities as the result of the revolution and the civil war. Well yes, Dad would say, first he murdered the parents and later he built dwellings for the orphans.

Dzerzhinsky, just like Piłsudski, was born during the second half of the nineteenth century to a family of Polish landowners in Lithuania. It was a profoundly patriotic milieu deeply entrenched in the traditions of the January Uprising. And what of it? One grew up to be a hero that Poland hadn't had for centuries, while the other became one of greatest villains of the twentieth century. American Sovietologists (after the empire's fall this term is falling into disuse, but there is nothing to regret in the end of either the term or the empire) insisted that Iron Felix should be placed in the select company of the most horrendous murderers of the twentieth century, next to Himmler[29] and Beria.[30]

If the return to the Spanish Inquisition is necessary for building socialism, it's better to do without socialism. These prophetic words were written soon after the Bolshevik revolution by no other than Włodzimierz Medem, a man

---

[29] Tr: Heinrich Lutipold Himmler (1900–1945): leader of the SS, one of the most powerful men in Nazi Germany, one of the persons most directly responsible for the Holocaust.

[30] Tr: Lavrentiy Pavlovich Beria (1899–1953): Soviet politician, chief of the Soviet secret police apparatus (NKVD) during World War II, deputy Premier (1946–1953). Beria administered the Gulag labor camps and carried out purges in which hundreds of thousands of people were arrested and killed. After the war he organized the communist takeover of Central and Eastern Europe.

respected by European and American Jews for his great intellect and moral authority and the most outstanding Bund activist at the beginning of the twentieth century. Already by 1928 Medem had written that Lenin's "socialism" without democracy not only made no sense, but that it would lead to dictatorship and crime.[31] Medem died young, in 1923. When I was a child my parents would tell me that I had been named after him—such practices were popular then. Even Rosa Luxemburg (an opponent of the Bund, although not a Lenin proponent), a fanatic who believed that nations subjugated by the tsars wouldn't need independence since the victorious socialist revolution would fulfill all of their objectives, said the following about the Bolshevik revolution: "The means invented by Lenin and Trotsky, that is, democracy's total abolishment are worse than the evil that was to be defeated by those means."[32] She continued: "Without general elections, without unrestricted freedom of the press and assembly, without a free expression of opinion, life dies out in every public institution and becomes a mere semblance of life in which only the bureaucracy remains as the active element. . . . Yes, we can go even further: such conditions must inevitably cause a brutalization of public life." We should add that Luxemburg, one of the tsar's subjects, was imprisoned in solitary confinement by the Prussians during World War I, without access to newspapers. She was freed after November 11, 1918—not immediately, as they were malicious—and only then did she learn about the so-called October Revolution, or Bolshevik coup d'état. The same Prussian military murdered her in a most horrific manner in mid-January 1919, less than two months after her liberation. Hence she had little time to write what I have quoted. But one cannot deny the clarity of her vision and intellect.

When I was in elementary school I belonged to SKIF (Sozialistischer Kinder-Farband—Children Socialist Alliance) circle (krayz in Yiddish). In fact, nearly all the students at this school were members of SKIF. Later in high school I joined Cukunft (Future), a young adults' organization. Both SKIF and Cukunft were connected to the Bund. My leader in SKIF was Josef Młotek, who after the war was a well known Jewish culture activist in New York, and in Cukunft—the aforementioned Victor Erlich, who was then a university student. This children's organization resembled the boy scouts and engaged in out

---

[31] Au: Quote from Irving Howe, *World of our Fathers* (New York: Harcourt Brace Jovanovich, 1976), 328–330 and 541–542; see also Emanuel Nowogrodzki, *The Jewish Labor Bund in Poland* (Rockville, MD: Shengold Books, 2001), 96–98.

[32] Au: Quote from Robert Conquest, *The Great Terror* (Warszawa: Michał Urbański Publishers, 1997).

of town excursions, games, singing (mainly folk Jewish songs), stage plays, a bit of historical reenactments like fights against tsarism, famous fighters who had perished in those struggles, and the like. What remained with me after several years in SKIF, besides a sentiment for Jewish songs, was perhaps some feeling of responsibility for others, maybe a little altruism. I suppose the organizers had nothing else in mind. Similar guidelines provided blueprints for the counselors at the Włodzimierz Medem Sanatorium[33] in Miedzeszyn near Warsaw, where I once spent winter vacation when I was nine or ten. Here the leading theme was the kids' self-government. Children themselves organized stage plays, various interest groups or clubs for chess, reading, art, etc. The counselors were wonderful pedagogues who in fact directed it all in a smart and subtle manner. It was a beautiful enterprise. The grounds and buildings were nice as well. Until the war, more than ten thousand children, mostly from very poor families, went through the Sanatorium. It was the Bund's pride and the apple of its eye. There is only one dissonant note in my otherwise idyllic memory—cod liver oil! Every day we had to swallow a tablespoon of that disgusting grease, from whale or perhaps cod? I don't know and I don't wish to know. It was then believed to be a panacea for all kinds of ailments and was a mandatory component of children's diets. I did all I could to weasel out from this abomination, but it wasn't easy. In August 1942, the Włodzimierz Medem Sanatorium ceased to exist. Teachers, children, everyone that the Germans could catch were deported to Treblinka. They all perished in the Holocaust.

Cukunft was a big organization for young adult Bundists from workers' families. Polish was spoken at meetings because many participants didn't know Yiddish. Here there was a lot of Marxist theory. Of course of the "good" one, and there were the two Karls (the second one was Kautsky),[34] and the theories of national and cultural autonomies, initiated in the nineteenth century mostly by Austrian social democracy (this was important in the Austro-Hungarian monarchy, populated by many nations); Bund principles. Such people as Lenin, Trotsky, and the like, without even mentioning Stalin, were the greatest enemies.

---

[33] Tr: The Medem Sanatorium: an educational and clinical facility for Jewish youth at risk for tuberculosis, established in 1926 by the Bund and CYSHO. Until World War II, it was recognized internationally by its reformist pedagogical approach and its leftist orientation. Closed in 1939, it was soon reopened. In 1942 the children and remaining staff were deported to Treblinka.

[34] Tr: Karl Johann Kautsky (1854–1938): Czech-German philosopher, journalist, Social Democrat theoretician, and supporter of Marxism who, after the war, became an ardent critic of the Bolshevik Revolution.

It took me a long time and I needed my American experience to talk myself out of that "good" Marxism as well. So nothing has been left? No, it has, but it cannot be called Marxism. But that's for later—everything in its own time.

In the years immediately preceding the war, when we were doing better, many people visited us at home. My parents were hospitable and liked to receive guests and Mom was a great cook. There was a variety of occasions for parties, from birthdays to all kinds of anniversaries. Traditionally my parents' friends gathered there on May 1, after the Bund rally. Yes, for my generation May Day and marching through the city streets in "People's" Poland was a hassle and everyone tried to get out of it the best they could. But for my parents it was a real holiday. Dad always participated in the march and Mom often did as well. I took part in it for two or three years before the war, together with my Cukunft group. Ten to twelve people, all close friends, would gather in our apartment at about five in the evening for some drinks after the march. In addition, some of the Bund's prominent activists including Emanuel Nowogrodzki, the Central Committee's secretary, and Shlomo Mendelson, an outstanding journalist, would stop by for a short visit. They all wanted to know how others assessed the march, whether it had been attended by more people than the year before, how it had gone in other cities beside Warsaw, where demonstrations joined those of PPS, whether there had been altercations with the police, or if the communists provoked anyone—it was authentic, deeply interesting, and lively, with loud arguments and good conversation. Communist instigators were typically groups of young people who would suddenly jump from the sidewalk to the street to join the Bund marchers, usually at the end of their line. They would shout pro-Soviet slogans and demand that the government be overthrown by force, which was illegal. The groups often carried signs, which they would quickly unfurl and hang on electric wires above streetcar rails where they were difficult to remove. Police just waited for this in order to intervene, hit random marchers with their sticks, and sometimes make arrests. The Bund safety protection service, sometimes called self-defense since its main aim was defending Jews against anti-Semitic violence, attempted to prevent such incidents. Its leader was my Uncle Bernard, widely liked and admired for his courage and composure. He was called "Bund General." Bernard was an activist in the porters union, naturally strong guys who made up his "army." They had no uniforms, but they could be easily identified as they all wore tight knee socks, knickerbockers, and cycling caps. They used canes with curved handles as their weapons. Those handles had a purpose. At numerous rallies and events, which were often held at the Nowości Theater on Bielańska Street, crowds would often rush to the entrance. Since there wasn't enough room for everyone, Bernard's army would hook together the canes' handles and form a barrier to stop people. When I was little they would let me through under the canes, knowing that I was "family." This used to make me very proud. Some of Bernard's men, for example Hershele Małymatek, became "heroes" of Warsaw folklore. Rumors had it that Hershele, a short, stocky, powerfully built man, was able to guzzle half a liter of vodka in one gulp while standing up . . . and on an empty stomach. It was called "little mother"; a whole liter was "mother." We won't inquire whether this story was absolutely true or not.

Cukunft had its safety protection service as well, called Cukunft-Shturm. Its members wore blue shirts and red ties and Sam Browne belts.[35] While "on duty" they lowered the strap of the cap under the chin to look very daring. At various demonstrations they carried flags with three parallel arrows, the Second International's symbol. Their leader was Berek Sznajdmil, one of my parents' closest friends, who was slightly younger than they were. I loved him a lot. When I was older he treated me as an equal and not as a nipper. Shortly before the war he invited me to share vodka with him at Gertner's, a popular dive on Leszno near Przejazd Street. This was the real proof that I was almost an adult. Berek was a bachelor. He had blue eyes and "good" appearance and worked at a travel agency in the Polish district. At work he was called Adam Młynarski (Sznajdmil=Młynarski). He joked that, when needed, he organized pilgrimages to Jasna Góra in Częstochowa. Berek was a cadet sergeant, which meant that he had received training at a military school and had finished the required military preparation after graduating from high school. He should have been promoted to second lieutenant in the military reserve, but these were the late 1930s and Jews were no longer given officer ranks. Berek felt that this was very unfair (which it was) and he felt hurt. In the ghetto he was active in the Jewish Combat Organization.[36] He was killed in Warsaw at the uprising[37] headquarters' bunker on Miła Street in 1943.

---

[35] Tr: Sam Browne belt, often a part of military or police uniforms, is a wide, usually leather belt supported by a narrower strap passing diagonally over the right shoulder.

[36] Tr: Jewish Combat Organization (Żydowska Organizacja Bojowa or ŻOB): World War II Jewish resistance movement, instrumental in organizing the Warsaw Ghetto Uprising.

[37] Tr: Warsaw Ghetto Uprising: April 1943 rebellion in the Warsaw Ghetto, the largest single revolt by Jews during World War II. Its aim was to oppose Nazi Germany's attempt to transport the remaining Ghetto population to the Treblinka extermination camp. The inadequately armed and poorly supplied fighters were defeated by the Germans, and the Ghetto was liquidated in May 1943.

In 1937 I had my thirteenth birthday, which typically was celebrated as a Bar Mitzvah in traditional Jewish families. But for me this was not an option because my parents had nothing to do with faith and I did not receive any religious preparation. Also, the Bund discouraged such activities. In fact, a prominent Bund member invited to my party announced that if Włodek's thirteenth birthday was going to be celebrated in a grander way than, say, the twelfth, he wouldn't attend! Today it sounds ridiculous and petty, but it was different then. A total rejection of religion or of tradition linked to religion was a reaction typical of people from his generation (Shloyme Mendelson was a little older than my parents) to what they perceived as rabbis' and melameds' backwardness.[38] Their atheism was a legacy of the Jewish Renaissance that took place in the second half of the eighteenth and the first half of the nineteenth centuries. It was the conviction of Shloyme Mendelson, a secular Jew and an atheist, a man who was promulgating Jewish culture—and doing it very well indeed—that he represented the true Yiddishkeit (Jewishness), and not those ignoramuses with clothes straight from the Middle Ages. In addition, he believed in democratic socialism. What could be better? In those days in Poland, just like now in the United States, in order to be a Jew one didn't have to belong to a religious congregation or a synagogue. As a result of Jewish integration, the Yiddish language and culture ended up here—perhaps irreversibly—in the realm of nostalgia and skansen. Even the great actress Ida Kamińska,[39] who emigrated to the States after the infamous March of 1968[40] (I used to meet her from time to time in New York), was not able to revive the Yiddish theater. Irving Howe wrote beautifully and wisely about these issues in his book *World of our Fathers.*[41]

I am now more forgiving toward the world of provincial, superstitious, orthodox Jews of those years because this world disappeared from Europe

---

[38] Au: Melamed: a teacher at a cheder, a religious school with elementary level teaching.

[39] Tr: Ida Kamińska (1899–1980): Polish-born Yiddish actress, founder and director of the Jewish Theater in Warsaw, she performed on stage and in films and achieved international stature.

[40] Tr: The Polish crisis of 1968, also known in Poland as March 1968 or as March events, was a major student and intellectual protest against the communist government. Security forces suppressed student strikes in major academic institutions; this was followed by repression of dissident movement. A mass emigration of Jews, a result of an anti-Semitic campaign disguised as an "anti-Zionist" government's stance, emptied Poland of most of its Jewish population.

[41] Au: Irving Howe, *World of our Fathers* (New York and London: Harcourt Brace Jovanovich, 1976).

suddenly and tragically, and no world should vanish in such a way. If not for the Holocaust, that society would have had to become emancipated; otherwise the young would have left it. One can see remnants of that world in Brooklyn or Jerusalem. Still, I feel disheartened when I read about the idolatrous adoration the Lubavicher Hassidim have for their rabbi, Menachem Shneerson, who died in 1994 in Brooklyn, declaring him the messiah. I also find the physical brawls they have between Hassidic clans truly depressing.

My thirteenth birthday was not celebrated in any remarkable manner, with one exception. Grandma Helenka, who had never been impressed by either the Bund or Yiddish, bought her grandson a beautiful Swiss watch with the money she saved from Ciechocinek. It was an expensive present and Grandma thus conveyed in her own way that this wasn't just any birthday. I had that watch until the fall of 1944, when I was wounded at the outskirts of Praga near Warsaw. When I regained consciousness while being transported during the chilly night to the hospital I realized that the watch was gone; one of the sawbones had stolen it (that's how all people connected with healthcare from paramedic up were called in the military).

Of all three sisters, my grandma Helenka was the most assimilated and truly fond of Polish culture. She read only Polish books. For years I slept in the same room with her and observed her reading habits. Every night before reading she would place a glass saucer filled with water on a chair at the head of the bed. In this saucer she placed a low candlestick with a single candle. There were electric night lamps at home so I asked Grandma why she wasn't using them. She answered that she had been used to this since her youth and she liked candle's yellowish light, and that she was going to keep it that way. To put out the candle, she wet two fingertips in the water and touched the wick. Then Grandma cleaned her fingers with a napkin, which was always lying on the chair. Among her favorite authors were Żeromski, Prus,[42] Orzeszkowa, and other classics of nineteenth-century Polish prose, mostly the positivists. We had many of those books at home. Sundays Grandma bought *Our Review*, a well edited paper for assimilated Polish Jews that espoused Zionism though without much enthusiasm. The Sunday *Our Review* published many death notices, which Grandma read diligently. And now I read a Sunday newspaper supplement with death notices. That's how the world turns. A member of *Our Review's* editorial staff named Regnis (that means Singer, read like in Hebrew from right to left!)

---

[42] Tr: Bolesław Prus (1847–1912), born Aleksander Głowacki: important Polish writer.

became one of best political commentators of the émigré press in London after World War II.

Grandma liked to tell various maxims, which she didn't spare her grandson, as she felt responsible for his upbringing. "Food shouldn't be thrown out because it's a sin and if you throw out bread God will punish you and you will always be hungry." Also, "Put on your plate only as much as you can eat, no more." I have been following it to this day and feel badly when I see the enormous amount of food that is wasted in the United States. If only they listened to my grandma, those rascals!

In Grandma's opinion, the basis of a dinner was soup and the most nutritious soup was beef barley, especially one made with bones. Now it so happened that as a child I didn't like beef barley, not because of its taste, but rather because of how it looked. I was repulsed by its grayish-brown color and its consistency. Usually when Grandma was baking a goose or preparing other delicacies she would call me to the kitchen—without words, just with a familiar gesture and a smile—where I would get some morsels to taste. I liked all giblets, pork cracklings, or cookies.

Grandma also had her opinions about clothes. We are not wealthy, she reasoned, therefore we should not buy shoddy things, because junk, although inexpensive, quickly gets worn out. Hence one should buy good quality things because they would last for a long time. She considered fabrics made in Lodz completely shoddy; those from Bielsk to be somewhat better; English-made, much better; but those made in tsar's factories, such quality existed no more. My beloved grandma Helenka perished in the Holocaust. Uncle Bernard, the only close family member who survived in the Warsaw ghetto, told me that Grandma was lucky because she died in her own bed at her home on Karmelicka Street. True, she died of starvation and cold, but she was spared Umschlagplatz, a cattle car, and Treblinka. Such was Grandma's luck. Bernard told me not to look for a grave at the Okopowa Street Cemetery because in the winter of 1942, when she died, bodies were thrown into common ditches. There was nothing to look for.

Both my parents were high school graduates. This placed them in the social group of those who read books and attended theater and concerts. For the previous generation, especially in Eastern Europe where the percentage of educated people was relatively small, a high school diploma was almost a guarantee of office-level employment. For their generation things were more complicated and, generally, additional professional education was required. I don't want to be misunderstood: in my parents' circles there were many self-taught people with the same or a better education and some more intelligent than high school graduates. My parents belonged to a private reading establishment (that's what libraries were called) and borrowed books for a monthly fee. When a book, usually a novel, became popular, or a writer was widely read and there were few copies avaiable, people had to enter their name on a waiting list (for example for Emil Zegadłowicz's[43] *Zmory* or Dołęga-Mostowicz's[44] *The Career of Nicodemus Dyzma*). Periodically they would send me to the library to find out if the book became available. Shortly before the war, however, we had a telephone installed and we could call the library. The phone was put in mainly for Mom's business, but it seems that it was most often used for conversations with Lutka. I hardly ever used it because very few of my friends had phones at home.

Popular novels by foreign authors in the original language were sometimes immediately available from the library. Books in Polish translation, however, were in great demand and there was typically a long wait to get them even if they were already in bookstores. A novel by the English writer Archibald Cronin, such as *The Citadel*, was a good example (after the war Cronin did not regain his former popularity in Poland). But Mom read it in English and didn't have to be on a waiting list. She knew English because she had spent about a year in the States. So how did Mom get to the States?

One day while browsing through our bookshelves I found a strange document deep behind rows of books, which turned out to be the key to this and a few other family secrets. It was a sheet of thick, handmade paper with numbers and inscriptions, possibly English, as well as some signatures and drawings. It was the first time that I saw something of this kind. Mom explained that these were worthless shares of a non-existent business, a manufacturer of fountain pens started in the States by her dad. At the end of the nineteenth century, my grandfather was an anarchist. In those days anarchism was a rather widespread but not very sensible revolutionary current. Many who participated in the 1905 revolution were exiled to Siberia. Grandpa escaped almost immediately to China and from there made his way to the States. Obviously he was an enterprising man, because once in the States Grandpa ceased to be a revolutionary (he wasn't the only one) and started a business. The business prospered. However, soon after Mom's return from America, the Great Depression started (toward the end of 1929) and Grandpa's business eventually went bankrupt. Like others who

---

[43] Tr: Emil Zegadłowicz (1888–1941): Polish poet, novelist, and playwright.
[44] Tr: Taduesz Dołęga-Mostowicz (1898–1939): Polish journalist and novelist.

experienced sudden failure, Grandpa killed himself; he drowned in the New York Bay. I also discovered that Grandpa not only had a business. He also had a second family. Although he didn't get married—this would have been bigamy—he had a daughter a little more than ten years younger than Mom who took her father's last name, Feinstein. And so I came to understand why we never mentioned this grandfather at home. Still, despite everything, Mom remained fond of him. He used to help Grandma before World War I by sending money for Mom's education. When the United States joined the war, or perhaps earlier, his help stopped. Grandma Helenka went to work in a mill making ribbons and lace, and Mom started tutoring. At the time she was in her last years of high school. This way they somehow managed to live through the war and Mom was able to graduate. Grandpa started helping the family again after the war. Mom went to see him in the States in 1927 or 1928 and she spent about a year there and learned to speak English. She brought home the money for our apartment's withdrawal fee and those worthless shares. I also learned from Mom that after Grandpa's death her half sister, who was already an adult, along with her mother, chose to end ties with her. Mom was bitter about this. My relatives from Argentina who located me right after the war knew the stepsister and stepmother's address (in California!) and tried to put us in touch. But nothing came of it. Most probably her descendants still live somewhere in the States, perhaps in California.

My grandfather on my dad's side died of tuberculosis when Dad was a child. Grandma raised her only son in a small Polish-Ukrainian-Jewish town, one of many such towns in the Ukraine at the time. In 1919 or 1920 she sent him west to Poland, just as my mom sent me east twenty years later. Perhaps it didn't, as in my case, save a son's life, but certainly it spared him many years of Soviet misery and terror. That's how the world turns; that's how moms are. Grandma and the rest of Dad's family remained behind the cordon, as the Soviet border was called then. In the mid 1930s, we got sad news from the Ukraine. Grandma asked to immediately stop all correspondence as Stalin's violent terror began raging throughout Russia. It's hard to imagine such a thing today, that for "contacts with foreign countries," that is, for writing and receiving letters and packages (and food packages were important because of starvation in the Ukraine), a person risked to be charged with spying or could be declared an "enemy of the people." Prison, labor camp, deportation, and often death were the experiences of millions of innocent people. All communication with Dad's family came to an end.

Dad often told us that during the 1917 Revolution and the subsequent civil war his town changed hands many times. There was ataman Pavlo Skoropadskyj with the army of a short lived Ukrainian government, ataman Symon Petlura, a Ukrainian nationalist, the "White" general Anton Dienikin, also ataman Alexey Makhno, a simple warlord, and few others. They all had at least one thing in common. Without exception, immediately upon entering the town they orchestrated a Jewish pogrom and often demanded a donation; that is, they extorted money. Polish and Bolshevik forces didn't organize pogroms. Poles treated the Jewish community with contempt and the Bolsheviks believed that Jews should be on their side, *per definitionem,* and so they conscripted us. That was awful and became the primary reason for sending my dad west. He fled with a Polish soldier, a legionnaire who had been given a place to stay in Grandma's house, and it so happened that he took too much time before deciding to flee when a different army suddenly entered the town. Grandma hid him at night and sent him together with her son to the neighboring town where Poles were still present. Dad never saw his mother again. He made his way to Poland and some years later married Mom in Warsaw.

Every year before Christmas, from the time of my early childhood until the war, we had a beautiful dinner at this legionnaire's home (I don't remember his name). Dad and the host reminisced about their mutual adventures. The apartment was pleasant and nicely furnished, but the district was not the best—Powiśle. The legionnaire wasn't overly successful in interwar Poland, but managed to land a cushy job at the State Liquor Monopoly. As Dad would say, much of the time "from morning until 5PM he farted in his chair and received a very nice salary." In the Second Polish Republic,[45] many members of Piłsudski's Legions occupied the most important positions in the administration and in the army. Those without great careers enjoyed good government jobs.

The rummaging behind bookshelves where I found my American grandfather's shares yielded another interesting (super interesting!) discovery. I didn't confer with Mom about this one. It was a recently translated copy of Theodoor van de Velde's *The Perfect Marriage*, perhaps the first modern sex manual in Polish. It's peculiar that my parents, although modern, never talked about sex with me. True, it is a difficult subject for parents to talk to their children about and perhaps they were counting on school to do it for them. And so it happened, but much later. Some older boys clued me in during a summer vacation. My sexual education, if we can call it that, was simple and crude.

---

[45] Tr: The Second Polish Republic refers to Poland between the First and Second World Wars (1918–1939).

My parents tried to have me spend as much time as possible in the countryside. When I was little they often rented a room in Urle on the Liwiec, east of Warsaw. Later, when we were doing better we would go to Zakopane. Janek and his mother came to Urle as well. I liked Urle; it was pretty there. I was not more than seven years old when one Sunday Dad arrived in Urle and brought me a bicycle. We didn't have much money then, and for my parents it was a serious expenditure. It didn't bother me that the bike was second-hand because I knew that a new one would have been too expensive. But there was a problem; the bicycle was a "strolling" one. This meant that the handlebars were pointing up like a girl's bicycle. Boys had mostly "racing" bikes with the handlebars pointing down. Perhaps a racing bike was more expensive; I don't know. Hence, my joy was not complete. I had to bite the bullet. I know this is ridiculous, but it stayed in my head. And it was the same with skates. I often went to the ice rink that was nearby on Ogrodowa Street. When I was little I had Turf skates, which were cheap and didn't require special shoes. One could attach them to regular everyday shoes. The other children had them as well. But older boys mostly skated on hockey skates that were much more expensive and required special shoes. There were also Salkhof skates that also attached permanently to shoes, but those were less expensive and, unlike hockey skates, didn't lend themselves to fast skating. I got Salkhofs, which, although not new, were in good shape. Because of that I couldn't race with other boys. They were better than Turfs, but . . .

I find it difficult to talk about the last pre-war years. On one hand, the upcoming tragedy was basically clear to every observer possessing even a bit of common sense. At the same time there was, perhaps unconscious, a feeling of total helplessness. Volumes have been written on that subject. But each story is different. My parents were faring better than before and one couldn't despair from morning till night because in a year or two, it wasn't precisely known when, Hitler would come. Or perhaps he wouldn't? Hope is a part of our psyche.

In the evening Dad liked to go to the Tabaczyński Café on Przejazd Street, which was close by and near the Bund's quarters. It wasn't necessary to rendezvous at a particular time because his friends always came there and sat together along with well known Bund leaders such as the aforementioned Emanuel Nowogrodzki and Shloyme Mendelson, Uncle Bernard Goldsztajn, and others. Tabaczyński Café was an institution, almost an extension of the Bund quarters. For the price of a "small coffee,"[46] not a costly investment,

---

[46] Tr: Pół czarnej (Polish), literally "half of a black": small coffee without cream.

they could sit as long as they wanted and have access to newspapers that were attached to wooden spines. There they discussed the fate of the world. What else could they do?

Shortly before the war Dad had a new suit made for him by a tailor: light tan pants and a somewhat darker tan checkered jacket. He looked nice, especially as he was already good looking. Mom seldom visited Tabaczyński. In addition to Lutka, she had several friends in Warsaw, mostly the wives of Dad's friends, whom she would meet at other cafés. They also saw each other at a hairdresser's, Mister Karol, on Rymarska Street, which was an extension of Przejazd Street south of Leszno. Hairdressers in those days used only first names; I think it's still the case. Dad would laugh that hairdressers and waiters were not part of the working class since they accepted tips. Dad's sayings, the "Folks-Zeitung" and all his socialism didn't please Grandma. If only this were PPS and not this Jewish socialism. She would have liked her daughter to marry the Prince of Wales. I believe that Dad's relationship with Grandma, although polite, was not particularly good. Lack of space in the apartment didn't lend itself to anything better. Well, it wasn't the first time in history that things weren't great between a mother-in-law and her son-in-law . . . and not the last one either.

Mom had acquaintances that she visited without Dad and sometimes she took me along. I remember best Mr. Wigdorowicz, who I believe was her high school teacher. He was much older than Mom. We didn't visit him often, but throughout the years those visits added up. Mr. Wigdorowicz had a wife and a daughter and lived in a nice apartment opposite us on Karmelicka Street. They liked Mom very much and treated her with great warmth. As I remember, he was the only person who, in the 1930s, tried hard to persuade Mom to emigrate. Mom thought Mr. Wigdorowicz was very smart and wise. Though usually amusing, he would become serious when he talked about leaving the country. He knew our relatives in Argentina and it seems that he was aware of what the anarchist grandfather was doing in the States. I don't know whether emigrating was a realistic option; probably not. I know that my parents never seriously contemplated it. But who did? The British didn't allow entry to their mandate, that is, Israel (then called Palestine), the States were blocked because of the so-called quotas, and other countries were not accepting Jews either. Nobody was.

Mr. Wigdorowicz was a hunchback and constantly made fun of his hump. The fact that he does it, Mom would say, doesn't mean that it is okay for others to ridicule his hump. A bit of this has stayed with me. Although I am not a hunchback, I have a big, crooked nose and sometimes I would make fun of it. I was able to convince Oleńka and Agnieszka, Ilonka's older daughters (we left

Poland when the youngest one, Joasia, was born) that Uncle Włodek had the most beautiful nose of the entire family. Both were smart and yet they believed this. They would often kiss me on the nose. There is nothing like indoctrination at a young age.

A year before the war, we were all on holidays in Zakopane. We lived in Krzeptówki in a room rented from a local highlander. We would wash in a brook behind the cottage. Krzeptówki is a village, or rather a part of Zakopane along Kościeliska Street, east of the town. Almost all the residents were named Krzeptowski. The place was very pretty and cheaper than downtown. Many friends lived here in the summer, Bund members and others. It was not far from there to the Pod Reglami Road and many beautiful valleys. Among the smaller ones I liked Behind the Gate and Little Meadow valleys. We also made longer excursions to Kościeliska Valley, to the Red Crests in West Tatra mountain, to the High Tatras, practically everywhere except for the more difficult trails high in the mountains that required special equipment and knowledge and skill of climbing. I have a picture of Mom wearing pants, so unusual then for a woman, climbing iron rungs up the Zawrat Mountain. She is looking down at the photographer—I think it was me—and she is smiling, clearly satisfied with her mountaineering achievements; so beautiful. One day we went with a large group on a day-long trek from Kuźnice through Hala Gąsienicowa to Kasprowy Wierch, then by Orla Perć toward Świnica and Zawrat, and further down to the Five Ponds Valley; finally through Roztoka we came out on the road leading to Zakopane near the Mickiewicz Waterfall. For us, ceprs,[47] it was a long route. Emanuel Nowogrodzki led the march and set its pace. He also made decisions about rest stops and carried the heaviest backpack with food for everybody. My Dad was there and Ilonka's dad, Michał, and Berek Sznajdmil and other friends. All was planned in a way that would allow us to catch the last bus from Morskie Oko to Zakopane. But it turned out that the bus had left moments before we got there and after a hard day's hike we had to walk all the way to Krzeptówki. My Mom had stayed home with Ilonka and was very worried as we were late and there was no phone to let her know what had happened. We sang all the way back and somehow made it home. It gave us a lot to reminisce about.

In the summer of 1939, war was in the air. Since spring, Hitler had been demanding a "corridor." My parents didn't want to go to Zakopane because it was far from Warsaw. Instead they decided to go to Kazimierz on the Vistula.

---

[47] Tr: Cepr or ceper is how highlanders (people who live in the mountain regions, especially the Tatra mountains) call anyone who does not live in their areas.

First they sent me by myself to Uncle Adam and Aunt Mania's guesthouse, so the "child" would benefit as long as possible from "fresh air." Dad arrived a few weeks later and Mom and Ilonka soon afterwards. After Mom's arrival, we rented an apartment because the guesthouse would have been too expensive for all of us. Lutka and Michał came a bit later on bicycles, yes, on bicycles. It was quite an achievement and I don't remember anyone from among my parents' friends who ever cycled such a long way. My uncle and his wife were supposed to take care of me as long as I was there alone, but they were too busy with the guesthouse and left "the child" to his own devices. For the first time I found myself in a new situation, neither at a camp, nor in my parents' or Grandma's care. In several of the neighboring guesthouses as well as my own, there were a number of young people, my age or a bit older, some of whom I knew. Many of them formed couples; boys "went out" with girls, but not in my case. Somehow no one found me attractive and I didn't impress them with anything. When I went to the beach on the Vistula with an entire group they tolerated me, but I had the impression that they looked down at me. And then I noticed Janka S. She wasn't a striking beauty and it so happened that we started to "go out." Janka was very nice and very smart too, I think. She was a child of divorced parents and had gone through a painful ordeal, which I couldn't begin to understand. Her family was wealthy. Later I often saw her in occupied Warsaw, until the moment when Mom sent me east.

All the boys in the group and some of the girls, although not Janka, smoked cigarettes. It was considered a sign of maturity. Nobody wants to feel inferior so I also began smoking. No one had any idea then that smoking was harmful; not us, not the adults. When Dad arrived and noticed that I was smoking, although I did not tell him, he took out his cigarette case and offered me one. Such was my Dad.

The news about the Hitler-Stalin pact filled the press in the second half of August. War was unavoidable. Poland mobilized and the trains were immediately confiscated by the military. We had to go back home by boat on the Vistula. Recently, Ilonka reminded me that our boat got stuck in a shallow bank and we had to be pushed from the bank. We made it to Warsaw a couple of days before the outbreak of the war. Grandma was already home with food supplies from Ciechocinek. Lutka and Michał came back on their bicycles, just as they had left. My parents were right not to go to Zakopane.

The world as I knew it had ended.

PART II

The War

For the first two or three days of war, Warsaw seemed calm. The radio played military marches and it wasn't clear what was happening at the front. On September 3, the western powers, that is, England and France, declared war against Germany. Crowds were demonstrating in front of embassies and enthusiasm was high. But the euphoria didn't last long. By the end of the first week of September, Colonel Umiastowski's[1] famous words were heard on the radio: "All men able to carry arms should immediately go east where a new defense line will be organized on the Bug River." The war was obviously going badly. Dad made arrangements with some close friends; all Bund members were to leave the next day, early in the morning. Mom thought that I should go with Dad to defend Poland. Even though I had just turned fifteen, I was tall and looked mature for my age. Of the eight or ten people in the group, I was the only teenager. We went in the direction of Mińsk Mazowiecki. The road was unbelievably congested. Crowds of people were on foot as were many of the military personnel. There were also people in horse carts, cars, bicycles, and some military trucks—all pushing east. When a German plane flew above, the people ran toward a ditch by the road or into the fields, lay on the ground, and waited for the pilot to shoot rounds from his machine gun and leave. Then they returned to the road and continued walking. Soldiers sometimes shot at the planes with rifles because planes flew very low. However, it wasn't at all effective. I don't remember any bombs being dropped.

After each raid there were wounded and killed, both people and animals. This went on for the entire day. It was a true war and it was waged almost

---

[1] Tr: Roman Umiastowski (1893–1982): colonel in the Polish army and head of propaganda in the Polish High Staff before World War II.

exclusively against the civilian population, a foretaste of what was to come. By the evening we reached Mińsk and spent the night at the home of a Bundist acquaintance. He had a spacious house located on the town through street at the back of a large yard that was separated from the street by a fence made of closely placed planks. The yard wasn't visible from the street. In the morning it turned out that only Dad and I were ready to continue. The rest either had blisters on their feet or weren't feeling well. People who live in the city are not used to walking great distances. So it was decided to stay in Mińsk for a day or two in order to rest before continuing. Our hosts were very amiable and hospitable and the weather was fabulous, a true Polish golden fall. On the second or third day, before we were ready to begin our march, our host came back from town with news that the Germans were seen in several neighboring towns east of Mińsk and were moving toward Warsaw from the east. There were countless rumors, chaos, and panic, as reliable information was nonexistent, but this news proved to be correct. The Germans attacked from the direction of East Prusy toward the south and were surrounding Warsaw from the east. This was completely unexpected. Unlike the battle lines of World War I, there were no trenches or fixed positions. This new type of warfare found the Germans covering great distances with mechanized forces, a Blitzkrieg. Going east now made no sense at all.

A day or two passed and we could see them ourselves; Germans on motorcycles, probably scouts, driving through the streets. They were indeed driving from east to west. Each motorcycle had a sidecar with a second soldier with a machine gun. We watched them through gaps in the fence. Not a living soul was in the street. Soon after they passed, there was a rumble of identical grayish-green trucks carrying German soldiers. There were a lot of them, equally spaced one after the other, traveling neither fast nor slow. Helmeted soldiers sat in two rows facing each other, rifles in their hands. There was a driver and an officer in the truck's cab. It looked a bit like a parade. A few days later, our prisoners of war walked down the same street in front of the house, unarmed and with uniforms unbuttoned and worn any which way. Many of them were wounded and needed support from their comrades. It was a very painful and pitiful sight. Perhaps the most tragic sight were the faces and the eyes of this defeated army. And the comparison with the victorious Germans in their cars was striking. Many of the locals, particularly the women ran from the sidewalk to the captives to give them bread or water or whatever they could. Germans on horses rode on both sides of the convoy. They chased the women away, but not in a brutal way; not yet.

Our journey had not taken us far. We were stuck in Mińsk. Since we were a rather large group, some of us sought out other friendly families in the town so as not to abuse the hospitality of our host. Dad and I stayed. And we waited, but for what? For nothing really, only to see how things would develop. News came first that the Russians occupied all of eastern Poland. Effectively our country had ceased to exist. The participation of "Western Powers" in the war had been useless. By the end of September, the Germans had defeated Poland. Immediately we began our journey back and arrived home without any trouble. The road was full of people like us. But these were not the same crowds as those that had been leaving the city several weeks earlier. I saw the first German on a bridge on Vistula River, but he took no notice of us.

It's difficult to describe seeing Mom and Grandma again. Everyone was crying. We had left Warsaw to fight only to find ourselves spending pointless weeks in Mińsk where we were in no danger and lacked for nothing. Meanwhile, those who stayed "safely" at home had endured the siege of the city; endless artillery shelling, aerial bombardments, lack of bread and other foods—this was the women's fate. It wasn't supposed to be that way, but that's what happened. There would be many other unforeseen—indeed impossible to foresee—occurrences to come in the lives of my generation, especially during the war.

After many consultations with friends it was decided that men should go east again, this time into exile. These were the same friends who left the city together at the beginning of September. Women and children would remain at home. I was also to remain at home. Why? I think the general opinion was that the men, especially the socialists, were in more danger than the women and children. Men in many of the families close to us were also fleeing east, to Russian-controlled territories or even further, to Vilnius, located in (then nominally free) Lithuania. Michał, Ilonka's dad, and his brother-in-law, Jona Joelson, also left their home in Miedzeszyn. It was a lemming-like rush. Ghetto, Holocaust—nobody was expecting that yet.

So I stayed home with Mom and Grandma. It was a different Warsaw. The Germans instituted a curfew. After seven at night the city seemed extinct. News or perhaps rumors—nobody was exactly sure—about enforced contributions and first shootings began to spread. This was a foretaste of the coming terror.

The telephones were working, so contact with friends continued. We learned by phone that my high school had reopened, so I immediately went to Żoliborz. I didn't get far. When the streetcar was going through Nalewki along the Krasińskich Garden, it was stopped by a group of soldiers who ordered all Jews to get off. We were about thirty or more. I wasn't yet familiar with German uniforms so I didn't know whether it was the army, that is, Wehrmacht, or some special unit. They made us form a column and we went to clean their quarters at the Krasińskich Palace annex. We also cleaned the toilets. Fun, their fun, began after the work was completed. They chased us back into the garden, ordered us to sing and to dance the hora[2] on the lawn. I knew neither the lyrics nor the melody so I moved my lips and imitated others. A few Germans stood in the middle of the circle, shouting at us to sing louder and to dance faster. For the culmination of the entertainment, they pulled several bearded Jews from the circle and started cutting off their beards, accompanied by our singing and dancing. Such was this show. To say that they were laughing wouldn't be enough; they were roaring with laughter. And we were jumping and looking at those frightened, mostly older Hassids. After couple of hours they let us all go. I returned home, no longer wishing to go to school. Still, the next day I went to school again, and the very same thing happened at the same spot, probably with the same military unit. It took place near Świętojerska Street, near Henia's and Mela's now non-existent umbrella business. After that Mom said enough, I was no longer to go to Żoliborz. And so my education at the Limanowski school had ended. Not only mine: soon after that we learned that the Germans ordered all Polish high schools to close.

New German announcements (*Bekanntmachung*) appeared on the walls. New prohibitions were constantly being imposed. We were ordered to hand over radios, furs, jewelry, and foreign money. At this time it was still possible to buy food, plus we had Grandma's provisions from Ciechocinek. However, the situation with coal was more problematic. One day Mom acquired a cartload of coal thanks to a former customer. This was a great achievement and we were all very happy. Grandma and I were standing at the window waiting for Mom. We saw her walking beside the cart as it entered the courtyard. She looked at us and smiled as though in triumph and then waved at us. I ran downstairs and carried the coal in pails to the apartment, not to the usual spot in the basement. Mom was afraid that people would steal it. At least during the first winter of the war, Mom and Grandma kept relatively warm.

I visited Janka almost every day. She lived on Leszno across from the court building not far from us. The apartment was fabulous: huge, beautifully furnished rooms, a big hall, and several bathrooms. In all my life I had never been in a place like this. Only two people lived here: Janka and her mom. The house had belonged to Janka's grandfather. Her mom wasn't thrilled by my visits;

---

[2] Au: Hora: a traditional Jewish dance.

I could see it on her face, although she never chided me. In any event Janka wanted to see me, which was more important. She always tried to be the one who opened the front door from the staircase so I would avoid meeting her mom. Several times Janka came to visit us. Mom liked her. Mom allowed me to visit Janka whenever I wanted, provided I came back home before the curfew.

Lutka came by several times in those days. I remember that she wore pants, something that wasn't commonly accepted in women's attire. Recently, Ilonka reminded me how Lutka came to always wear pants: she used to ride from Miedzeszyn to the city on a bicycle! I cannot imagine any woman we knew, including Mom, who would go to Warsaw on a bike—and under German occupation no less. Lutka was exceptionally courageous and energetic. These qualities allowed her to save not only herself and Ilonka, but Michał's family from the Holocaust as well. She arranged for the four of them to escape to the east across the Bug River. Hers was an authentic heroism.

At the end of November, a *Bekanntmachung* appeared on the walls requiring Jews to wear armbands with the Star of David. Because of this my Mom decided that I should leave immediately to join Dad in Baranowicze. I begged her to come with me, as did Lutka, to no avail. Mom said that I need to go because I was just a teenager and for her just a child. She had to stay because Grandma was not able to make such an arduous journey and also she feared that if she left we would lose the apartment. My arguments had little influence, losing out to duty, devotion, and perhaps a certain lack of determination. Our uncertain financial situation made the apartment an important part of her decision making. Yet Lutka had chosen to abandon her own house even though it was not a modest apartment like ours. Of course, Lutka's mom was no longer alive. Still, we had considered having Grandma move in with Aunt Ewcia. In that case the apartment would also have been empty and we would have lost it as well. Or I could have said, but I did not, that "I will not leave here without Mom and Grandma and that's final." After all, I had seen firsthand the cruelty and sadism of the young Germans at the Krasińskich Garden, even though they hadn't killed anyone then. Still the coming Holocaust was not possible to imagine. And so it happened. Mom died because of a wretched apartment.

Together with a neighbor we knew, we went to a railroad station in Praga and continued east by train. One of the last stations I remember was Mordy,[3] although we got out several stops later, closer to the Bug River, where we met with smugglers who had been previously engaged. There we went to a shack

---

[3] Tr: Mordy (Polish): muzzles.

where a number of other people were assembled. The plan was to cross Bug at night by boat. The shack was dirty and the smell was awful and poverty was in evidence wherever I looked. This was Poland B. I had heard about it, but had never seen it up close. When evening came I got hungry and was given a slice of black sour bread with lard. It made me sick to my stomach. I just had enough time to run to the yard and vomit. I was sitting on the floor in the shack's corner starting to doze off when I heard a baby's whimper. Within our group of more than a dozen was a family with a tiny child. Late at night, the neighbor woke me up and we went to the river. The bank on our side had woods; the eastern side was sandy. Near the river I noticed the silhouette of a German and I became frightened. It turned out that he was the one who took the bribe. He stood by the boat's entrance counting people—the neighbor explained all this to me. We crossed the river quickly. There was a bit of ice, but not much. Before going back across the river, the smugglers gave us detailed instructions about what to do on the Soviet bank. We were to get away from the river as soon as possible, find a country road that ran parallel to the river, and turn right. There was supposed to be a village and then some kilometers farther down a small town with a railroad station. And indeed it was just like the smugglers said. In the confusion after leaving the boat, I lost contact with the neighbor. I looked for him when I got to the station, but I never saw him again. He was a kind man. Mom had asked him to take care of me during our escape and he did so faithfully. In front of the station, I saw a Red Army soldier for the very first time. He was wearing a hat with a preposterous peak protruding in the middle, similar to what Prussians had on their helmets in old paintings. The hat had ear flaps. He had a bayonet on his rifle and his coat almost reached his ankles. He made a strange impression on me.

I got on the train—the rides were free—and arrived at Baranowicze without any problems. Dad was at the office, but the people he was renting a room from gave me his address and I met him there. It was an emotional reunion. Dad had a job at the District School Administration. I think he had a rather important position in the financial division and he worked hard. He told me that he owed his job to his knowledge of Russian and bookkeeping. One funny and one serious thing happened the first day. Dad gave me money and told me where to find a restaurant. He was not allowed to leave the office, so I ate alone. I ordered borsch and another item featured on the menu several lines below, a dish called "ukha," which I was sure was an entrée. But it was a type of fish soup. I had eaten two soups and thus my study of Russian began. That night Dad and I discussed schooling for me. Since Dad worked for the school administration, he knew the best place for me to go. It turned out that in Baranowicze the Russians had established schools that taught in four languages: Russian, Polish, Yiddish, and Belorussian. These schools were perhaps the remnants of a rather liberal educational policy of the 1920s. At the time I didn't see any Russification,[4] but I did observe it three years later, when I was graduating from high school among a small Finno-Ugrian nation of Mordvins. Of course I wanted to continue my studies in a Polish school, but Dad disagreed. You know Polish, he said, you have learned Yiddish, and now you need to learn Russian. This war could last a long time and it might prove useful. And that's what happened. The next day he brought me a Russian-Polish dictionary and a very famous novel by Mikhail Lermontov,[5] *A Hero of our Time*. I struggled with my head alternately in the book and in the dictionary. In this simple way, thanks to Dad I learned a second foreign language. For those who don't know, Lermontov was great Russian romantic, a little younger than Pushkin.[6] Just like Pushkin, he didn't write much prose. I have a nice set of his collected works published in Russia, which I bought just after the war. I still enjoy his poems a great deal.

I wasn't particularly impressed with the new school. I remember neither the teachers nor the other students. But some things I do remember. I had trouble with math at the Limanowski school and I was an average student. This suddenly changed in Baranowicze. Somehow everything became clear and math ceased to be a struggle. I could grasp concepts quickly and repetition and memorization were no longer necessary. In fact, I couldn't wait for new material and liked to study it from the textbook even before we got to it in class. My math teacher from the Limanowski School, Mr. Poprożenko, would have been surprised. I don't know how to explain it. Maybe it was due to hormonal changes linked to my growth or perhaps to the shock of war—or both?

Other interesting details from the Baranowicze school have to do with history and politics. For decades, from the beginning of the nineteenth century, the Russians engaged in wars at the Caucasus in order to absorb the mountain territories and indeed the entire Central Asia into the tsarist empire.

---

4   Tr: Russification: an assimilation process whose aim was to replace the culture and language of non-Russian communities with the Russian one, in order to ensure Russian domination over nations and territories that were first part of the Imperial Russia, and later of the Soviet Union.
5   Tr: Mikhail Yuryevich Lermontov (1814–1841): Russian romantic writer, poet, and painter, one of the greatest poets of Russian literature.
6   Tr: Alexander Sergeyevich Pushkin (1799–1837): Russian romantic writer and poet, recognized as the greatest Russian poet and the father of modern Russian literature.

Throughout this entire period, they encountered strong opposition from the local, almost entirely Muslim populations, especially those of the mountain regions. The most prominent leader of Dagestan's mountain inhabitants in the mid-nineteenth century for over 25 years was a certain Shamil. He was considered there a national hero who led a righteous fight against the tsar, the oppressor of nations. Although he lived before Lenin, Shamil was a sort of Bolshevik, although naive and politically ignorant. Had he lived later, he would have been a Bolshevik—that was the unspoken implication. Yet all that suddenly changed. The teacher gave us a text, I think it was typewritten, which recast Shamil as a loathsome cutthroat, in fact, a bandit and a nationalist as well. And this was his main sin and that his fight against the tsarist army was—objectively speaking of course—unjust and contrary to the interest of his own nation. And why? It's very simple: because—again objectively and dialectically—in those times and in those territories Russia and its army represented progress in contrast with the Muslim backwardness and ignorance. And Shamil, the scoundrel, didn't seem to understand that historical necessity. Therefore it was only fair for him to be exiled to Siberia after he was caught, where his life, like those of so many other "terrible criminals," ended. (I cannot imagine how Russians would manage to deal with their history without Siberia). When I was learning this sinister nonsense during the 1939-40 school year, I didn't know about George Orwell. But when I read his works later I had a solid background for understanding his books.

There were other absurdities as well. We received a textbook on the history of the Soviet Union. This was nothing special except that it was solidly made, in hardcover, and printed on good white paper, which made it stand out from the other textbooks, which were printed on newspaper quality paper. Of course this was for propaganda reasons: the importance of the subject had to be reflected in its physical attributes. I noticed here and there sheets of white paper glued together. But if you held such pages up to the light you could discern either a face or text that was otherwise invisible. Once I remember taking a great deal of time to carefully remove the glued paper. Underneath was Marshal Mikhail Tukhachevsky—the "former," now plastered over and therefore non-existent, hero of the Bolshevik revolution and of the civil war. He was now portrayed as a Nazi "spy" (no portrait in the new version) who was executed for his crime (murdered together with his entire family). When the textbook was originally printed, Tukhachevsky had existed in his first incarnation and his second incarnation was glued over it to make the book more up to date. Textbooks by their nature have large printings, so all that gluing necessitated a lot of manual work. But so what? For new historical truths every-thing and anything goes. In the mid-1930s, Russia had five marshals, three of whom they executed almost immediately after sham trials. According to west-ern historians, those three were outstanding military experts. Tukhachevsky became a German spy, Vasily Blücher a Japanese one, and Alexander Yegorov an English spy. Thus the alleged spying—how should I say it—was nicely and proportionately divided. (American imperialism hadn't become important as yet). The two who survived the slaughter, Kliment Voroshilov and Semyon Budyonny were men first and foremost loyal to Stalin. They were fit to be corporals rather than high ranking officers. The purges affected all levels of the Soviet military leadership, from the heads of the army, its corps and divi-sions, to the leaders of battalions and even regiments where in some cases the purges were even worse. They were all accused of being spies and enemies of the people; madness. Among the victims were a disproportionate number of officers of Polish descent. The army purges were one of the main reasons for the unprecedented defeat in the war's initial period, when not thousands but millions of Russians died or were taken captive. The officer cadre had been hollowed out and was of inferior quality. It was a tragedy not just for Russians, but for all of us. These are matters from the past, but I am unable to pass over them lightly. Was it truly some idiotic "historical necessity" for those two "isms" to annihilate my generation as well as several other generations of Jews and non-Jews, anyone, whoever was there?

The only friend I had then was Krzysiek, our landlord's son, who was a great guy and my contemporary. He went to the Polish school and he intro-duced me to his friends and to the girls. Soon there was a friendly group in Baranowicze made up mostly of Warsaw Bundists who knew each other from before the war, or at least had known about each other. Among them was Fiszka (Felek) Najman, who was a bit older and later became my close friend. Tobcia Geber was also there along with her entire family, husband, mother, and step-father. The Russians referred to us as "bezhency."[7] In general the locals didn't like us and we lived from hand to mouth. A well known joke was: "Sleep faster, I need the pillow" (in Yiddish: shlof shneller, ich darf hobn dem kishn). Our room could accommodate two beds and not much more. In any case we didn't have much more, so that wasn't a problem. We were not allowed to use the kitchen, so we cooked on an electric cooker. Dad's wages weren't bad, but the shops were generally empty. This is when I became acquainted with a common

---

[7]   Tr: Bezhency (Russian): fugitives.

Soviet and later Polish phenomenon, having enough money, but there being nothing to buy with it.

News from both sides of the Bug River was worse and worse yet. It turned out that the arrests of Erlich and Alter were followed by detentions of less important Bund activists in the Soviet zone. Everybody was afraid. News came through the grapevine from people we knew who traveled to Białystok, Lida, Volkovysk, and other places. Of course there was nothing in newspapers about this. They devoted what space they had to pictures of Stalin on the front page followed by idiotic nonsense. Utterly terrible things were happening in Warsaw. Dad wrote to Mom that she absolutely had to flee and he went to the border to make arrangements with smugglers and wait for her. They swindled him out of a lot of money and did nothing. In the spring, Dad again went to the border and again achieved nothing. The border was probably tightly closed by then, so Dad decided to go back to Warsaw. Rumors, which later proved to be true, said that the Russians were making lists of "bezhency" who wanted to go back west and informing the Germans, who would intercept them in Brześć on the Bug. At an appointed time people would cross the bridge and find German soldiers waiting on the west bank and Russian troops on the east bank. My cousin Mietek Fajnsztein, some years ago one of the Saski Garden's "kings," visited us before his return. We were supposed to soon follow suit. Mietek perished, together with his parents, Aunt Mania and Uncle Adam, in the Warsaw ghetto.

Almost all the families we were friends with in Baranowicze, with the exception of Tobcia Geber, registered to return. I can neither understand nor explain why the families including the Najmans, the Babics, the Kormans, the Grundlands, and Dad and I were soon exiled to Siberia, while the Gebers and a few others decided to stay. Many times these turned out to be life and death decisions, although no one suspected that then. Such are the accidents of fate.

In the spring of 1940, probably at the end of May, NKVD agents came to our house and told us to get dressed, pack as much as we could carry, and wait in the street in front of the house. We were not the only ones: there were people standing in front of several other houses. As the night was ending, the agents made us form a column and rushed us in the direction of the railroad station. Krzysiek tried to help us carry our things, but they chased him away. There were many people, all or mostly all Jews at the branch line, who like us were refugees from German-occupied Poland. We started to look for friends and it soon became clear that all the families we were close with and who had registered for the return to the German occupation zone were there. The Babic family, Bund members with whom fate had joined us for the entire war period, had a baby only a few months old with them, born in Baranowicze. (Józef Babic is now a grandfather in Israel.) The Korman family, Bundists, had a daughter as well, Hania,[8] a bit older, who now is a grandmother in Australia. We found both Najman brothers with the wife of Jakub, the older one, and other acquaintances as well.

A freight train—with so-called cattle cars—was waiting with its engine idling. We formed a tight group in order to get into the same car. The inside was crowded and smelly. There were a few sleeping bunks. Women hung sheets in front of the parasha[9] that stood in the corner. From time to time the train, called in Russian "echelon," would stop at a branch line and they would let us out to get boiling water (the famous railroad "kipiatok," which sometimes stank of machine grease). We received very meager food rations, bread and some soup. That was all. Generally people had their own food from Baranowicze.

Nobody said where they were taking us. From the stations we passed it was easy to figure out that we were going east. It wouldn't have been difficult to escape from the train, despite the NKVD escort, but life in Russia was so strictly regulated that escape made no sense. Every person needed to have a document, a kind of internal passport (udostoverenye), had to live somewhere, and also had to have a "pripiska," that is, to be registered by the police ("assigned," Latin formula for serf's legal status in feudal society: *glebae adscriptus*; attached to the soil, comes to mind!). Without registration you couldn't get a job, and you couldn't get registration without a job—a vicious circle. Getting an apartment without backing "from above," for example from some party committee, important institution, or factory was simply unthinkable. And with the housing shortage, when each apartment (or rather room), usually shared (called communal), was registered and allotted by some municipal authority, renting an apartment was not an option. In addition, everyone was afraid of everyone else, since anyone might be, and many were, informing for the NKVD. No one has described the realities of everyday life in Soviet Russia in the 1930s better than Anatoly Ribakov in *Children of the Arbat*, as well as other volumes of that series.

After about a week of travel, we passed the city of Sverdlovsk (before the Bolsheviks and now Yekaterinburg) when someone noticed, through the car's little barred window, concrete poles with signs: "Europe to the left and Asia to the right." We crossed the Ural Mountains, which are beautiful, vast, and not very high, and we were in Siberia. After one or two more days of train travel

---

8 Tr: Hania or Haneczka: diminutive of Hana.
9 Tr: Parasha (Russian): a covered chamber pot, often enclosed in a wooden stool.

along the trans-Siberian main line, we arrived at Tavda. From there we spent a day in open barges on the Tavda River heading north and a day marching through virgin forest. To our surprise, we found a big, uninhabited village in the middle of the forest. There were wooden houses made of thick, identical, equally spaced logs and two or three streets crossing at right angles. This was clearly a planned settlement, not an old village built haphazardly. The area was not fenced. We lived there for sixteen or seventeen months, from May-June 1940 until the end of September 1941. It was not *sensu stricto*[10] a prison, but rather exile. In Soviet terminology it was called special resettlement (specpieresielenye); we were deportees without the right to leave our dwelling place. The exact location was Sverdlowskaya Oblast, Taborinskij Rayon, Uvyerenskoye Pochtovoye Otdelenye, specposolok Kurenyevo, about 500 kilometers northeast of Sverdlovsk, western Siberia.

On the first day, Dad received a "promotion" that proved useful for me, but didn't turn out well for him. Sakharov, the NKVD commander, gathered us at the square in the middle of the village and announced that we would stay in Kurenyevo forever, or at least until the end of our lives, and that we should not fool ourselves into thinking that we would ever get out. After this lovely introduction he tried to explain to the newcomers, we were a thousand or more, that we would clear the forest and share each house among twelve of us (there were about hundred houses in Kurenyevo). He also said that we would be allowed to send one or two letters per month (I don't recall which) per family. He was speaking Russian and a commotion began because very few people understood him. Dad translated into Polish and Yiddish for the people near him. Sakharov must have noticed, because he called Dad over and ordered him to translate for everyone gathered in the square. That evening or the next day Dad was summoned to NKVD headquarters, where he was appointed "village elder," and immediately everyone began calling him, both to his face and behind his back, the "elder donkey." Soon afterward, in June or July 1940, Dad told me that I would go to high school in the district city of Taboryn and that I would live in a school hostel during the school year. I don't know how he arranged it. It was a significant achievement; I would be able to continue my education. Favoritism exists everywhere.

Each house had one big room without interior walls and a Russian stove suitable for cooking and baking bread and on which people could sleep to keep warm; nothing more. Four families of friends from Baranowicze who traveled

---

[10] Tr: Sensu stricto (Latin): in the strict sense of the word.

in the same car took up quarters in our house. All were connected to the Bund: Chaim Babic with his wife Rywka and baby Józio[11] (born in Baranowicze), Judel Korman with wife Edzia and their slightly older baby Haneczka, Judel's unmarried brother Mendel (Chaim and Judel were carpenters, Mendel was a shoemaker), the two Najman brothers: Jakub, the elder, with wife Fela Celemeńska, and Fiszka, a bachelor and my future friend, as well as Dad and me. Before the war, Fiszka was studying and Jakub was a "półkownik": not a pułkownik (lieutenant), properly spelled with "u," but rather with "ó"[12] to suggest the word "półka" (shelf). This was the name for salesmen in textile shops who did nothing all day but remove bales of fabrics from shelves, show them to customers, and then put them back on the shelves again. This name was a bit ironic because Piłsudski's rule—or rather the rule of the "reform government" after his death—was often described as the "reign of lieutenants," those from the Legions. The "półkowniks," together with other salesmen, had a separate section in the Bund's Commerce Employees Union (Handls-Ungeshtelte Ferein), a big trade union located on 5 Zamenhoffa Street. Dad belonged to that union as well. He was part of the bookkeeper's section management.

We examined our new accommodations and found German names carved on the walls, as well as three arrows—that was the Second International's symbol—and inscriptions in honor of Austrian social democracy and its leaders. It wasn't hard to guess what this meant. In the 1920s and at the beginning of the 1930s, Vienna was governed by an Austrian social democracy, which built large housing estates for the workers and named them in honor of Karl Marx. These were nice, inexpensive, modern apartments in free standing buildings with lots of greenery that didn't form narrow and constricted streets. The most outstanding architects of these times participated in designing housing developments that still exist today. The Warsaw Housing Cooperative in Żoliborz was built according to the same architectural models. In 1934, Chancellor Engelbert Dollfuss' fascist Austrian government came out against social democracy. Violent fights, which were eventually suppressed by the police and the military, took place on housing estates. It was known that part of the developments' defenders made their way to Russia. Kurenyevo was their fate in the country of the "victorious proletariat." It was they who most probably built the settlement, since we didn't find any inscriptions in Russian or in other languages on the logs. What had happened to them and when had they

---

[11] Tr: Józio: diminutive of Józef.
[12] Tr: In Polish both letters: u and ó sound the same.

left? No one knew. Perhaps they had been forced out? They may have been sent to forced labor camps, or possibly they had been murdered; Stalin didn't like foreigners. It was a painful and tragic discovery. And it wasn't good news. They had been people just like us.

Very many, maybe most of the deportees in the settlements were families who had registered to return to the west, to the other side of the Bug River. There were also a large number of escapees, who had no intention of going back to the Germans. So why in that case didn't Tobcia's family end up in Kurenyevo? I don't know the answer. We were unable to understand what criteria guided the NKVD, and one has to remember there was widespread chaos in Russia as well. Anyway, there were almost no local Jews here and only a few Catholic Polish families.

In our house, in one common room the little ones slept on the stove and three couples had spaces separated by some sheets. Fiszka, Mendel, Dad, and I slept in a row on the floor. It was warm inside because there was plenty of wood for heating and the gaps between logs were well sealed. When I think about this house now, I admire the people who were able to maintain a harmonious coexistence in that incredibly confined space, in primitive conditions and scarcity. No doubt the bond created by our Bundist past was a major factor.

The three women had the greatest impact: Rywka Babic, the epitome of sensitivity, who was very pretty, with full lips and big olive eyes, delicate, and an extraordinarily good person; Edzia Korman, who was the most energetic, enterprising, and cheerful of the three; and Fela Celemeńska-Najman, who was slim, very lively, with dark complexion, pretty, always smiling, and well read.[13] They kept house and we gave them our meager wages and rations: black, underbaked bread, a bit of groats, occasionally oil, and once in a blue moon a special treat, one herring per family. The women did all they could to be fair and not give their husbands preferential treatment. Our house was the ideal of collective property. I remember all three with great warmth. Of the three, only Edzia survived the war in Russia. After her return to Poland and immediately after the Kielce pogrom,[14] she immigrated to Australia with her husband and daughter.

---

[13] Au: Fela's brother, Jakub Celemeński "Celek," was Bund's courier on the so-called Aryan side, responsible for contacts with the resistance movements in other ghettos or with leaders of the Polish underground. He survived the war and left extremely interesting memoirs, *Elegy for My People* (Melbourne: The Jacob Celemeński Memorial Trust, 2000).

[14] Tr: The Kielce Pogrom (July 4, 1946) was an outbreak of mob violence against Jews in the city of Kielce, Poland. It followed a rumor o child kidnapping and murder, disseminated by Polish communist armed forces, and resulted in the killing of about 40 Jews.

Rywka and Fela died tragically soon after their release from Siberia. Rywka contracted typhus in 1942 in Astrakhan while nursing a nine-month old baby, her second childbirth during the war. The newborn, Vyera, survived by a miracle, or rather thanks to many miracles. She has been living in Israel for decades and is a grandmother. Fela died at the end of 1942 in the Volga Region, where many families from Kurenyevo lived, including me and Dad. A local country "specialist" aborted her pregnancy. She suffered greatly before dying. It is a fact that Soviet backwardness, anti-abortion laws, and wartime destitution all contributed to their deaths. But there is also this truth: they perished because they were women. No man has ever died after an abortion or after giving birth twice within seventeen months in the inhuman conditions of wartime Russia. I liked them both a lot. If they gave preferential treatment to anyone in our Siberian room for twelve, it was perhaps to me because I was the youngest.

In Kurenyevo we had two additional sources of food, both irregular and uncertain. One was the parcels we received from time to time from friends in the eastern part of Poland, from where we had been deported, that was occupied by the Russians. And after a while we also began to barter with peasants, the so-called kulaks. Kulaks had been deported from the European part of Russia in 1929–1931 during collectivization, that is, the compulsory creation of kolkhozes. They lived in local villages, kolkhozes, generally from several to more than a dozen hours' walking distance from us. Shirts and other articles of clothing were worth their weight in gold. They could be exchanged for good bread or flour, potatoes, and other foodstuffs. Such were our deals. These contacts, although forbidden, happened all the time and weren't difficult, as the taiga almost reached our homes. Evening meetings took place in the forest, where we would bargain with visitors from the "free" world. Both sides were very interested in the exchange. Sakharov had three or four assistants, who didn't watch us closely since escape was not easy. The kolkhoz people traded mostly with produce from their small private plots. Those little plots allowed peasants as well as others to survive. Although they did not have ownership titles, each kolkhoz family had a small piece of land where they grew vegetables, fruits, whatever they wanted, whatever was needed and worth cultivating. These crops belonged to the family and the surplus could legally be sold at the kolkhoz market in the neighboring town. Each household was also allowed to own one cow—not more, God forbid—as well as couple of pigs and some fowl. The plots were tolerated, although the authorities didn't look upon them kindly, since the entire arrangement didn't go together with "socialism." After all, didn't Lenin himself say that small-scale property gives birth to capitalism every day, every hour? And if millions of people didn't have enough to feed themselves, well, that was not nearly as important as whatever that fanatic had to say. Of course the plots were carefully cultivated. People took far better care of their private plots than of the collective kolkhoz farms.

The forest allowed yet another clandestine activity. It happened that among the sizable number of educated people in the settlement, there was a radio engineer. He managed to rig up a primitive radio with some spare parts. In the evening, a small group to which Dad belonged would meet in the forest and try to find a foreign radio station. Often the sounds came and went and it was impossible to understand anything. Ultimately they settled on the BBC's signal, which introduced its broadcast with the first notes of Beethoven's Fifth Symphony. Even if the voices were garbled, the sound of the notes meant that England was still holding on. In the summer of 1940, after France fell, such news was very comforting. Official "information" came from a broadcasting station controlled by the NKVD. Each house had a loudspeaker and nothing more. All we could do was to modulate the sound or turn it off. All day long, the station broadcasted idiotic propaganda, suitably doctored news, and Soviet songs, some not too bad, for example, "Katyusha."[15]

One day in the summer before I went to school, Dad came home beaten up. His nose was bleeding and he felt awful. The women somehow patched him up. It turned out that for some time the authorities had pestered him to answer questions about people in the settlement, their origins, views, etc. He kept dodging them as best as he could, but finally they got fed up, punched him couple of times, and removed him from his "job." Dad's authority, as well as his popularity among the settlement ladies in Kurenyevo, went up dramatically. As his replacement, they appointed as "senior donkey" a porter from a village near Baranowicze, a powerful guy whose name I don't recall. Clearly he had no qualms about snitching on people.

Because of Dad's demotion, we wondered whether the permission to go to school in Taboryn would be withdrawn. But it wasn't. Perhaps the NKVD people hadn't seen the connection or hadn't bothered to take care of it. Perhaps it was the result of their usual mess?—there was so much of it! They weren't particularly bright. Was it again by chance? Most likely it was. I was lucky once more.

We worked in twos in the forest. After Dad had lost his "post" we worked together. Each of us had an ax and there was one big two-handed saw for each

---

[15] Tr: Here, "Katyusha" is the name of a popular Russian song. It is also the name of a rocket launcher, as mentioned elsewhere in the book.

pair of lumberjacks. First we had to cut the tree trunk about half a meter above ground, something like two sides of a triangle open in the direction in which the tree was even minimally leaning; it was supposed to fall that way. The triangle's depth was about one-fifth of the trunk's diameter. The base cut was parallel to the ground and the angle was acute. Then we would begin to saw the trunk on the opposite side of the triangle at the height of its base. When the saw was nearing the triangle, the tree would begin to creak and we had to immediately jump several meters away, or better yet behind another tree, since the falling tree could hit one of us. After the tree fell, we had to cut the branches with an ax and continue to the next tree in order to meet the daily quota that was always difficult to achieve. It was the healthiest work I ever did in my life. The forest was beautiful and the air clean. The only thing that was lacking was adequate food. I was always hungry.

The sections of forest destined to be cut were outlined and individual trees were marked by expert forestry engineers who from time to time came to the settlement. They were prisoners (in Russian: zakliuchyonnyi, that is, people under lock and key, called "zeks") with long-term sentences. These were generally very intelligent and interesting people. Sometimes prisoners who were doctors or other specialists also came to the settlement. They arrived on horseback, without an escort, since there was really no chance of escape. They were reconciled with their fate. It was said that the system had taught them *kak svobodu lubit*, that is, "how to love freedom." Dad soon got to know them. He possessed a natural ease in initiating contact with people, and his perfect erudite Russian, the result of graduating from high school in tsarist times, helped him as well. Of course all these people were innocent, victims of blind mass terror, just like us. One could learn many interesting things from them. In the Soviet legal system and prison regime, the category of political prisoners didn't exist. Whoever ended up in the dock and therefore in jail was, *ipso facto*, a felon. Of course there were real criminals in prisons, bandits and thieves, in their slang "urks" or "shpanas," and it was they who held sway, informed on others, and robbed and mercilessly tormented the allegedly non-political inmates. But the imprisoned intellectuals were able to organize and oppose the thugs and brigands. Generally this required strong people with years of prison experience. We got to know a few of them and I enjoyed talking to them. We also learned from them how to make various Siberian prison "delicacies." The one I remember best and like to this day are fried potatoes (zharyonaya kartoshka). The potatoes have to be cooked (but not too soft—they need to be a bit firm), then sliced and fried on both sides in a skillet. Fantastic! The peel should not be removed. It's edible and should not be wasted. Two conditions were needed for this delicacy; one had to have potatoes and fat as well. It didn't happen often.

At the beginning of September, I walked—yes, over 25 kilometers on foot—to school in Taboryn. I quickly saw that the town, or rather the big village, was an administrative center. It was from here that the NKVD ran the entire region's prisons and labor camps as well as settlements such as ours. This region was truly an island, like those described by Solzhenitsyn in *Gulag Archipelago* (Glavnoye Upravleniye ispravitelno-trudovyh Lagerey; Chief Administration of Corrective Labor Camps). The hostel where I lived was awful: dirty, cold, and without adequate nourishment. In the morning and evening there was black bread barely spread with jam and also some suspicious dark hot liquid in an aluminum mug. The main meal was a lump of groats (hulled grain) with a hole in the middle where a bit of oil had been poured in the kitchen. Some boarders insisted that it was machine oil. Several children from the post-kulak villages, two from my Kurenyevo, and three or four from the special settlement Chosh also lived in the hostel. The remaining students, the majority of whom did not live in the dorm, were the children of NKVD employees. They looked at us as if we were hardened criminals and didn't want to associate with us. That was fine with me. The existence of Chosh, another special settlement in our region, was known to us through our business contacts with the former kulaks. In Taboryn I learned that, just like in Kurenyevo, almost all of the people there were Jews, "bezhency" from the part of Poland now occupied by the Germans. They had been deported from various towns in the Russian zone about the same time as we had. It was an enormous "operation" which took place in the spring of 1940. According to historians, Russia deported about 250 to 300 thousand Jews from the eastern part of Poland they occupied. This represented a much higher percentage than the ratio of Jews to non-Jews in these areas. Doubtless many of the deported died in exile or were killed in the war. However, after the repatriation to Poland in 1945-46, it turned out that this was the largest group of Polish Jews to survive the Holocaust. Was it an irony of fate? Of course it was. The Russians didn't deport us to Siberia in order to save us, but to isolate us and put us to work in the forests.

I am unable to recall even a single teacher from the Taboryn school that I could say anything good about. It was all hopelessly dull. But from the textbooks I was able to pick up useful knowledge; even the NKVD was unable to falsify mathematics, physics, and chemistry. Still, it was an unpleasant period in my life. I hated school, my school hostel, and Taboryn and I made no friends there. I fled to Kurenyevo, to our house, to Dad and our friends as often as

I could. On Saturdays for as long as the days were relatively long, I walked the 25 kilometers home after school and then walked back the 25 kilometers on Sundays. I was sixteen and strong enough to do it. Once on my way from the settlement to school I encountered a convoy consisting of many sleighs, which were transporting goods from the Taboryn railroad station. The coachmen asked me to join them, which I did willingly. But it was too cold and I couldn't sit for long. The coachmen were bundled up in enormous sheepskin coats. I needed to walk, to move. I would have frozen sitting there in my miserable fufaika (a sort of wadded jacket). I wore valenki, boots made of felt, on my feet, which were perfect for the freezing cold. Without them one couldn't venture outside in the winter. Under the socks or, rather, under the pieces of fabric wrapped around my feet was a layer of paper. This made surprisingly good insulation.

Siberian cold can be very harsh and minus 30 degrees Celsius is not unusual, but the weather is dry with almost no wind, which makes the cold more bearable. Winters are long. By September there is frost and the ground freezes. Coming home was always more pleasant than the return walk to school. I will never forget how it looked as I emerged from the forest and entered the clearing where Kurenyevo was situated. Smoke rose straight to the sky from all the chimneys. I felt warm and comfortable knowing that in a couple of minutes I would be among my dear ones. Later, when days were short and nights fell early, I wasn't able to undertake such escapades because of a real danger—wolves. They were not dangerous in daytime, but if it was dark and they were hungry the pack would attack a person traveling alone. At least that's what people said. Although I had never seen a wolf, I was haunted by a scene from *"Ashes,"* where wolves attacked Rafał Olbromski at night and ate his horse! So in winter I would spend every Sunday in the hostel. It was awful.

Dad and his friends planned an escape from Kurenyevo for November 1940, during the "holiday" commemorating the Bolshevik revolt. It was then called the great October Revolution. The plan was to go back to a big city in eastern Poland like Lvov or Białystok, or if everything went well, to Vilnius. There would be three free days without morning roll calls before work, the duration of an energetic walk to the nearest railroad station. We left before dawn in order not to be noticed. The group consisted solely of men who had no families. From our house there were: Fiszka Najman, Mendel Korman, Dad, and me, as well as Gerszon Fiszman, an acquaintance from the Bund, who before the war had worked in a slaughterhouse. He was an exceptionally good and helpful man. In the evening we arrived at an ex-kulak village situated along the way. We were planning to spend the night with Yermolay, a peasant we knew and with whom we had bartered. This man was friendly, smart, very experienced, and understood us. We trusted him. He was tall with wide shoulders and a huge beard and he looked like an Old Testament prophet from a Renaissance painting. There were religious icons in his house, which was unusual for those times in Russia. Yermolay immediately and decisively objected to the entire project. He said that if we got to the station unnoticed—and that wouldn't be easy—and if we bribed the cashier with, say, a watch to get the tickets, the cashier would take the watch (then worth a great fortune) with one hand and grab the phone and call the NKVD with the other. And he would have no choice in this, because if we were later caught on the train (which was very likely since the trains were checked frequently) he would otherwise be punished. And us? For trying to escape they would have the right to shoot you right away or, if you were lucky, they would send you to a place much worse than Kurenyevo; and there was no lack of those. We stayed the night at Yermolay's and, in order not to be noticed, made our way back before dawn. No doubt this was the right decision. Yermolay had helped us. You can find good people in this world, even in Siberian hell or perhaps precisely in such a hell.

When the 1940-41 school year was over in early summer I returned to Kurenyevo. There I began working in a brickyard and "gained" one more wartime profession. If I'm not mistaken it was the only job at the settlement other than cutting the forest. The Kurenyevo brick factory was a classic eighteenth-century factory dating from before the Industrial Revolution. The work consisted of consecutive steps all performed by hand. There were probably enough exiles and prisoners who worked for almost nothing, so that machines were not needed. First we dug the clay with shovels in a nearby clay pit. Then we transported it in carts through a path lined with planks to a wooden shack. At the shack we forced the clay, by hand of course, into wooden molds shaped like bricks. We placed these molds one next to another on planks, which were positioned on wooden racks a meter or a meter and a half above ground. We then left them there for several days to dry out. Afterward, when the clay had hardened, we took the bricks out of the molds and placed them upright next to each other on the same planks, where they continued to dry out. From the shade and color of the bricks—light yellow-brown—one could see whether they were ready to be fired. From these unbaked bricks we would build a kiln on a totally flat piece of ground lined with fired bricks. They formed the kiln's base, which was set adjacent to a hill. The hill's slope, which was leveled out perpendicularly to the base, constituted the kiln's back wall. A wall of red, that is, fired bricks adhered to the hill. The kiln was about seven meters high, four to five meters deep, and perhaps seven to eight meters wide. Bricks were placed in a "herringbone" pattern (like the fabric of some men's jackets). The first row faced left at about a thirty-degree angle, the next faced right, and so on. All the bricks in each row were of course parallel to each other with small gaps between them. This is how the first layer of bricks was formed. The next, higher layer was placed on the first, but the second layer's first row had the "herringbone" facing right, the second left, and so on. In this manner the kiln was filled with bricks. It had either three or four hearths with semicircular vaults, as if in Roman style. There were empty spaces for the hearths left in the bottom layer of bricks. We continued placing the bricks closer in subsequent layers until they formed a semicircular roof about a meter and a half in height from the hearth's base. Next we spread clay on the kiln's exterior to seal it, leaving only a few openings on the top for the smoke to escape. The hearths were heated with wood and the fire had to be kept burning day and night. Surprisingly, this created a meeting place in the evening and at night where the boys and girls from the entire settlement would gather. Our social life flourished in this place. We sang and composed little poems about the better times to come after the war when: "we will talk of the war and how here we hung out; and of Kurenyevo that we will spit out" (some said: "and of Kurenyevo that we will puke out.") When we had potatoes we would bake them in the hot ashes. It took several days for the kiln to cool down and then we faced a serious problem. Although all the bricks came out fired and red, some of them, sometimes as many as half, were cracked or broken in two or three pieces. Sakharov shouted that it was sabotage and that he would send all of us to a labor camp. These were not necessarily empty threats and the results could have been tragic. I don't know what our mistake was. There were no experts either among our people or among the zeks who could have taught us how to make good bricks. We tried various changes to our "technology," especially during the firing, but nothing helped. It might have ended badly, but we were released from Kurenyevo in September 1941, three months after Hitler's attack on Russia. And so my career in brick making came to an end without any accomplishments.

Suddenly, and without a word of explanation from Sakharov or other NKVD people, they allowed us to leave Siberia. But we knew from official news broadcasts by the radio station that a treaty had been signed between the Soviet Union and the Polish government in exile in London, the Sikorski-Mayski Agreement. Beginning in July 1941, there was a great deal of excitement as we anticipated a change in our circumstances. In September 1941, the Germans captured a large area of European Russia. The country, especially the railway system, was an incredible mess. We fled south to be as far as possible from the Siberian cold. The trains were unbelievably crowded and chaotic. They ran however they wanted and whenever they wanted. Masses of desperate people camped at the bigger junction stations. There were people from the west who were fleeing the Germans, and those like us, recently freed from exile. Entering, or rather forcing one's way onto a train, was difficult. We became separated from some families we were friends with during our escape, among them the Babics and the Kormans, who ended up in Astrakhan on the Caspian Sea. Dad and I and other friends and acquaintances from Kurenyevo, about ten families all together, ended up on the Volga's shore, where we settled in the small district town of Baranovka near the city of Syzran. Why there and not somewhere else I cannot tell. The Baranowski district adhered to the autonomic region of Mordvins, a small nation of Finno-Ugrian origin. I lived there from September or October 1941 until the beginning of 1943, when I joined the army. Dad stayed until the end of 1944, when he was again arrested by the NKVD.

All in all, Baranovka was not very different from Taboryn. It was a district center, really a big village. Although many Mordvins lived in the district, there was only one high school which was taught in Russian. The area was typically agricultural. Within a few kilometers around Baranovka were a number of villages, each one a kolkhoz. The villages were either Mordvian or Russian, but none had ethnically mixed population. Both Russians and Mordvins lived only in Baranovka, where there were some district offices in addition to the local kolkhoz. The villages were depopulated since most of the men had been drafted into the army. Only the women, older men, and teenagers remained. Mordvins generally spoke in their own language in the villages, although it seemed to me that they all knew Russian.

Immediately upon our arrival I started school. I was in the graduating class. Perhaps it's strange, but high school in this rural and seemingly backward part of Russia was very good. This was because of three excellent teachers. The class counselor was Genrikh Alexandrovich Raycyn, a physics professor at the Moscow Polytechnic Institute. He hadn't been drafted since he had been lame since birth. It was purely by chance that he ended up in Baranovka during the evacuation in the first months of the war. He taught physics and chemistry. One day Mr. Raycyn entered our classroom during German class—it was the only foreign language taught at this school—sat in the last row, and listened to how the local teacher, a young woman, was reading with great difficulty from a piece of paper, mispronouncing each word. He said nothing, but from that point on he taught us German as well. Literature was taught by Mr. Kazayev, who did an excellent job. Having been educated by Kreczmar, I was able to appreciate his skill. I owe him my knowledge and fondness of classical Russian literature. Mr. Kazayev came from Petersburg. He was no longer a young man and belonged to the generation of the pre-revolution Russian intelligentsia, which had been almost entirely decimated by the Bolsheviks in the 1920s and 1930s. Thanks to hiding in this God forsaken place, he had avoided the same fate. I owe equally as much to our excellent mathematician, Mr. Mishin. It is enough to say that three years later, in my first year at the university's chemistry department, I was already familiar with a great deal of material which had been included in the mathematic lectures for chemistry students. Mr. Mishin came from the same background as Mr. Kazayev and his life had worked out similarly. I didn't know much about it then, until Dad explained how these two found themselves in Baranovka. All three were fabulous pedagogues. Dad quickly became friends with them, especially with Mr. Raycyn.

In Baranovka, my father and I and a few other families took quarters at Yegor's, a peasant who owned two houses, an old one where he lived with two adult daughters and a new larger one next to it that he had built for his son, who was getting married. But then his son left to fight in the war, so the house stood empty. Yegor let us live in that larger house. It soon became clear that there was not enough work for the newcomers in Baranovka and that we could manage better in nearby kolkhozes, where they lacked laborers and food was less scarce. So Dad, the Najmans, and two or three other families moved about 15 kilometers to the village Tshirkovo, which was inhabited by Mordvins. Other families from Kurenyevo also settled in nearby villages. I remained in Baranovka at school.

With respect to comfort and cooking, the school in Baranovka was very similar to the previous one in Siberia. The graduating class consisted of five boys and a dozen or so girls. Vladimir Zevnin, who had left Smolensk with his mother and a younger sister, was one of my closest friends. His father had been shot as a saboteur or some other kind of "enemy of the nation" in 1937, during the Stalinist Terror's most rampant period. Although Volodia[16] was then only thirteen, he was his sister's great protector and support for his mother. He was remarkably intelligent and energetic. He was a natural leader and people were drawn to him. To say that he was liked is an understatement. He was also very good-looking and all the girls in our class were crazy about him. His family was very cultured. Even while fleeing Smolensk in a great hurry, they

---

[16] Tr: Volodia: diminutive of Vladimir.

nonetheless took some classical music albums with them. Sometimes we would listen to them. There was one in particular that I liked a lot, but I was unable to find it either after the war in Poland or even in the States. It was Beethoven's "Zastolnaya Piesnya" (Banquet Song), which began with the words *"Nely, naley, boka polney"* (Pour, pour a glass full of wine) and was sung by a baritone. I can still hear this melody in my head. Another close school friend was Pavel Kazayev, who in some respects was Zevnin's opposite. Pavel was the youngest child and the apple of our elderly literature teacher's eye. He also had a mother and two or three older sisters. Pavel was an excessively modest and delicate boy and the best student of all three of us. He was shy and never even looked at girls (they weren't interested in him either), but he could recite Pushkin by heart, including his indecent poems, probably from his father's pre-war library (since such "dirt" wasn't published under Soviet rule; the Bolsheviks were very prudish). And that is how I first heard them. In this respect Pushkin is equal to Aleksander Fredro. We were inseparable. I have a picture of the three of us in an old photo album that I sometimes look at. It is all that is left of them.

The two other boys in our class were Naum Malin, who was lively and always smiling and was evacuated from Moscow with his mother (she had become our school's principal when her predecessor got drafted), and Vasily Shumkin, who was very calm and quiet and the only Mordvin among the five

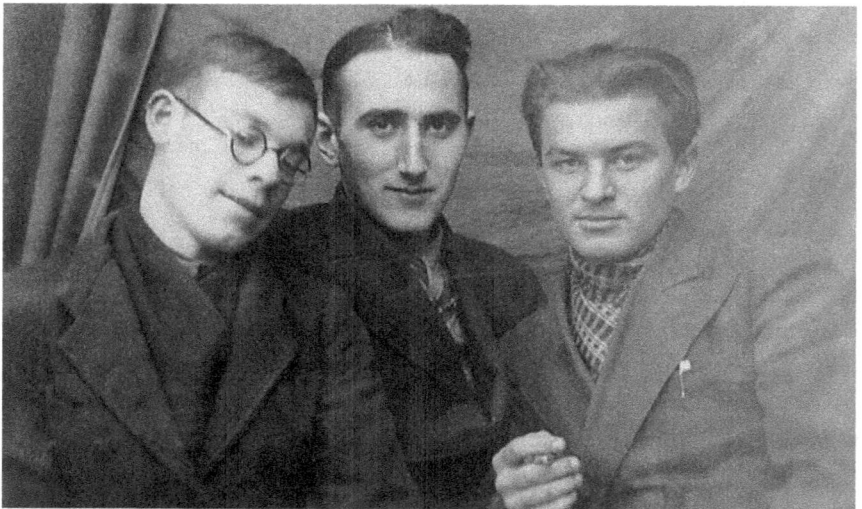

Figure 7 My closest friends from senior year of HS, in Baranovka, Russia, November 1941. From left: Pavel Kazayev, author, Vladimir Zevnin. Both were killed during the war.

of us. Both were great boys. Immediately after we took our high school exams in the spring of 1942, all the boys were drafted except for me. I was a foreigner. In addition, I had been freed from a recent deportation to Siberia. It was very painful to be left behind. I wanted to be on the front lines like my close school colleagues. My friends were gone and the girls ceased to pay attention to me. In March 1945, after I recovered from wounds I suffered in combat, I went to Baranovka and visited my old school. There I found out that all four of my graduating class friends had been killed. Today their names don't mean anything to anyone, but for me they were very close friends. Of the five, I was the only one to survive. Perhaps this is a good way to realize what dreadful losses Russia suffered in World War II. At school I talked with Mrs. Malin. It was hard for me, but worse for her. I recalled that Naum, after high school graduation, was called to the army's armored division. It was considered a good assignment, a bit safer than infantry. Despite the rather low status a high school principal occupied among the Soviet district elite, Mrs. Malin had been able to arrange that for her son. Volodia had joined the artillery. Pavel, Vasily, and later me, the infantry. Mrs. Malin told me that Naum died in a burning tank. She suggested that I should see my other friends' parents, and that's what I did. I visited Volodia Zevnin's mom and Pavel Kazayev's parents. I am unable to describe it. They seemed happy to see me and were warm and no doubt sincere, but were they able to not think: why is he the one who is alive and not my son? Perhaps they could. Who knows? I was not able to see the Shumkins, as they lived in a far away Mordvian village.

I'm going back to the winter of 1941-42. Dad was working in a kolkhoz in Chirkov and was able to visit me from time to time in Baranovka and bring some food when possible. I tried to go to Chirkov as well. During one of my visits, I found out that Mrs. Hela R. had left her husband and, along with her son Jerzyk, had moved in with my father. It had already been known in Kurenyevo that this woman and Dad were "romantically inclined." Still, I wasn't ready for this new arrangement and the impression it made on me was not hard to notice. Dad kept babbling on that after the war we would of course go back to Mom in Warsaw and that he was sorry not only for this situation, but also for having to explain himself to his son. Mrs. Hela, for her part, tried very hard to be nice to me. She was an attractive woman who came from an impoverished family in Sosnowiec, located in Silesian region. Before the war she was married to a man who was much older, wealthy, and dull. I knew this family from Kurenyevo. She was a bit younger than Mom and her son Jerzyk must have been about six or seven. But I kept thinking about Mom and could not accept this arrangement. I went back to

Baranovka and stopped going to Chirkov. I refused to meet with Dad. Although Dad continued to bring me food to the dorm, we did not see each other.

Sundays were no longer as sad or as solitary as they had been in Taboryn because I had friends and because of Lidka, a girl from my class. Lidka was from the Russian village of Slavinko, which was located about five kilometers from Baranovka. Almost all the families in that village were called Zakharov. To tell the truth she liked Zevnin more than me, but what could she do—he already had a girlfriend. Besides, I wasn't that terrible and, in addition, I provided the benefit of giving her cheat sheets during math tests. I think that this peasant girl from a tiny village buried in enormous Russia was also attracted to my "otherness" and the idea of having a forbidden and dangerous relationship with a foreigner. She was a lively and intelligent girl, curious to learn about Poland, about life outside the Soviet system, as were Volodia and Pavel. This was the result of Stalinist Russia's complete isolation from Europe and the world. During the week, Lidka lived in the dorm and generally went home on Sundays, but sometimes she stayed with me in the almost empty building. I liked being with Lidka. It was truly young love, but it ended badly a couple of years later.

In late winter of 1942, we received the news, I don't remember how, that the Polish Army, under the aegis of the Polish government in London, was being formed in Buzuluk in Kazakhstan. It was General Anders' Army, though it was not yet called by that name. Almost all the men from the families that came from Kurenyevo, including Dad, immediately decided to go to Buzuluk. Dad and I were reconciled—we couldn't do otherwise—and both of us felt greatly relieved. Of course, I wanted to join the army with all the others, but Dad thought that I should stay, graduate from high school, and go to Buzuluk right after the exams. He said that it made no sense to drop out of school shortly before the end of the last year of studies, since final exams were supposed to take place early that year, in a month or two, especially since the army was in need of boys with high school diplomas. He was right and I agreed. Most of the men from Baranovka and the neighboring villages left for Anders' army and, to our great astonishment, all except two came back about two weeks later, not having been accepted. Dad said that at the Buzuluk camp they were confronted with hostility and contempt for being Jews. Only Gerszon Fiszman, who had served in the military before the war, and Jurek Koprowski, who had graduated from high school in Warsaw in 1939, were accepted. The others were rejected for all kinds of alleged reasons. Non-Jewish Poles, including those with families, were accepted without exception. Everyone who came back was very bitter. I suggested that perhaps they would take me just as they took Jurek because I would have a high school diploma. But Dad answered right away that my diploma would be worthless in Buzuluk and that I shouldn't delude myself. And even if they did accept me, I would clean latrines. It is only in retrospect that one sees the tragic consequence of the then Polish army authorities' refusal to take Dad and the others. Three years later, in the early winter of 1945, those same nine men, all of them fathers of families from Baranovka and all of them Jews and Polish citizens, were arrested by the NKVD and spent many years in prisons and camps. The eldest, Mr. Koprowski, couldn't withstand the harsh conditions and died in prison. My dad, who was accused of being one of those terrible counterrevolutionary ringleaders, came back to Warsaw only in September 1956. All those people were completely innocent. It was a savage, blind, and senseless terror. That was the war's fate for our small group of friends and acquaintances from Baranowicze and Kurenyevo: the Holocaust created by the Germans, rotting in Siberia and later in Soviet prisons, and the disgusting anti-Semitism of some, though not all, Anders' army institutions. And those were "our" London government's official organizations. The two Najman brothers and I avoided the second Soviet jail because we were in Berling's Army[17] since 1943.

In 1942, in Baranovka, I read the letters that Gerszon sent from the army to his sisters. The letters were in Yiddish (his sister Danka G. knew how to speak Yiddish, but neither how to read it nor write in it). They were very sad. He wrote that, while he had served in the army in the pre-war Poland in the mid-1930s, he had never been as mistreated as he was now. Gerszon was killed in the war. I do not know what happened to Koprowski.

All the hopes in connection to Anders' Army were over and all was as before. Final exams were drawing near. There were three kinds of high school diplomas in Russia then: Gold Rim for those with straight A's, which practically guaranteed acceptance to university; Silver Rim for A's and B's, which was also important for university acceptance (but one had to have mostly A's for subjects that were part of final exams, like Russian, math, physics, chemistry, and biology; good grades in physical education or art were not enough!), and

---

[17] Tr: Polish First Army, also known as Berling's Army, was formed in 1944 in the Soviet Union from the former Polish I Corps, as part of the People's Army of Poland (LWP), a formation of the Polish Armed Forces in the East. Subordinated to the Soviet first Belorussian Front, it participated in the offensive against Germany that ended in the capture of Berlin in May 1945.

Figure 8 Father, on right, with his friend Chaim Babic, after labor camp in Siberia, Russia, 1942.

diplomas without any rim if one had C's. I couldn't count on getting a Gold Rim if only because Mr. Kazayev was very demanding and it was doubtful that my Russian, although not bad, would merit such a grade. From the five of us, only Pavel got the Gold, which he well deserved. I was counting on Silver, but it turned out that the military training instructor stuck me with a C even before written and oral exams! I don't pretend to be especially strategically gifted, but I wasn't worse than others doing drills with fake wooden guns and other such formidable deeds. It was an injustice and all four friends, who had received better than a C grade, interceded on by behalf and spoke to Mr. Raycyn, our class counselor. He talked about it with the principal, the grade got raised to a B, and I got a Silver diploma. It turned out that the instructor, a disabled war veteran, for some reason didn't like "Polaks" and I had become his scapegoat (*Vsio byvayet,*[18] as the Russians say). After a year of studies with Mr. Mishin, the written math exam was not difficult. First I did Lidka's problems—she was sitting in front of me—and then mine. There were three topics to choose from on the Russian exam; all three came from the school superintendent's office. I wrote about Tolstoy's *War and Peace*. We had to analyze and

---

[18] Tr: *Vsio byvayet* (Russian): everything is possible (literally: everything happens).

compare the book's heroes with those who represented, in some measure, the author's views, and they were not the same characters. This was a topic one might have encountered on Mr. Kazayev's tests. The next one was not. One had to analyze an article by Friedrich Engels about the role of work, or rather, of work tools in the "humanization"—literally—of monkeys. The article was interesting and in hindsight quite naive (It was written in the second half of the nineteenth century—it couldn't have been otherwise) and was part of our mandatory readings. Engels was a proponent of Darwin's theory and, in general, an enthusiast of the scientific achievements of his times. All that was nice of course, but what did it have to do with a Russian literature final exam?

When school ended, my friends joined the army. According to Russian tradition there were farewell parties for them. I remained in Baranovka and Lidka moved to the city, apparently to stay with relatives. We didn't part amicably, certainly not at all the way I wanted. She couldn't forgive me for being the only one of the five friends who didn't join the military. She knew that it wasn't my fault, but Russian girls were like that. After the failure with Anders, my efforts to join the Russian army as a volunteer remained fruitless. Dad suggested that I move to Chirkov and work there, but I didn't want to. Finally I settled in a small Mordvian kolkhoz, two or three kilometers from Baranovka, where several families I knew from Kurenyevo lived. There I shared a house with an elderly Mordvian couple whose children had gone to war. The only middle-aged man left among village locals would be the kolkhoz's head, usually a party member who possessed *bron*, literally an armor protecting him from being drafted. This was a typical state of affairs in Soviet villages during the war. An eighteen-year-old young man with a high school diploma was, therefore, something of a "star" on the local scale. I worked mainly in the fields and in outbuildings and the women even taught me how to milk cows. The kolkhoz's head also employed me for administrative work, making various simple measurements, doing accounts in the evening, writing reports, etc. Food was scarce, since whatever could be transported was sent to the military. Despite this the situation was better than in cities, where people were receiving starvation food rations. Bread was very difficult to obtain, especially in the early spring when I started work. There was no lack of milk, however, and sometimes we had potatoes and mushrooms from the forest. The beekeeper introduced me to cucumbers with honey. They were not too bad . . . when one was hungry.

Several times in the summer and fall of 1942 I traveled to the VoenKomat (it's an abbreviation of Voennyi Komisariat, district recruitment office) in Baranovka to remind them, with no effect, about my request to join the military. Finally, at the end of 1942, as the Germans were approaching Stalingrad, I was called up (everyone qualified then) and was sent to a nearby town of Penza to attend a shortened course for infantry officers. For the first time in many months I met with Dad, who threw a traditional farewell party for me. He organized it in Baranovka rather than in Chirkov to spare me an encounter with Mrs. Hela R. Some friends from Kurenyevo came, as did a few of the girls from my graduating class and Mr. Raycyn with his wife. I was sad because neither Lidka nor Volodia nor Pavel were present. There was a lot of vodka, that is, moonshine.

I arrived at the school located near Penza at the beginning of 1943. The red brick barracks had been built in the nineteenth century or maybe earlier, and apparently hadn't been used before the war. They were very cold. I had to wait some time for the next session to begin. Penza mass-produced second lieutenants (mladshih leytnantov). After being commissioned, they were sent to various infantry divisions at the front as platoon commanders, platoons being the smallest military units lead by an officer. We were told that the front stretched from besieged Leningrad in the north to the Black Seat in the south and that every couple of minutes a platoon commander "dropped out" of the line. We were needed to fill in. Later, when I was already at the front, I tried to determine the ratio of killed to wounded. My incomplete and admittedly small statistics sample showed that for each person killed during attacks—and only attacks—there were six or seven wounded, two or three of them seriously. I was assigned to a large group trained to operate the 82 millimeter mortars, called battalion mortars, as each infantry battalion had a group of such light cannons with a smooth, non-threaded barrel.

The first thing they instilled was drill and discipline. Later came exhausting physical exercises, such as overcoming an obstacle course that included crawling under barbed wire, digging trenches and the like, as well as sharpshooting. Next we learned how to use infantry weapons, especially "our" mortars. We were taught the principles of offense and defense, how to the use maps, compasses, and field glasses, situational awareness, and how to maintain proper relationships with subordinates. All this was rather sensible. I also learned many other practical things in Penza, such as how to iron pants, which at night had to be placed under the mattress to keep the crease.

Obtaining a pass to leave the barracks and go to town on Sundays depended on two people: the company's head (*starshina*, usually sergeant major) and the platoon's deputy commander (pomkomvzvod, abbreviation of pomoshchnik komandira vzovda). Hence, a poem:

> Sluzhu sovietskomu narodu—
> Starshinie i pomkom vzvodu
>
> I serve the Russian people—
> Sergeant majors and deputy commanders.

I don't remember if I ever went to Penza. I didn't know anyone there, times were difficult and I didn't feel like visiting the city.

In 1942 there was an almost continuous series of German victories. The Germans were besieging Leningrad and were still near Moscow, although not as near as in December 1941. In the south they occupied the entire Ukraine, a great part of southern Russia, and were also besieging Stalingrad. Again, just as in 1941, countless numbers of Russian soldiers were killed or taken prisoners. The Russian government was evacuated to Kuibyshev (called Samara during tsars' times, and again now; a big city on the Volga River north of Stalingrad). Apparently, according to rumors, since reliable information and true analysis of the situation in Russia were non-existent, only Stalin remained in Moscow. Even if untrue, such disinformation had a positive influence on people: tsar-batiushka[19] is not afraid and is staying with us, with the people. It was also evident that as the Germans continued pressing forward the generally primitive party-line propaganda tried to change the war's character. The point was no longer the defense of Soviet rule, communism, and the Bolshevik party—those words were now seldom heard—but a mortal danger threatening Russia, our mother and common homeland (*matushka Rossiya*!), our nation and our country. And that was true. The exalted songs broadcasted all day long spoke of the holy national war (*idziot voyna narodnaya, svyashchennaya voyna*)[20] that was being compared, and rightly so, to the invasions of Napoleon's military expedition in the nineteenth century as well as Polish invasions of the seventeenth century. Later, after the victory at Stalingrad, every daily newspaper communiqué from the front ended with the words: "For Stalin and for the Motherland." It sounded just like: "For the tsar and for Russia." Suddenly orthodox churches opened in many towns, according to the principle: "When in fear, God is dear." Dad told the story about a little church in Chirkov, which for years had been

---

[19] Tr: Tsar-batiushka (Russian): tsar-father, here: the leader-father.
[20] Tr: Idziot voyna narodnaya, svyashchennaya voyna (Russian): The national war, the holy war is coming.

used as storage for fertilizers and other materials. An order arrived from the district party office in Baranovka to throw out the fertilizers, clean up and renovate the building, and get it ready for becoming a place of worship again. Dad knew about it from the kolkhoz's head, with whom he was friends and drank vodka. I don't know where they found a priest. People joked, or perhaps these were not jokes, that church paraphernalia were brought from some big city's Atheism Museum. New military medals were created, some of very high prestige, named for Kutuzov and Suvorov, famous military leaders of past centuries. This would have been unthinkable before the war, when only Bolsheviks were honored. Kutuzov was greatly responsible for the victory over Napoleon in 1812 and Suvorov, Catherine II's favorite field marshal, was known for his many victories during her reign. Suvorov is especially memorable for us, since it was he who was in charge of the 1794 Praga slaughter when he was suppressing the Kościuszko Uprising.[21] In the fall of 1942, the Germans came close to capturing Stalingrad. This would have had immense and tragic consequences, somewhat like cutting a living organism in half. Petroleum, grain, and other raw materials were coming from the north along the Volga River, the longest river in Europe, which was and still is Russia's natural transportation main line. Additionally and perhaps more seriously, this would have been a major blow to the morale of the military and indeed the entire nation. The battle lasted until the end of January 1943. In Penza we followed all the news from Stalingrad with bated breath. It was clear that we would be sent there at the end of the course. The entire previous class was sent to Stalingrad. Suddenly, in February 1943, there was an announcement that the German Sixth Army under field marshal Friedrich von Paulus' command, which was besieging the city, had been surrounded, had capitulated, and had been captured by the Soviets. It's hard to grasp the magnitude of the triumph this signified. It was the first truly great Russian victory of the war. The entire country breathed a sigh of relief. Hitler proclaimed national mourning and Stalin did something really smart under the circumstances (atypical for him). He ordered a parade of the captured prisoners of war at the Moscow Red Square near the Kremlin wall. They marched, led by their field marshal and generals, and cast the flags of the regiments, squads, and divisions—an army was a huge unit then—under the feet of Stalin, who took the salute. All the papers published photos

---

[21] Tr: The Kościuszko Uprising (1794) against Imperial Russia and the Kingdom of Prussia was a failed revolt, lead by Tadeusz Kościuszko, aiming to liberate Poland and Lithuania from Russia after the Second Partition of Poland of 1793.

of this extraordinary parade. Stalingrad was the true turning point of the war's eastern front. Although human losses would still be enormous for the next two and a half years, the end result had already been determined. The remainder of the war would be an almost constant Russian offensive, all the way to Berlin.

My course was coming to its end—I don't recall having been informed of the date of our promotion—when I was called to the headquarters and told that the Thaddeus Kościuszko Polish Infantry Division was being formed in the town of Sielce on the River Oka near Moscow. I was to go there instantly, before the course ended. They gave me assignment papers (*komandirovka*) and a written order to travel to Sielce. And this is how I found myself in General Zygmunt Berling's[22] division. I preferred to serve in the Polish army rather than in the Red Army. Still, nobody had asked me what I preferred—another decision was being made for me during my war years. That I would remain in the military many years after the war was neither my intention nor foreseeable at the time. I will talk about this later.

In Sielce I was sent to a military academy where I was assigned to the 82 millimeter mortars section. This was like an old friend, since I had already trained on these weapons in Penza. The routine was the same as in Penza, but perhaps easier the second time around, plus this time it was in Polish. This last statement is not totally true, as the instructors were almost exclusively Russian officers called "pop"[23] (acting as Poles). They were mostly officers of Polish origins transferred to Sielce from the Red Army. They had lived "behind the cordon," that is, either in Russia, Soviet Ukraine, or Belarus in the time of the Second Polish Republic. Some of them spoke Polish rather well with the so-called Lvov accent, but there were others whose speech was full of awful mistakes. One of them, who spoke beautiful, refined Polish, was an education officer—they weren't called political yet. His name was Jerzy Putrament. He was a Vilnius native and a pre-war communist activist. No one could foresee that in the near future, in post-war Poland, he would become a minor writer and a generally disliked communist party mole in writers' circles. For years he acted as the head of the Polish Writers Union' party chapter and was a member of the communist party's Central Committee. He was very important and, according to what I have read about him (for example in Stefan Kisielewski's *Journals*, the best and the truest book about communist Poland),

---

[22] Tr: Zygmunt Henryk Berling (1896–1980): Polish general and politician, commander of the First Polish Army, important member of the post-war Polish government.

[23] Tr: POP: acronym for Pełniący Obowiązki Polaków (Polish): performing the duties of Poles.

a truly disgusting individual. But, for the sake of honesty, he merits a good word. The Kielce pogrom of July 1946 was, in communist Poland, an absolutely taboo subject; it wasn't mentioned; it just didn't exist. It ought to have been eliminated from history and from human memory, period, the end. But twenty years later, in July 1966, I read in *Życie Warszawy*[24] Putrament's memorial article about the Kielce pogrom. I think that Putrament was the only person among all Polish writers and journalists who wrote something about it. Perhaps it was because he was a member of the Central Committee that he could take a chance to write about it without interference from the censors.

Życie Warszawy was the official party line mouthpiece, but, as the saying goes, to insist that it always lied wouldn't be accurate, since it did have two completely truthful sections: small announcements and death notices. The former might be "I am looking for a Singer sewing machine" or "Would like to sell a pedigree miniature Pinscher." One of the death notices I still remember to this day: "A member of the 1944 Warsaw Uprising, grandson of a January 1863 insurgent, great-grandson of a November 1830 insurgent." At the cadet school in Sielce, Putrament was lecturing about future Polish democracy, about social justice, but never used words such as socialism and communism. He talked a great deal about agricultural reforms and about Lvov and Vilnius not being Polish cities, as they were surrounded by Ukrainian and Belorussian "sea" and shouldn't be ours. "They," the future owners of "People's Poland"—and Putrament was one of them—already knew at that time about plans to alter the borders after the war.

Upon my arrival in Sielce, I immediately wrote to Dad. Soon afterward he arrived at the camp, along with both Najman brothers: Fiszka and Jakub; this was after the death of Jakub's wife Hela. Fiszka was assigned to the second infantry regiment and later to the regiment's investigation unit. Jakub, if I'm not mistaken, also ended up there. Both survived the war. Cousin Bernard Fiszer was also placed in the same division, but I learned about it much later, totally by chance, when I was already at the front. Dad stayed at the camp for several days. We saw each other every day and with each day he became more and more gloomy. Finally he decided that I could stay here because before the war I was a boy, but for him this army wasn't acceptable. There were too many communists. Dad knew the names of many high-ranking people of the division who ran the place. He was afraid, and perhaps rightly so, because war or not, Bund members were still being jailed in Russia. I myself, however, never

---

[24] Tr: Życie Warszawy: "Warsaw's Life," a Warsaw daily newspaper.

heard of any Bund activist in the Polish army who was arrested in the 1943–45 period. Dad spoke rather negatively about Wanda Wasilewska, who, together with Zygmunt Berling, was behind this venture and for reasons I don't understand, spoke in obscene terms of her chastity. But he had positive things to say about her father, Leon Wasilewski, a historian and a prominent activist of the Socialist Party. Wanda Wasilewska, a communist activist and a writer of modest talent in pre-war Poland, was now the president of the Union of Polish Patriots, an organization with an Orwellian name. It was created by communists and was the army's sponsor. The army, in turn, was conceived by Stalin to be one of the tools for assuming power in post-war Poland. All this is true, but it's also true that most of the privates, non-commissioned officers, some pre-war officers, and young people like me who ended up in the division's military school wanted to fight the Germans; that was it. I knew many who didn't make it in time to join Anders (Anders' Army left Russia at the end of 1942) or, like the Najman brothers, weren't accepted.

That's what happened to Dad: one Polish army didn't want him and he didn't want the other one. So he went back to Chirkov, which proved to be a very important decision with unforeseen consequences. Did Hela R. play a role in his decisions? I don't know. These are not simple matters, but probably she did not. After all, he did not go to Buzuluk to join Anders and again a year later to enroll in Berling's army in Sielce just to go back to Chirkov.

I graduated from the cadet school and in accordance with an old Polish custom was "knighted" by Berling, who touched my arm with a sword. I was assigned to the second baon (battalion) of the first infantry regiment, as platoon leader in the 82 millimeter mortar company. I was the company's only Jew. There were eighteen or nineteen of us in the platoon; that was my entire domain. Most of the privates and non-commissioned officers were older than I, but hardly anyone had completed more than four years of elementary school. The situation was similar in my company's other platoons and in other units as well. There were some people who had held regular service in the pre-war Polish army. I believe all the platoon commanders were from Poland and posts such as company commanders or higher were staffed by many "pops"; who I think were the sole battalion commanders. There were about sixty people in my company (three platoons with three mortars each) under the command of Lieutenant (later Captain) Boris Cypuchowski, who hailed from Soviet Ukraine and spoke Polish rather well. At first I thought him to be morose and sulky, but with time I realized that he was a good, decent person and a good leader who—and this was very important—had a great deal of front-line experience.

In addition to the mortar company, which was small in size, but with considerable firepower, there were three rifle companies, each twice as numerous as our own, a CKM (heavy machine gun) company, an anti-tank gun company, and several smaller units: 45 millimeter anti-tank cannons, a communication platoon, a support platoon and a medical station with a combat medic and paramedics. All together it totaled about six hundred people. Infantry baon was the smallest separate combat unit. The anti-tank gun company had a nice name, but the weapons were useless because their bullets would bounce off the German tanks like ping pong balls. Instead this company was often used as an additional rifle company. Our 45 millimeter cannons were not good as anti-tank weapons. It wasn't until sometime in 1944 that they were replaced with the same caliber guns with longer barrels. This allowed for greater accuracy and for the missiles to travel with greater speed and impact, increasing their effectiveness.

We held division maneuvers before we left the Sielce camp. I had no opportunity to get closely acquainted with people from my platoon before we marched to the nearby railroad station and rode westward toward the front. The departure date—easy to remember, September 1, 1943—symbolized the continuation of the fight against the Germans. Two months earlier, after the battle for Stalingrad, Russian forces had achieved another great victory on the central front, on a section of the so-called Kursk salient. This was a summer victory, so Goebbels' propaganda machine was unable to blame "General Frost" for its defeat, as it was the custom.

Our train was slow and it was a couple of days later that we arrived at the Moscow suburbs. We entered the areas just recaptured from the Germans on the newly reconstructed rails. Right away we noticed that railroad stations and towns had been completely destroyed and burned, part of the German "scorched earth" policy. The names of the towns we were passing, such as Mojaysk, Gjatsk, and Vyazma, made me realize that Napoleon's La Grande Armée had marched this way—back and forth—in the fall and winter of 1812-13. We were going in the direction of Smolensk, northwest from Kursk. At night, one could see the glow of fires in the west and hear the dull roar of explosions; the front was near. In the evening, well before we reached Smolensk, the division left the train and walked the remaining distance. Since the Germans still had air superiority, we marched only at night and rested in some forest or thickets in the daytime so that we couldn't be seen from above. After a couple of days of marching, we stopped for several days in a forest east of Smolensk. This was to be the routine during "my" entire war; after a few days of intensive marching, we had a long break of several days in one place where we would set camp and with shovels, saws and hatchets, build dugouts and position guards. (From the spring of 1944 onward we had tents.) In daytime, officers conducted exercises so the soldiers wouldn't be bored and would go to bed tired, and they would learn as well. The dugouts were rather big, covered with a "roof" made of logs, branches, and soil. When it was possible, we constructed stoves in the dugouts, complete with chimneys made of American canned meat tins. For the infantry soldiers and officers this canned meat, *svinaya tushonka* (braised, or rather smoked pork), was the only visible sign of American aid. The weapons and ammunition were solely Soviet. The tins were square across and half a meter or more long, and we connected them to form a chimney. The canned meat was excellent—for those times—delicious, fat, and nutritious. It was the best part of our menu, which mostly consisted of thick soup, bread, and chicory coffee. Every day the company provided the platoon with several loaves of bread, which were divided, when the circumstances allowed, according to an established ritual: everybody would sit on the ground in a tight group with one man sitting in front and facing them. Often although not always, this was the *zapyevaylo*. Behind him one of the commanders would cut the bread in equal pieces. He would then raise a piece in the air so everyone could see it and shout: ready! Then the *zapyevaylo*, who didn't see the bread, called a name at random until everyone got his share. My platoon thus had an absolutely fair distribution system for the most important material possession, with no possibility of cheating or of "exploitation of man by man." This same procedure was followed in the other units. The *zapyevaylo* was a soldier who, at the command "platoon (or company, or army in general) sing!" would begin a song while we were marching. Other times he would start singing spontaneously, without the command. I liked collective singing. It was good and uplifting, brought people closer, and helped to battle fatigue.

I think that it was then or perhaps a bit later that I got my own orderly. Orderlies were, in fact, officers' servants. Such a function had been generally accepted before the war. It wasn't quite appropriate for the Kościuszko Army, but the higher ups didn't oppose it, perhaps because it was a pre-war tradition. I was actually one of the last to get an orderly. Almost all my platoon commander colleagues had orderlies, so while I didn't feel I needed one I also didn't want to be seen as having inferior status. Then a private came to see me and declared that he wanted to be my orderly. Mikołaj Caban was considerably older than I and had performed his military service before the war. He came from a village near Stanisławów, spoke Polish well, and was probably of

Ukrainian origin. I did not have a lot for him to do. Mostly he prepared my meals in the field kitchen and helped me to take off my boots (with canvas tops). He was quite devoted to me, especially after I ceded "my" five hectares to him. The origin of this is as follows: a rumor spread among the men that, after the war and following the agricultural reform, every Kościuszko Army soldier would get five hectares of land, for free of course. I have no idea where this rumor originated. But since everybody in the company was talking about it and since I had no intention to live in the countryside and farm after the war, I told Caban that I would give him my land. He took this declaration in an odd way. On one hand, strong peasant mistrust made him doubt that this was true. On the other hand, he wasn't sure that it was pie in the sky either. For that matter, neither was I. Putrament kept talking about all this. The whole thing was too appealing to be totally rejected. And so it remained. Meanwhile, our life consisted of marching and stopovers and it brought us closer together. Sometimes we slept on the ground next to each other, covered with two coats and a canvas raincoat, a so-called coat-palatka. Unfortunately, after his four years of school Caban was a secondary illiterate, and hardly the only one in the platoon. With time I learned that he was a decent man. I liked him. He was also a sort of link with platoon's men. I would find out from him what they were talking about and also what they were saying about me. Unfortunately, they didn't respect me much. I turned nineteen while in the cadet school and for most of them I was just a kid. In addition, there were a few non-commissioned officers in the platoon who had served in the military before the war. To them I was less than nothing. I don't believe it had anything to do with my being Jewish. I felt no anti-Semitism in the military. Certainly at that time I wasn't a good leader. I wasn't firm or assertive enough. I suppose that, with time, this changed for the better because the situation demanded it. And besides, even at the very beginning of my military career people could see that I knew what I was doing, particularly during maneuvers and exercises, and that I was familiar with mortars and other infantry weapons. I also helped to carry heavy equipment while we were walking, although I didn't have to, and they appreciated that. And there was a lot to carry. An 82 millimeter mortar weighed about 60 kilograms and had three parts. The crew consisted of five people who formed a squad: a leader, usually a non-commissioned officer who carried the tripod; a gunner who carried the barrel; an assistant-gunner who carried the base, and two ammunition bearers who hauled very heavy boxes with ammunition. This had to be carried in addition to personal weapons, usually automatic PPSh guns (I don't know where this acronym

comes from. I think that these are the designers' initials),[25] a helmet, a sapper's spade attached to the belt and very useful, and a gas mask that everyone
cursed. Far from the front we would load mortars and ammunition on several
of the horse-pulled carts, which the company had. When we were conducting
exercises closer to the front, the carts would stay behind and the equipment
ended up on our backs. The mortars had a five kilometers range, far for infantry. During attacks, our place was among rifle companies. When fire from the
nine company mortars was centered in a small sector, there was a lot of noise
and destruction. The mortars' drawback was their lack of accuracy, especially
at the distances of more than one and a half to two kilometers. Another problem was the delivery of the ammunition, which was heavy. During attacks, the
ammunition bearers had to work like crazy.

At the end of September, we received orders to break camp and begin to
walk west. We were in the front-line zone and had been warned about the existence of mine fields and various kinds of traps. We were told that we were
going to the front, which had become stabilized west of Smolensk following
a Red Army offensive. We were supposed to get our sector and take over the
positions left by one of Russian infantry divisions. The view at night as we
passed through recently captured Smolensk was chilling. The city was burned
and totally destroyed. There were no houses, just ruins. Here and there charred
remains were still smoldering. I had never seen anything like that before. I saw
a lot more of it later.

After crossing the city early in the morning, for the first time in my life I
encountered several dozen German captives. They were walking in the opposite direction, escorted by several Red Army infantry soldiers. They were in
disheveled uniforms with expressions of uncertainty on their faces, and some
of them were wounded. It brought to mind the scene from Mińsk Mazowiecki
in September 1939. We veered left to let them pass. Suddenly a single Russian
tank, going fast toward the front lines, appeared as if from nowhere and seemed
to have no intention of slowing down as it approached the Germans. A commotion erupted as the Germans jumped to the road's edge. The escort started
shooting into the air. The tank crewmen were laughing and the escort members
started screaming at the tank crew, but they were already far ahead. Nobody
actually got hurt. It was a sort of joke, but at one point the blood in my veins

---

[25] Au: PPSh 1941 or PPSh-41 (Pistolet-Puliemyot Shpagina), commonly called pepesha or
pepeshka, is a Russian 7.62 x 25 mm caliber submachine gun designed by Georgi Shpagin
and introduced into the Red Army's weaponry in 1941. It became part of the Polish Army
armament in 1943.

ran cold watching the tank run straight towards living people. Yes, I hated the Germans, but I wasn't able to bear such a sight.

A few times as we came closer to the front we found ourselves under German artillery fire. At those times, Cypuchowski and the battalion's commander, Captain (and later Major) Dziewanowski, demonstrated class and courage. They were able to tell from the missile's sound whether it would fall far enough in front or behind us so as to pose no danger or close enough so that it would be necessary to throw oneself immediately on the ground, preferably in some hollow or ditch. The rest of us quickly learned this as well. And it was absolutely necessary to wear a helmet and cover one's neck with a sapper's spade for protection from the shrapnel. If possible, it was best to jump into the hole made by the missile itself, since there was only a slim possibility that the next one would fall in the same exact spot (as Gauss has proved). That's how we got our experience. The platoon suffered no losses.

Finally a few days later we learned that we would take over Russian positions that night. Our battalion as well as the entire first infantry regiment would go first. We were to begin to attack the German defense lines early in the morning. The other platoon commanders and I spent a lot of time that day at the briefing with Cypuchowski, the company's head. We received detailed instructions about the location of Russian positions we were supposed to take over and we drew all this on our maps. The maps were, in general, 1:25.000 to scale: one centimeter corresponding to 250 meters. There was a tiny river called the Mierzeja between the Germans and us. We were told that on our stretch it was little more than a small wetland area. And the next day it was apparent that it would not, in fact be an obstacle. The positions we were supposed to take were no further than a few hundred meters from the Germans. I passed the information to my three squad leaders and to the mortar crews.

We pushed off after dusk. At first I was able to navigate. I knew where I was and where I had to lead the platoon. After awhile, though, I got lost in the dark. The map and the compass didn't help. The only possibility was to stay close to Cypuchowski and not take my eyes off him. But Cypuchowski was short and coming too close to him with the entire platoon made no sense because if other platoons in the same situation did the same thing then the whole company would become a closely packed group, which was both unwise and prohibited. Finally I made a "strategic" decision. I ordered Caban, who was a strong guy, to stay halfway between Cypuchowski and me and to signal with his hand; and I told the squad leaders in turn to keep their eyes on me. We advanced in this manner. Was I afraid? And how! I was simply petrified. But so what? I couldn't hide or flee. And there wasn't much time to be afraid since all I could do was to think about the platoon. I couldn't let us get lost. I had to take the men to the designated spot, position the mortars, and wait for further orders. It was the same all over again: duty and determination to do what was necessary and definitely not to be worse than others. These are perhaps the most important motives of one's behavior in such circumstances. I wasn't the only one to be afraid. Many of those around me made the sign of the cross.

We hadn't yet reached our main position when the Germans began firing flares. Possibly these were burning phosphorus, which slowly descended and illuminated a small area. The light was extremely powerful, making everything as clear as in daytime. It all seemed very strange and somewhat unearthly, since the illuminated circle was surrounded by darkness. After a moment machine guns began to rattle and we saw volleys of luminous bullets. We fell to the ground and continued to advance by crawling or quickly jumping from place to place as we had been taught. Both the flares and CKM volleys weren't unexpected and we had experience with them in our maneuvers and exercises. Of course it wasn't the same as exercises, but at least it was familiar. Suddenly the Germans ceased firing flares and the CKMs went silent. There was total darkness and quiet. And then something totally unforeseen and unexpected happened. From the direction of German trenches came the sound of a lively folk dance, oberek or something like that. A moment later, the music stopped and a loud man's voice in perfect Polish told the Tadeusz Kościuszko First Division soldiers to stop listening to the lousy Jews and the Bolsheviks who controlled them, since they were enemies of the Poles, and to join the Germans. The voice gave assurances that the Germans would not shoot them and gave the password, which had to be given when approaching German positions, as well as the appropriate response. The voice promised that those who did this would go back to their homes in Poland and the war would be over for them. And this repeated: music and then this speech over and over again. All this lasted quite some time. Yes, the Germans had good espionage and good loudspeakers. To me this was frightening. I froze. This was and has remained the most terrible memory of my first front-line night. Then I kept doing what I was supposed to do. We reached our positions and placed mortars according to the predetermined plans. With the first daylight, we could see that no one was missing from either the platoon or the company. I felt relieved. It's difficult to say what happened in other units, but it seems that very few men defected. Immediately after the war, I heard rumors that in the fall of 1943 the Germans drove two soldiers around the General Government[26] boasting that they were Kościuszko soldiers, defectors from our division. Not many out of about ten thousand, assuming that it was true to begin with. I don't know whether any historians were ever interested in this matter and have tried to clarify it.

At dawn preparations for the artillery offensive began. The bombardment of German positions lasted about an hour, followed by a fifteen-minute pause, during which time artillery observers evaluated the damage and selected additional targets, whereupon the cannonade would continue for another hour. This was an established procedure prior to an infantry attack. The cannonade was truly intense as the Russians were providing us with artillery support. To this we added what small amounts of our own mortar fire we could. Then airplanes joined in, flying over us in several waves and dropping bombs on the German positions. Finally, on cue we, the infantry, jumped out of the trenches and ran forward, shouting as we went. To tell the truth I am unable to recall this and replay it in my head. Nor can I recall how we crossed the Mierzeja River. I know that on a few occasions, when the firing was more intense, I fell to the ground and looked around to see if all my men were there; it seemed so. Finally we jumped into the trenches and, to our surprise, found them empty. The Germans were gone. Losses in my sector were small, since there was not much firing. The trenches were well built and deep. Most likely the Germans had forced the local population to make them, as was their habit. There were also dugouts where we found some food, maps, and other odds and ends. The first line of trenches was linked to the second and to the subsequent ones with transverse trenches. We quickly jumped over them. I kept in contact with the company's leader visually or through messengers. It seemed that we had advanced by some two or three kilometers, perhaps more, without meeting any serious resistance except for sporadic rifle shots, when we received an order to stop and reinforce our positions.

The next day, all hell erupted. Planes bombarded us ceaselessly, nose-diving and shooting at us with machine guns. They came in waves, one after another. Anti-aircraft guns from our side fired with little effect. I did not see any Russian planes engaging the Germans in the air. In spite of very intense bombardment, there was not one direct hit in my sector. We remained in German trenches two or three days when we received orders to retreat.

---

[26] Tr: The General Government or General Governorate: part of Poland under Nazi Germany's administration during World War II, from 1939 to early 1945. It comprised most of central and southern Poland, western Ukraine, and eastern Galicia and included major cities such as Lodz, Cracow, Warsaw, and Lvov.

Russian troops were to take over. I don't know why the offensive didn't continue. I didn't expect any of it. I was looking at this war with a platoon commander's eyes. I only know as much as I myself saw; our superiors were not at all prone to supply more detailed information, neither then nor later. Perhaps higher-ranked officers knew more than I did. Company losses were minimal. It must have been worse in other sectors because when we were retreating from the front I saw many wounded soldiers.

This was my baptism of fire, and this is how the October 1–12, 1943 Battle of Lenino has remained in my memory. I demonstrated neither great courage nor commanding ability. I did what was needed, what I was told, and I hope that I did it no worse than others. Lenino was the name of a nearby small town that I never visited. After the war, October 12 became the Polish Army Day.

Several days later, the division assembled two or three kilometers from the front. I spent my time doing little more than observing the second battalion of the first infantry division. We spread out in a grove near a destroyed village. Despite it being middle of October, the weather was still mild and one could wash up thoroughly outdoors at a well, wash one's underwear, and get some rest. At the next briefing I learned that we would soon deploy farther away from the front as part of army command's rearguard. That meant that if the Germans began an offensive and threatened to sever a nearby section of the front we would move to stop them. High ranking officers usually kept a large number of troops in the rearguard. At the briefing, I asked Cypuchowski to exchange my officer's TT pistol with an eight-cartridge magazine (I also had one or two spare magazines) for a PPSh gun, equipped with several dozen rounds. I had noticed, even before approaching the first front line, that both he and Dziewanowski had automatic pistols. After a while all platoon leaders had the PPSh guns. I felt more secure when I received my PPSh gun. They let me keep the pistol as well.

And so the already familiar routine began: marching, then several days of stopover, and again "soldier is marching through the forest, through the woods." First we encountered a poor Belarus village, but as soon as we got settled we were told to leave. We walked for about a week to the next village, which was very similar. I don't know why we stopped in the first one and I don't know why we went to the next one, which had just recently been recaptured from the Germans, but that's how it is in the military. It was already November and the weather was awful with rain and mud. Soon the cold and snow arrived. It wasn't an easy life.

The most repulsive memory of my wartime dates from this period: lice. Even after the many years that have gone by I can think of nothing more revolting. One becomes disgusted with oneself. In December 1939, I came back to Warsaw from Baranowicze covered with lice. I don't know whether I contracted this filth in the house on the Bug River or whether it was perhaps in one of the crowded trains, either on the German or the Soviet side. In any case, both Dad and I got to work and the lice disappeared. From time to time they would appear during our excursions in Siberia and the Volga region, but we always found soap, hot water, and an iron. We ironed our clothes and underwear under steam and managed to get rid of that scourge. But when the army was marching in the winter it was not possible to do this. One night I got so mad that I jumped out of the marching formation and took off all my clothes right there in the snow, put on clean underwear, which I still had in the bag with my personal belongings, and threw the old clothing out. I was aware that the relief would be short-lived, as the vermin hid in the seams and nooks of the clothing, but even this was fine. I couldn't get rid of my pants and the uniform because I didn't have any extra ones. Sometimes, but infrequently, special laundry cars would arrive; we called them "voshoboyki"[27] in Russian because they first washed and then kept clothes under steam. That helped. But unfortunately there were so many soldiers who wanted to have this done that it was difficult to recover our own clean and lice-free rags. Unfortunately, there was yet another kind of lice that were small and flat and they lived not in the clothes, but on the body, primarily in the crotch. We called them nits or louse. But enough! I had to be wounded to get into a hospital and get rid of this filth once and for all.

There were no more than a dozen houses in the village where we stopped. My platoon got one house for quartering. An elderly woman with several teenaged grandchildren lived in it. They slept on the stove, my soldiers on the floor while I slept on a bench, a bit like in Kurenyevo. The villagers were as poor as church mice and we shared our food with them. The borderland between Belarus and Russia probably had never been rich, but now, after the Germans' departure, it was totally devastated. We spent the 1943-44 winter there. Other units were distributed among neighboring villages while the division staff was stationed in the somewhat larger village of Lyaptievo. The name is not a sign of wealth, since it comes from the word "lapotye," or peasant footwear made of wicker, material used to make baskets.

---

[27] Tr: Voshoboyki (Russian): lice killers.

Some notes I made in those times still exist. They are mostly about my everyday activities with the platoon. They show that I planned our exercises in detail and prepared them conscientiously. One day I wrote—clearly with satisfaction since I ended the sentence with an exclamation point—that while marching each of my squads was able to position the mortar and aim it from above at a specific target in 40 seconds; it was a good result. My watch, which Grandma had given me for my thirteenth birthday, came in handy. Ammunition was distributed sparingly and target shooting rarely took place. That winter we were given skis, sleds, and white camouflage clothes and we started to learn how to fight in the snow. However, we never did. We also had classes in politics, which, since I was a battle officer, I didn't conduct. People from the entire company had to attend these talks, where "experts" from the battalion would speak. Apparently my company wasn't large enough to have its own education officer. In the evening, officers from my unit and adjoining units often played cards for money, mostly poker, but that didn't interest me. I was sending my officer's wages earned in the army's front-line zone to Dad in Chirkov. The wages weren't worth that much. I went to Lyaptievo a few times for briefings with higher rank-ing officers. I remember Berling well because he liked to gather all the young division officers together at crowded meetings and because he had a colorful way of speaking. Once, when evaluating each regiment's achievements at the maneu-vers in which the entire division had participated, he said that in his opinion the second infantry regiment placed first, next was the first infantry regiment, then for a very long time nobody, next was sh-t . . . and then the third infantry regiment! Another time he devoted his entire speech to the need for self-study. We are, he said, a cadre division. He explained that after entering Poland the size of the army would increase greatly, and that within a few months each platoon leader would have the chance to become a battalion leader. He, on the other hand, even though he was a Piłsudski legionnaire (this was true), had to wait almost twenty years for such an opportunity. But, he continued, rather than hitting the books in the evening to study, our officers prefer to grab a bottle of vodka with one hand, a woman by the lungs with the other, and have fun! There was a lot of truth in what he said about vodka, or rather, moonshine, but not so much when it came to the gentle sex. Some higher ranking officers did, in fact, have girlfriends, for example telephone operators from communication services or nurses from the division hospital, but people like us, ordinary guys of lowest ranks, did not. The ladies were called *polevaya podviznaya zhena* (mobile field wife). After the war I saw happy marriages that had originated as such unions; one can never tell. Such things were not only happening on the eastern front.

Eisenhower lived openly with his female driver as did many other great men. I read recently that such things went on every day in the Israeli army.

I heard the name Katyń for the first time that winter in Belarus. One day, the company received an order to send a few people to the regiment as part of a larger delegation that would go somewhere nearby to see the graves of Polish officers, inmates from 1939 at a Soviet prisoner of war camp who were murdered in 1941 by the Germans entering these territories. Our lodgings were near Katyń. At the time I was completely unaware of the scale of the crime; nor did I know who its perpetrators were. When I asked Cypuchowski to send me with the group, he answered that he had received a different list telling him whom to include and my name wasn't on it. At the time I didn't pay much attention to this. However, I kept it in mind, since it seemed odd. Did "they," the division leadership, already know the truth and were manipulating us? What criteria did they choose to determine whom to send? I don't know. People came back from Katyń and told us that they had seen open graves and the remains of corpses, Polish personal military documents, various uniform parts, eagle buttons, and other things. They believed beyond a shadow of a doubt that the Germans were responsible. I believed that as well. It seemed to me that mass murder wasn't Soviet style. Instead they would have sent them all to Siberia, let them chop the forest and slowly die of starvation and cold. After all, this had been my experience. Many years after the war, after Stalin's death but before Dad' return from prison in September 1956, in a chance conversation with his peer, a Bund member (after the war in Warsaw there were still several—literally—such specimens whom I would meet from time to time) I told him my "theory" and was told point blank and with a raised voice that I was a fool and that I didn't know what I was talking about, since there was irrefutable proof that the crime had been committed by Russians. It was mass murder of innocent people. They died because of who they were, like Jews in the Holocaust. Among Katyń victims, there were approximately 8 percent Jews, although there were very few Jews among professional officers. The explanation is simple: when mobilization was announced in September 1939, many reserve officers found themselves in prisoner of war camps. There were many people with higher education among them: large numbers of Jewish medical doctors, pharmacists, and engineers. One doesn't hear much about it, even now; perhaps it doesn't fit the stereotype of "żydokomuna."[28] From the group of our closest friends, the one who died in

---

[28] Tr: Żydokomuna (Polish): Judeocommunism, a pejorative anti-Semitic term coined in the interwar period. It blames Jews for introducing communism in Poland, identifying communism with a Jewish-led conspiracy to seize power.

Katyń was Janka Pogonowska's father, who before the war was a professor of the Pharmacy Department at the Warsaw University.

In the spring of 1944, we were transferred to Soviet Ukraine. At first we stayed in villages between Żytomierz and Berdyczów. Although I had never visited them, I knew those villages' names from classic Yiddish literature. Our life was just like in Belarus. The area was perhaps a bit wealthier, but the moonshine, made from beets, was worse. I never drank such stinking stuff in my entire life.

One day we discovered that we had one horse too many; this was called "above quota." Nobody knew, or in any case wanted to admit that they knew, where the horse came from. The horse existed unlawfully. Cypuchowski made it clear that he didn't wish to know anything, but that we had to get rid of the horse. And it had to be done quickly so the higher authorities wouldn't take it away. Private (or perhaps corporal) Pilecki, the best soldier in my platoon, arranged to exchange the horse for a bucket of moonshine and some food. The transaction took place in one of the neighboring villages, where kolkhozes were being reestablished after the departure of the Germans. Pilecki was much older than I. Before the war he used to live in Lvov and claimed to be a professional pickpocket. However, in the company nothing was ever taken from anyone. But, as they say, thieves never steal from friends. He was extremely smart and was great as an area reconnoiter—sometimes better than Mister (second) lieutenant with his map and compass—and had fantastic eyesight. Later that summer, when we were in Poland, Pilecki was unparalleled when we came upon minefields. He was able to perceive each thin wire or other suspicious object hidden in grass. This was very useful, as if a sixth sense: my men just followed his trail.

We hadn't been in Soviet Ukraine very long when we were transferred farther east, near Kovel. Before the war, this used to be Polish Volyn. We set up camp in the forest instead of staying in villages as we had before. They were hostile to Poles and allied with German Ukrainian partisans' units in the area—the Ukrainian Insurgent Army.[29] We were forbidden to leave the camp alone or even in small groups. Sentries stood day and night at the camp's border. We didn't stay near Kovel for long. The Soviet offensive was advancing quickly, the Germans were retreating, and military doctrine says that the enemy cannot be allowed to break away from the attacking army. The idea was not to let the

---

[29] Tr: Ukrainian Insurgent Army: Ukrainian Nationalist Partisan Army, which used guerrilla tactics in its fight against Nazi Germany, the Soviet Union, Czechoslovakia, and the Polish population of western Ukraine during World War II, and against communist Poland after the war. It stopped its activities in 1949.

Germans stop and reinforce their positions. We experienced this doctrine on our own feet when strenuous marches began.

One night, when we were walking through a large village I noticed that, without exception, all the houses in one part of the village had been burned. Only the stove stumps were still standing. About half of the houses in the village were totally destroyed. It was strange. When the same sight was repeated in another village, I asked Pilecki, who was from this region, what had happened. He told me that the burned houses belonged to Poles who had been savagely murdered—women, children, and men—by their Ukrainian neighbors. Their possessions had been looted and the houses burned. The Volyn slaughter, which resulted in tens of thousands innocent people being killed, had undoubtedly been provoked by the Germans. But so what? "Seeds fell on fertile soil"; such was the conclusion of the Kielce pogrom discussion published in Parisian *Kultura* in the 1970s. After all these years in the States it is hard to imagine, and even more difficult to explain, how such evens had been possible. Christianity had existed for a thousand years there and for fifteen hundred for the Germans. Pilecki was sure that the Ukrainian houses were empty—there was no light in any of them—because people knew who we were and were afraid of us and had fled to the nearby forests.

A few days later—it was daytime—we were passing through a small town (I don't recall its name) when I noticed that the main square was almost empty. Something struck me—where were the Jews? I never saw such towns before the war, but I knew there were Jewish "shtetls," especially in eastern Poland. There was a small stall in a little square where an older, non-Jewish woman was selling food and moonshine. I stepped out of the column, made a small purchase, and asked her about Jews. She looked at me as if surprised, shook her head and said "gone, gone" and that was all I was able to get out of her. I had to return to the platoon. Several minutes later we had left the town behind. That was my first encounter with the Holocaust. I understood nothing. I was left with a vague feeling of horror.

Afterward, events moved fast. We crossed an undamaged bridge on the Bug River near Luboml and continued in the direction of Chełm. I didn't know that, in the future, the Bug would constitute the border with Russia. Chełm hadn't been damaged. It seems that my regiment was either the first or one of the first Polish units to arrive after the Germans had retreated. The population welcomed us in a friendly manner and kids ran after the soldiers. Things were the same several days later when we passed through similarly undamaged Lublin, the first major Polish city on our path. I would lie if I insisted that it was the same unrestrained enthusiasm that welcomed the French army or the Americans in freed Paris. There was reticence. But I didn't understand any of it then.

Several times on the way from Kovel we were able to travel in trucks for a day or two, which helped us move westward more quickly. The trucks were either Soviet ZISs or American Studebakers. I would sit in the cab next to the driver, trying to learn how to drive. The Studebaker was easier to drive, as it had a synchronized transmission and more comfortable seats. The ZIS was less comfortable, but sturdier. In this way we arrived at the shore of the Vistula River, which lay between Puławy and Dęblin, in the second half of July and we stopped at the shore. There were German positions on the other side of the river. Farther north in the direction of Warsaw, from Karczew and beyond, east of Praga, the Germans kept a well fortified bridgehead on the Vistula's eastern shore.

My battalion was assigned a significant stretch near the estuary of the Wieprz River to the Vistula. Tall poplars had been planted on both sides of a beautiful country road that ran along the river. It was summer and the tops of the poplars were crowned with thick leaves. We placed an observation point on one of the trees. On its eastern side, which could not be seen from the river, we attached a rope ladder and pulled a telephone cable to its top. Each day before dawn a platoon commander dressed in leafy camouflage would climb up to direct the company's fire and he would come back down at dusk. Through binoculars, one could clearly see CKMs slots, trenches, all kinds of fortifications, and people on the opposite shore. But the binoculars could only be used before noon, when the sun was behind us; in the afternoon the sunrays would have been reflected in the lenses and betrayed us. We noticed right away that the soldiers on the other side of the river were not German, as they were wearing different uniforms. It turned out that they were Slovaks. This stretch of the front was not as dangerous, since we were separated by the Vistula River, and German lines were held by allies whom they didn't fully trust in those days (summer 1944). Most probably this saved us, because the Germans would have understood where the fire was coming from and would have cut the poplars with their artillery fire. As always, the ammunition was given to us sparingly. Cypuchowski was very cautious and didn't want us to be discovered; hence he didn't let us shoot much and often changed our positions. And then a miracle (almost) happened: a message from the battalion informed us that the Germans had left train cars on the railway siding near Dęblin full of ammunition, including missiles suitable for soviet mortars. The company's head immediately went to Dęblin and brought back much of the captured ammunition. We couldn't have dreamed of such amounts from our sources.

The company head, usually an experienced sergeant or sergeant major, was an extremely important person, almost like a company commander. He took care of all supplies, from ammunition to provisions.

The caliber of German mortars was one millimeter smaller than ours: 81 millimeters. They couldn't use our ammunition, but we could use theirs, provided that we compensated for backlash and the loss of energy by adjusting the barrel's angle of elevation. We had special shooting charts for using German ammunition. At Cypuchowski's briefing we deliberated about how to employ this accidentally acquired "treasure" to the best advantage. We knew that a mobile field kitchen stopped more or less at the same spot each day, arriving around noon at the unit on the opposite shore. Soldiers were drawn to the food like flies to honey. But there was a problem. The site was at a good distance from the Vistula, at the limit of our mortars' accuracy. So far we had been shooting at the position on the shore. Shooting further made sense only if done by volley fire from the entire company. We decided to do it after first practicing discreet target shooting. For several days we meticulously noted the mortars' parameters and places where the missiles exploded until Cypuchowski felt that we knew enough to start "the fun." I was supposed to direct firing that day. It wasn't an honor; Cypuchowski simply believed that I would be the quickest to do the necessary computations and to adjust the firing when needed. I wasn't at all happy about it. It was late summer 1944; the Allies, landing in France, had finally set up the long ago promised second front and were pushing forward. The war had been won, so it was important to preserve one's life. A year or two earlier, I wouldn't have had such thoughts. Well, I was free to think whatever I wanted, but orders were orders. It turned out that, indeed, adjustments were necessary, and I believe I was able to transmit them rather quickly by telephone. It was truly gratifying to watch from above the little figures scurrying away in panic, some falling on the ground and either not getting up or getting up but limping. I still see it as if in a photograph. I was sorry they weren't Germans. After having used the German rounds, my company moved to a different place while I sat until dusk in a tree. It wasn't my life's most enjoyable afternoon. Still, sometimes things were worse.

One day we were told that three soldiers from the division who had committed robbery, rape and murder in a nearby village had been condemned to death by a military court and that the execution would be public. Several thousand soldiers stood at three sides of a rectangle with the place of execution situated at the foot of a small hill across from them. A military chaplain accompanied the condemned and gave them last rites. They were then blindfolded and shot immediately. It was the first—and the last—time that I witnessed such spectacle. It's not easy to keep the discipline among tens of thousands of men armed to the teeth, some of whom may have been bandits and murderers. There are people who become savage in a war and a warning such as public execution, although primitive, could be effective. After seeing great numbers of people killed and wounded every day, death becomes ordinary, even trivial. The Germans left well camouflaged minefields and we often saw our mutilated soldiers. Corpses were also a common sight, especially in the first days in the new region; they floated in the Vistula and Wieprz rivers. Mostly they were German, but sometime they were ours.

I remember another public execution in our division, although I didn't watch it. It took place shortly after the battle of Lenino; a soldier was condemned for treason. I'm not familiar with the details and cannot recall how it happened that I wasn't present to witness the execution. For lesser crimes, military courts condemned soldiers to prison terms and, without exception, changed prison sentences to service in penal companies.[30] These units were sent to exceptionally dangerous places. For example, in the previously described two-part artillery preparation, a penal company—sometimes a battalion—attacked in the interval between the first and the second cannonade. They took the fire from the remaining CKMs as well as other firing points. During this "scouting by attack"—what a beautiful euphemism—gunners observed the undamaged targets and then tried to destroy them in the second firing. This was followed with bombing from the air. Only then did we attack. Losses among the "penals" were enormous. Those who survived such events received an automatic reprieve and went back to a regular unit or were sent to a hospital. They were led mostly by officers who had been sentenced as well. I suppose all this followed the Red Army model. I don't recall the younger officers being ever informed officially of the military justice system's principles. I twice observed "penals" in action. The first time, I believe they were attempting to capture a bridge on the Vistula, near Dęblin; they didn't succeed. The second time it took place in September, when our offensive from Karczewo toward Praga began; there they were attacking during the interval of artillery preparation.

When the Vistula was the front line, we were called to the division for a briefing. A high-ranking Russian general told us about his stay in France

---

[30] Tr: Penal companies or battalions: military units whose members were convicted men either assigned to serve in them as punishments, or for whom such formations were an alternative to incarceration or capital punishment.

and about the combat of the Allies, especially the Americans, he had seen. Apparently people of his rank were able to fly to France over Italy or Africa in the summer of 1944—I'm not sure. The general had many very large stars on his shoulder straps and even more medals. There was also a general in a Polish uniform on the stand as well as several colonels. Berling, who was no longer commanding our division, since he had been promoted to be the Corps or perhaps the Army leader (after our departure from Sielce, other Polish units had been formed there), wasn't present. The briefing took place in a meadow. At first the general talked sensibly about American weapons, comparing them to ours. For example, in his opinion their airplanes were good, but not their tanks. I have heard a similar estimation from our tank crewmen. As long as the general talked about weapons, it all made sense. But suddenly he began to talk about their military, about infantry, and it all changed. It's not an army, he said. They don't know what an offensive is. They attack as if they were going for a walk since there is nothing and nobody left on the German side, as everything has been destroyed and crushed into powder and dust by artillery and aerial bombardment. The general laughed loudly at this pathetic army. The presumption was that we would be able to defeat it without any trouble. The nitwits on the stand laughed with him. What crudeness and stupidity. I was very young and my critical skills hadn't ripened yet. I was rather inclined to believe what my superiors were saying. However, it still struck me as odd. Certainly I wasn't the only one to have this reaction, but I don't recall talking about it with anyone; self-censorship was already at work. Yes, the Allies respected human life. What was funny about that? But they fought and died when it was necessary.

Later I understood that it was a typically Russian, yes, Russian, but not necessarily Soviet contempt for people, for human life. It was the same contempt for life that Tsarina Catherine and other tsars had toward serfs and all the "lower levels" of the social ladder. This remained in the Bolshevik era, only wrapped in hypocrisy and continued even after they left.

It was the end of July or the beginning of August when I was summoned by Major Dziewanowski, the battalion's leader. My good friend Romek Czerkies, also a platoon leader, was called in as well, and in the major's tent we found several other lower-ranking officers. Dziewanowski informed us that his chief of staff had been seriously injured in a minefield and that he needed a replacement, but wouldn't get one from the regiment. He wasn't able to assign any of his companies' leaders to this position, since they were much more experienced and thus needed to command their companies, especially now that the offensive was about to begin. Therefore, one of us was to leave the tent as the chief of staff. It was an unprecedented jump and promotion. The previous chief of staff was a captain. Dziewanowski and all the others called him "chief of staff," but technically the battalion had no staff and therefore he couldn't be a chief of staff. The point was that this position's formal name was long and particularly clumsy: battalion's older adjutant, so nobody used it, but the duties and the authority of the officer carrying this function were similar to those of a chief of staff. First Dziewanowski talked with each of us separately. Afterward we had to solve written problems. These, duplicated on a hectograph, had to do mainly with artillery fire. They required knowledge of geometry and, in some cases, of some trigonometry. The reason for it was as follows: in an attack, an infantry battalion leader for a brief time was assigned a great number of artillery units, and the older adjutant was responsible for coordinating their actions. After this exam, Dziewanowski chose me. I think that to a great extent I owed this promotion to Mr. Mishin, since I still remembered what he had taught me.

My most important daily duty was keeping contact with the "top," that is, the regiment's leader and the headquarters, as well as with the "base," the battalion's subunits. I talked with the regiment by radiotelephone—that was the name of a heavy box with an antenna and with a cable and a phone sticking out from it. There also was a second box, heavy as well; I think that it contained batteries. This device worked within a distance of no more than five kilometers, and not always well. The two signalers who carried them followed me constantly. It was our battalion's only radio. The difference between this and today's cell phones is incredible. Communication with the company was by phone, and during attacks—through signalers, like in the times of Alexander the Great. Still, the telephones worked well. Even during night attacks, the radiotelephone operators were sometimes able to pull phone lines to the area where leaders of some rifle companies were located.

With the new post, my life became totally different than the relatively tranquil existence as head of a mortar platoon. All day long—and at night as well—I had much more to do. For example, I had to write numerous notifications and reports, indicating the number of people in the battalion, the amount of provisions and ammunition needed for the following day, etc. Orders and all kinds of instructions kept coming non-stop from the regiment. I had to forward them to the companies' leaders and to Dziewanowski, who was mostly absent from the battalion's commanding post, since he preferred to visit the companies. Dziewanowski was an excellent leader. He worked hard and was generally liked and well respected. Like any chief of staff, I could not issue orders on my own, but only "on behalf of the battalion head." My "being a boss" lasted a very short time. Less than two months later I got so banged up that I had to leave for a long time, but it proved a very interesting and instructive period of time. I should add that I suffered no shortage of good food and vodka. A battalion wasn't an economic unit for nothing.

Soon after getting the new post, I was ordered by the regiment's chief of staff to get him "the skinny," that is, live captives from a unit on the Vistula's other side. The regiment wanted to interrogate them. This order was addressed to me personally, not to the battalion or to Dziewanowski. Such was the order of things. I had no clue how to go about it. Fortunately, Dziewanowki helped me. First he told me to send a message to each company asking for several brave and strong volunteers for a dangerous mission, and that only those interested needed to respond. "You will see, you will get more men than you require." Of course the old-timer (old? Dziewanowski was only 37) was right. I talked with each of them, selected five or six and invited them to the tent for a meal with some vodka. Also present was the major. He further reduced the number of volunteers to three and promised the others he would send for them when the next opportunity arose. Then we began to discuss the mission's details and the weapons they were to take with them. I was familiar with the Vistula's shoreline. Our section was typical of much of the river. It had sandbanks, that is, entirely exposed empty small islands of sand and a few islands with thick, low vegetation where people sometimes prowled. These could only have been soldiers from the unit from the opposite shore, and that is where we decided to send our scouts. They left in the night in a small dinghy. I stayed on the shore with a rifle platoon of over thirty men positioned there just in case and we had at our disposal small boats if help was needed. After a short time they came back with two Slovaks who didn't put up any resistance, as they preferred to surrender to Poles rather than continue fighting for the Germans. All ended well.

Not many soldiers were needed for the front on the Vistula, so most men participated in various maneuvers. My first maneuver after assuming my new post was called in military jargon "overcoming water obstacles" or, in human language, crossing a river. The river was the Wieprz and both shores were under our control. Even without the Germans, it was a complicated procedure which lasted from dawn till dusk and required cooperation with sappers and artillery. We were convinced that we did everything we were ordered to do correctly. Dead tired and very happy with ourselves, we were going back to our tent together with Dziewanowski when suddenly a Willys, a convertible American jeep, stopped in front of us. Only generals used such cars, and not just any generals. General Wojciech Bewziuk, who had assumed the division's command after Berling's departure, stepped out of the car and without any greeting began to assault our major with absurd and groundless criticism of the battalion. This took place in front of me, a second lieutenant (or perhaps I was already a lieutenant), which made it all the more unpleasant and inappropriate. We were both standing stiff at attention. I was a half-step behind Dziewanowski, who kept saying "yes sir" (in Russian of course). I don't remember if Bewziuk spoke Polish; I didn't know him. But I knew the plan of the maneuvers and our tasks by heart and I also knew that we had done all that we were supposed to do. I was about to tell the general all this when I felt Dziewanowski imperceptibly squeezing my hand. He felt somehow that I was getting ready to answer. I understood from this that I was supposed to keep quiet. After a short time the general got back into the Willys and was gone. I learned from my boss—in Polish—that I was a lunatic, since one doesn't talk back to a general. Their role is to yell at us and ours to say "yes sir." I learned a lot that evening. We went to the tent and drank some vodka, ate a bit, and a moment later fell asleep.

Soon afterward, we subsequently had maneuvers called "infantry attacks behind a fire wall." The point was that the artillery ought to direct its fire in front of attacking infantry and, as the line advances, move the fire forward in order to form something like a wall. It wasn't a bad idea, provided that the artillery functioned faultlessly and with great precision and that the unavoidable dispersion was smaller than the distance between the "wall" and the line of attacking soldiers. In practice these conditions were not easy to fulfill. The commanding officers walked ahead of their units and the person who led the entire mass of troops, a good fifteen or more meters in front of everyone else, was no other than Bewziuk—the same who earlier had yelled at us. With a helmet on his head, a rifle with his bayonet pointing forward, he marched with spring in his step straight into the explosions. This was no joke. The shooting was done with live bullets. I had to reevaluate my opinion of him. What can I say? He didn't have to do this, but he was setting an example.

At the end of September we handed over our defense line on the Vistula to Russians and the division relocated to the Karczew-Otwock area. This is where we believed the attack on Praga and Warsaw would begin. It was in Otwock that I learned that an uprising in Warsaw was in progress. I didn't grasp either the significance or the extent of the uprising. We took positions somewhere between Otwock and Karczew. My regiment was at the front. On the right we had the third infantry regiment, Russians on the left, and the second regiment in reserve. Tanks accompanied us in the attack. We didn't have a continuous front, that is, an unbroken line of trenches in front of us. Rather it was a well armed, deep defense. It consisted of minefields, barbed wire fences, anti-tank obstacles, and concrete bunkers with shooting positions. We were told that we didn't have to capture the bunkers; that in fact it would be better to go around them and leave them behind, together with their crews. That sounded nice but wasn't simple, as firing from CKMs could come from all four directions from each of the bunkers and the neighboring bunkers; the fields of fire overlapped. The Germans knew how to wage war. We spent several days or perhaps as much as a week before the attack on continuous consultations with regimental and divisional staff officers, and later on transferring information to our companies' leaders as well as familiarizing ourselves with the terrain. One of the instructions I received from the regiment was to make three bonfires at night, two directly in front of our positions and 15 to 20 meters away from each other, and a third 70 to 80 meters in the direction of the Germans. These acute triangles were to indicate to low flying night bombers where to drop bombs. We made two or three such triangles in front of the battalion. It was a primitive but effective method. At least the planes didn't drop bombs on their own troops. They bombed every night for two or three nights before the attack.

In Otwock, just before the attack, I received unexpected visits from two close friends. The first was Cousin Bernard, one of my three cousin-defenders from the Saski Garden before the war. I was very happy. He served in the 1st Division as well and was told about me by chance. His parents, Uncle Natan and Aunt Andzia, had been deported deep into Russia, just like Dad and I, and were both alive. His older sister Ewa had died. He didn't know more than I about the fate of Jews. Next Fiszka Najman, my friend from the entire Russian period: from Baranowicze, Kurenyevo in Siberia, and Baranovka in the Volga region turned up. I knew that he was serving in the 2nd Division's intelligence unit, but until that time I had no opportunity to see him. He was going to visit a Jewish family that had been hiding nearby in Otwock and he wanted to take me along. We were to go there after dusk, after meeting a family member who would take us to their apartment. We didn't want to arouse any suspicions; it was best not to be noticed by neighbors. The young man who took us there as well as his sister and her husband were hiding in the apartment. They were very cultured people who spoke Polish without the slightest accent and didn't look Semitic. It was the first time that I heard the expression "on the Aryan side" and "good," that is, "Aryan" appearance. I felt their incredible fear. They were afraid of practically everything, even the faintest noise. I told them that since both the Russians and we were here, the Germans wouldn't come back. That assurance was met with the woman's unbelieving smile and her reply that the Germans were powerful and could come back. And even if they didn't, there was no need to hurry with the disclosure of their presence. It was that evening that I found out about the Holocaust. I just read this sentence to myself and I do not think the shock of it really sank in at the time. I found out, but I still didn't know. I couldn't believe it. It was too horrifying. It didn't register that Karmelicka Street was no more, that neither Grandma nor Mum existed, that our friends and the world we lived in were gone. This disbelief stayed with me for a long time; perhaps even to this day. Fiszka and I left late that night. The next time we saw each other was in Lodz after the war. I never saw this family again.

Right before the attack, I was busy communicating and pointing out targets to the artillery men who were to help us with our offensive. I felt strange—even unit leaders much higher ranking than I were arriving to receive my instructions. Among them was the head of a "katyusha" division, a colonel with a chest covered in medals, a Russian. We ourselves had no katyushas, new short-range rockets with launchers mounted on trucks. Today, Hamas bombs Israeli border towns with similar missiles. Then they were considered very powerful weapons. The noise they created made them even more frightening; it sounded like howling. The Germans had something similar that we called "cows," but ours were louder. The colonel and I settled what was to be settled and I told him that I wanted to take a closer look at this new weapon. He smiled as if in agreement and we began to walk in the direction of a katyusha standing nearby, which looked like a loaded truck covered by a tarpaulin. But before we got close enough to inspect it a guard armed with an automatic rifle jumped at me, screaming: *nye lzya* (forbidden). The colonel spread his hands as if he were helpless, although he had known what would happen. He made fun of an ally.

The attack began early in the morning on September 10. All happened *lege artis*:[31] cannonade, "recognition by fighting" by the penal battalion (it suffered great losses), artillery again, the air force, and finally us. Right from the start on the first day, it was extremely hard to advance. I don't know what was worse, the minefields or the fire. Romek Czerkies was killed that day. He was blown to pieces in a minefield and died instantly. Not so long ago, we had both taken Dziewanowski's exams. Had he passed our fates might have been reversed. I often thought about that. Romek was my age and graduated from high school in Russia just like I had done. His family had been deported from

---

[31] Tr: Lege artis (Latin): literally: by the law of art; here: according to pre-planned or approved rules.

Lida in eastern Poland to Siberia in 1940. It was a military family, which was probably the reason for the deportation. He looked very young, almost like a boy with his rosy cheeks. He was very kind and considerate. In the military he was the only contemporary with whom I was friends. He had no chance to enjoy life.

Against all odds we had captured considerable territory that first day. Despite their very good fortifications, I think the Germans lacked enough people. The night was rather calm. We received food and ammunition and I spoke again with artillery soldiers. The next day the attack continued. We tried to walk in the tracks left by tank treads so as not to step on a mine. Of course there also were anti-tank minefields. My major was killed that evening in the second attack. We were sitting in a ditch a couple of steps from each other when he was hit by a bullet; perhaps more than one. He lived after being shot. His wounds were immediately dressed and he was sent to the rear. I couldn't believe it when, a week later, my battalion comrades who visited me in a hospital brought the news that he was dead. After the war, I checked a certificate in the archives that "Major Dziewanowski Longin, son of Wiktor, born in 1907, died of wounds at the Independent Medical Battalion on 09.11.1944." Another close and exceptionally decent person was gone. It was quite painful. I learned a lot from him and I owe him much.

That night I was visited by a captain, the leader of the Russian battalion placed to our left. I don't know how he found me—and after the initial fuss and a couple of vodkas he explained the purpose of his visit. He insisted that, within my battalion's attack line—and those lines were very clearly marked on his map as well as mine—there were men from the Vlasov army,[32] a small group of no more than 20 to 25 men. He and his people wanted to "do away with them," even though they were not inside their "map." The presence of Vlasov army members in our sector made sense. The Germans preferred to use them against Poles rather than against their fellow countrymen. I had no idea how to deal with this problem. I tried to think of what Dziewanowski would do. Surely, I reasoned, he wouldn't notify the regiment. He would consider himself competent enough to make a decision on his own. I made it clear to the captain that we would gladly help and that it should be a shared operation. He wiggled out of it, saying that his men would manage very well

---

[32] Tr: Russian Liberation Army, or Vlasov army, were Russian forces subordinated to Nazi Germany during World War II. Organized and led by Andrey Vlasov, a former Red Army general and a Nazi collaborator, it attempted to unite anti-communist Russians who opposed the communist regime.

by themselves. They were planning to surround the Vlasov people at night and to attack them in the morning. So we agreed. He didn't want to have us as witnesses. The next evening, my men told me that they had passed an area where they saw many dead Vlasov army soldiers. They could identify them by their uniforms. That's how it was in the war.

The following days of the offensive became more and more difficult, as we had fewer and fewer men. I calculated then that for each man killed there were six or seven wounded. I was well informed, since every night I received an account of the number of soldiers in each subunit. Companies' heads were asking me for supplements and I wanted to ask the regiment's leader to send us additional men, as I knew he had reserves. I also knew that there was no chance this would happen. My counterpart from the first battalion had warned me that he had done this, but got nothing and, in addition, had been accused of "spreading panic." They even threatened to shoot him. He got off, but in his opinion it could have ended badly. Supposedly—again, we weren't told about such things—a regiment's or division's leader had at his disposal an NKVD group authorized to shoot "alarmists" and all kinds of defeatists on the spot. I don't know whether this was true, but it was enough to make me keep my mouth shut and not be a "scaremonger."

The regimental commander's orders were transmitted through a radio-telephone. A typical message, always in Russian (I don't know whether he spoke Polish), went as follows: *Yesli ti mnie nye vzmoshnish vysotu X v 30 minut, to ya tiebya sobstvyennorushno razstryelayu* (If you don't take over the X hill in thirty minutes, I will personally shoot you). And that wasn't all, because at least three times, at the beginning, in the middle, and at the end of the sentence, my poor mom was called the worst kind of names. We were both looking at the same map and we knew full well which hill it was. A regimental commander was supposed to communicate his messages in a code. Yet during defensive maneuvers this was seldom observed, and never by him. I was now well taught and so I answered everything by saying "yes sir" and that was all. And then events took their course. My major never behaved this way toward his company heads. He hated the regimental commander for speaking like this, especially because he always arranged for his regiment command to be placed five kilometers behind us, that is, at the end of radiotelephone's audibility, as far from the front as possible. But Dziewanowski fought alongside his soldiers. And died. After the war I learned that our regimental commander had survived and became a general. Well, we cannot blame anyone for surviving, can we?

Many years later I read that such crass behavior and issuing these types of orders was quite typical of the Red Army. And the person who did it best was none other than Marshal Georgy Zhukov, no doubt the main architect of the victory at the eastern front and the de facto commander-in-chief (the great Stalin formally carried that title). Zhukov was also known for his total disregard for losses and for human life, especially during operations he directed himself. The example for this came from above.

It was the fourteenth or fifteenth of September and the map showed that we were near Praga, very close to the Vistula (although I couldn't see the river), when we encountered German tanks. I was lying in a shallow ditch in the meadow together with my two radiotelephone operators, counting the tanks—there were seven or eight of them—and sending the information to the regiment. I knew we had nothing to fight them with. The commander of the battalion's armor-piercing guns, an excellent sergeant (unfortunately I don't recall his name), had been wounded the previous day and not much was left from his company. The tanks seemed to turn a bit and instead of continuing in our direction veered to the left. One of them was very close, probably not farther than twenty or thirty meters away. And then I was wounded. The missile exploded not far from me. The left side of my body was hit by shrapnel and my left hand suddenly felt lifeless. My boys were lying to my right and were safe and sound. They dressed my wounds as best as they could and stopped the flow of blood. As soon as the tanks disappeared, they carried me from the battlefield. I was only half conscious. To this day I remember only a few fragments. I suppose that those I have retained were the significant ones. First of all, I recall the line of our infantry, soldiers who were walking in the direction opposite to ours. While the three of us were going back, they were heading toward the front. I don't know how to describe what I was feeling. It was like complete bliss; in that moment there was an awareness, that our soldiers would stand between me and the Germans and that I was safe. Such happiness is probably felt only by a soul that learns that it will go to heaven and not to hell. The soldiers moving forward were subdivisions of the second infantry regiment, kept in reserve by the commander and now sent by him to help, or rather to take over. I also remember that I was lying in a big tent in a field hospital among many wounded and was found by Stefcia Koprowska, who was a nurse in that hospital. I had no idea she was working here. Stefcia was my age and we knew each other well, since she and her family had been in Kurenyevo and Baranovka. Stefcia told me that I would lose my left arm if I stayed there because the only thing they were doing was amputating arms and legs. She said she would try to send me to the rear, to a better hospital where I would have a chance to keep my arm. I woke up later, in the middle of the night, on a cart, semiconscious. There were several of us, wounded and lying on some straw. The driver was a soldier and we were going east. I don't know why, but I imagined that we were heading toward the Germans instead of east. I began to scream, but the driver assured me that he knew where he was going and that there were no Germans on the Vistula's right bank, that they had escaped to Warsaw and had detonated all the bridges on the river. I noticed then that I no longer had my watch, a gift from Grandma. The next time I woke up completely, I was in the hospital after surgery. First, a great relief: my fingers were sticking out from the plaster. The fact that I didn't lose my hand I probably owe to Stefcia. She married a pharmacist whom she had met at the field hospital. Soon afterward, they left Poland and we lost touch. Unfortunately, such losses happened often in my life and later on in my life with Felusia as well. What a pity.

The hospital was located in Otwock. Several of us were placed in a large room on the first floor. Soon after I woke up, my companions made me aware of why I had been put on this floor: the mortuary was in the basement. Those expected to end up there were placed in this room to make carrying them down easier. Wound infections and gangrenes were common. We had sulfonamides, but no antibiotics (the Allies had penicillin, it seems). But all went well. After a couple of days, I was placed on a higher floor. I stayed in Otwock for several

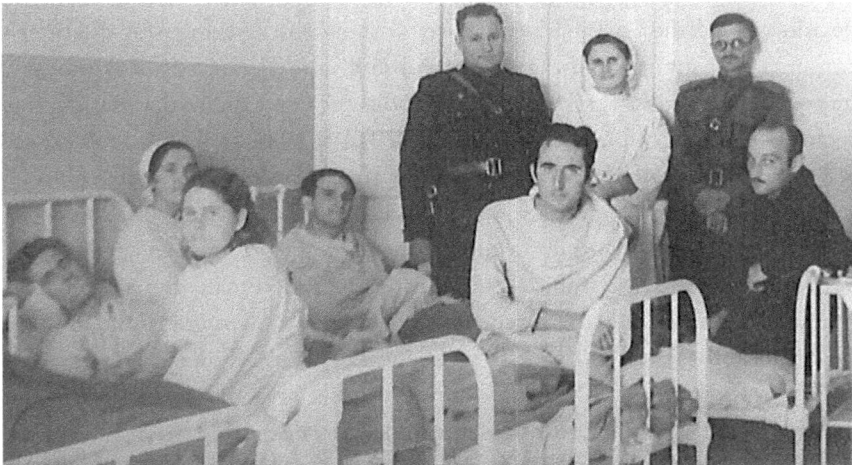

Figure 9 Hospital room in Otwock, late September 1944. Sitting 4th from the right, author, after first surgery (left arm in a cast).

weeks. Cypuchowski visited me at least twice at the hospital. He had learned about the stolen watch. When he came to visit me the second time, he brought me a gift, a German "captured" one (trofiejny). I wore it for many years. He told me that the battalion had been decimated, but that reinforcements would arrive soon. The battalion would be almost new, different. My first photo from the military service came from there; Cypuchowski is in it.

In Otwock I learned more about the Warsaw Uprising, as always not from official sources, but rather from conversations. However, we were still neither aware of the magnitude of the tragedy for the city's population nor of the extent of the devastation. We heard some news about Berling's attempts to help the uprising. Just after our division approached the Vistula, he sent several units of his 2nd and 3rd Divisions by boat straight from Praga to Warsaw. Such a frontal attack from the river had no chance whatsoever without serious help from the Russians. The losses were enormous and the aid for the uprising nil. One didn't have to be a strategist to understand that if the Russians had truly wanted to help the uprising, they would have continued to attack by encircling Warsaw from the south, from the bridgehead on the Vistula's left bank by the Pilica's estuary. They had captured that bridgehead, called Magnuszewski, in the summer offensive at the end of July. Most major operations in that war were conducted by encirclement. Stalin intentionally allowed this calamity for purely political reasons. These are known facts. What I'm particularly interested in is the elucidation of Zygmunt Berling's role in the affair. I don't believe we have heard the final explanation. It's hard to imagine that Berling made the decision to aid the uprising on his own, without the agreement of the front's commander—the Russian marshal of Polish origin, Konstantin Rokossovsky, one of this war's most outstanding leaders. But the fact remains that Berling was removed from his military command in the fall of 1944 and, against all expectations, never assumed any important post after the war. What was behind it? Looking for a "real," before-the-war general to replace Berling, our rulers did something almost grotesque. I don't know where they found, in 1945 or the beginning of 1946, a certain Michał Rola-Żymierski, a man who actually had been a legionnaire and later a general, but who got thrown out of the military by Piłsudski for financial fraud! To make the story comical or, rather, tragicomical, he was promoted to marshal—after Piłsudski only the second one in the twentieth century—and army's chief commander; disgusting.

I was transported from Otwock to a hospital in Lublin. It was located on the grounds of a nunnery near the city center. All the doctors, mostly women, were Russians. In addition to our military nurses, there were nuns, who were much better. After the plaster had been taken off it turned out that my elbow was stiff. I was able neither to straighten my arm nor to bend it. The elbow joint was impaired. I soon began a series of operations to correct it. I had at least three or four of them in Lublin; they didn't help much. When I was leaving the hospital at the beginning of February, I had a non-functioning left arm. In addition, the wound opened up two or three times a year, oozing pus and blood. It was annoying and dangerous. I was very weak after each return of the illness. This continued until the beginning of 1952, when, after the wound had opened yet again, I was told to see Dr. Władysław Chimiak, who was working in a well known military hospital in Lodz on Żeromskiego Street. At that time we were living in Rembertów outside Warsaw. Karusia was three and Dzidzia[33] had just been born. At that time, there was a mandatory convalescence following a hospital operation. This meant a much longer absence from home than it would happen today. I didn't want to leave Felusia with two little children, but she insisted. Dr. Chimiak did the operation and from that time on (more than half a century!) the wound hasn't opened even once and I have been able to bend and straighten my arm almost perfectly.

I spent several months at the Lublin hospital. For me a hospital stay was, on the scale from one to ten, in the realm of low minuses. I assess it more or less the same way Berling had assessed the 3rd infantry division.

A priest, the nuns' confessor and elderly, was an unusually nice man who frequently came to the hospital. He visited the wounded and often talked to us. I found that he was an avid chess player. First we played in the hospital room by my bed. Later we moved to the monastery's library, and after a while the priest gave me a key to the library so I could play chess when he was absent. It was a big sunny room with a high ceiling and soaring, recessed windows. There was no librarian. The bookshelves were filled almost exclusively with religious works, including, of course, the lives of saints. There were also some chess manuals that belonged to the priest and to his predecessor, who was a chess player as well. The manuals were mostly in German. Some were very old, written with Gothic characters. In my entire life I have never spent so much time playing chess as I did then. I had plenty of time and I liked the library. There were five or six young men in my hospital room and our conversations mostly revolved around intimate details of female anatomy and—probably more imaginary than real—my hospital companions' erotic triumphs. I suppose that this was true of all military

---

[33] Tr: The names of Karusia and Dzidzia refer to Karina and Ilona, the author's daughters.

hospitals in the world. Given such conditions, maybe it wasn't the worst thing, but after a while it got repetitive and boring. I would then go to the library.

In addition to books about chess, the library had a publication that made a major impression on me. It was the daily newspaper *Mały Dziennik*,[34] which was published by the church. Before the war it was the cheapest newspaper, costing 5 grosz. I had heard about its existence, but never read it. Complete editions, from the 1930s up to the war, sat on the shelves stitched together. I read them one by one. For years and years there had not been one single day without vile anti-Semitic propaganda, often on the front page. It is hard to believe that such texts, so filled with hate, were published by the Catholic Church, but it is true. Not much changed after the Holocaust and after several waves of Jewish immigration from Poland in the late 1940s, 50s, and 60s, which, practically speaking, left Poland almost devoid of Jews. There was a newspaper that began to be published in Toruń after the fall of communism and whose title invoked that rag from before the war: the *Nowy Dziennik*. Here's an example of the *New Journal*'s virulent anti-Semitism: "According to Talmudic traditions killing non-Jews ethically equals the killing of cattle . . ." (July 27, 2006, 174), starts an article in the section "Thinking is a weapon." Shame, nonsense worthy of Goebbels. This is much worse than Dmowski.[35] This tragedy has been enhanced greatly by the attitude of Polish church leaders who didn't have the courage to control this situation. What to do? For centuries the Church has been anti-Semitism's source and disseminator. Clearly the decisions of the Second Vatican didn't reach Polish church leaders. For me these things are especially painful. It is different in the States. All the religious institutions, without exception, emphatically oppose any signs of anti-Semitism and all racism. In the 1970s and 1980s, the archbishop of New York, Cardinal John O'Connor, and the city's mayor Edward Koch, a Jew, were two popular and well liked celebrities who participated together in TV and radio shows. Of course they didn't agree about everything, but their conversations were always friendly and often witty. They even published a book together: *His Eminence and Hizzoner* (New York: William Morrow & CO, 1989).

We got a letter from Helena Gold from Baranovka at the end of December 1944 and a new family tragedy began. My father had been arrested by the NKVD. This news was written at the end of the letter, following great praise for the Red Army and socialism in general. It was very brief: your dad is visiting

[34] Tr: Mały Dziennik (Polish): Little Journal.
[35] Tr: Roman Stanisław Dmowski (1864–1939): Polish politician and statesman, co-founder of the right wing, anti-Semitic, National Democracy movement.

his old friend Sakharov. It was the name of NKVD's commander in Kurenyevo. Helena was a good friend. Together we survived Kurenyevo and Baranovka. She was one of the people with whom we used to spend evenings and nights warmed by a brick oven. She was beautiful, very smart and nice, and lived with her parents and a younger brother. Helena's dad had connections to the Bund and soon shared my father's fate. The family lived in Upper Silesia before the war and was assimilated. She lived in Wrocław for several months after returning to Poland, got married, and soon afterward left for Israel. She is another close friend with whom the connection ceased to exist.

In January, after the capture of Warsaw, Uncle Bernard came to see me at the hospital. It was a great and truly joyful event. Other than my father, he was my only living relative from before the war. Following the Warsaw Uprising, Bernard hid in a bunker and survived in this manner until the middle of January.[36] He told me about Mom. She had worked in a Bund soup kitchen, serving soup. The soup kitchen's activity ceased when there were no more resources. After Grandma's death, Mom was given an opportunity to be taken to the "Aryan side," but she didn't accept. She was afraid that her Semitic face would endanger the Polish family who would hide her. This was very much like her. He saw her for the last time in the summer of 1942, when she was walking in the middle of the street toward Umschlagplatz in a group escorted by Germans or Ukrainians and Jewish policemen. Treblinka was the next stop. He was standing on a sidewalk and told me that their gaze met for a split second.

Uncle Bernard came to the hospital each day for the next several days. Once he took me to a photographer and we had a picture taken together. He was in his war uniform with a moustache and beard that he never had before the war. I was in an army winter coat, smiling but haggard, with my arm in a sling, obviously after yet another operation. We talked in Yiddish. Bernard spoke Polish poorly. On the Aryan side he pretended to be deaf-mute and his papers bore the name of Bronisław Malinowski. I know at least one other case where the father of a close acquaintance, a well known Jewish painter and sculptor, Mr. Willenberg, pretended to be a deaf-mute on the Aryan side and survived. He supported himself by painting religious images for his clients. My dad's arrest by the NKVD had a great impact on Bernard and hastened his decision to travel or rather to escape to the west, as far as possible from the Bolsheviks.

---

[36] Au: Bernard described his life during the war in an extremely interesting book: Bernard Goldstein, *Five Years in the Warsaw Ghetto* (Garden City, NY: Dolphin Books, Doubleday & Co, Inc., 1961).

Figure 10 With Uncle Bernard, Lublin, January or February 1945. Uncle Bernard pulled me out of the hospital for this photo.

Bernard was a well known Bund activist; Dad was not. If they had locked Dad up, he had no chance whatsoever. Bernard asked me what I was planning to do after the war and I told him that I hadn't decided, but that I was interested in history or perhaps law. He was emphatically against these choices; anything was fine except for the humanities. You need to have a specific profession, he argued, one you would be able to take overseas in your head, because ultimately you will have to leave since there is no family left. You will have to take care of yourself and your future family to have *parnose* (that's Yiddish, difficult to translate, it more or less means prosperity, security for the family, something like that). He suggested pharmacy or chemistry; and that's what happened. Bernard was in touch with a small group of Bund members in Lublin and introduced me to them. He gave me addresses where I would be able to find him after my return from Russia, since it was obvious that I intended to join Dad after leaving the hospital. He left me about 20 dollars. US dollars were very valuable then and 20 dollars was a lot of money.

In February 1945, the doctors declared that they could do nothing more for me. I got a sixty-day-long leave, plus couple of days for the journey "home"

Figure 11 Józio and Vyera Babic, Lodz, Poland, late 1940s. Their mother, Rywka, died in Russia, in horrendous circumstances during the war. Their father, a bundist, sat in prison (see text).

and back. I immediately left for Baranovka. There I found that not only Dad, but all the men, including men who were fathers of families, had been arrested: Chaim Babic, Motel Gold, Saul Segal, Heniek Grundland, Motel Rowiński, Parasol (I don't remember all the first names), Koprowski, Ber; nine people in all. Only one or two of them, in addition to Dad and Chaim, could have been considered Bund followers or enthusiasts. The others were Jews from various social levels who had nothing to do with the Bund. All these families had been with us in Siberia, in Kurenyevo. Before their arrest some of them had lived in Baranovka, the rest in the surrounding collective farms. When I arrived, all the wives and children had moved to Baranovka in order to be together. They lived in three houses that stood next to each other. The worst off were Chaim Babic's children: Józio, who was about four, and two-year-old Vyera. Their mother Rywka had died two years earlier, and now the father was in jail. There's no doubt that if Jews had something like sainthood, a rabbinical council would bestow that honor on Mania Segal, a native of Gąbin. She spoke Yiddish and peasant-style Polish without an accent, but not sophisticated. She was no longer young and had gray hair, blue eyes, and wore long, large skirts, a scarf on her head, and another one on her shoulders. She looked like a Polish or Russian peasant, certainly not like an old Jewish woman. Her husband Saul was a carpenter, a good, very calm and taciturn man, who submitted to her in such a natural way that it could not be called being under the thumb. They had no children. When I arrived, Saul had already been jailed and Mania was taking care of the kids. She was the one who saved the siblings and later took care of them and gave them a good preparation for the future—that's what happened, without any exaggeration. How she did it during the war in Baranovka, only she knew. When she had to go to some office—one little one in her arms, the other held by the hand—she wouldn't leave the manager alone until she received either food coupons or something else vital for the children, HER children. And she did all that with an almost nonexistent knowledge of Russian.

After a couple of days, I went to Ulyanovsk to inquire after my dad. The NKVD building was located at the corner of Karl Marx and Lev Tolstoy streets; fabulous. Both certainly were turning over in their graves. Well, they had more serious reasons to turn in their graves than this coincidence. The entrance to the building wasn't visible. There was a gate in a high fence on one side, and behind it more than a dozen people bustled in a yard totally invisible from outside. The point was not to let passersby see ordinary people trying to get access to the NKVD. The suppliants were almost solely peasant women, bundled up in all possible ways because it was winter. There was a small window in the building, usually closed. Occasionally it would open, bark at someone, and close after a moment. Why be civil, since we all were enemies of the Soviet authorities? The person who succeeded in getting a visit through the window was immediately surrounded by other women and an animated exchange about what "he" had said and how "he" had behaved would follow. Everything here was direct, devoid of falsehood or fear. The acquaintances I had seen in Baranovka had turned their heads in order not to see me, the villain's son. Here, on one hand, one was anonymous in the little crowd and on the other—perhaps desperate enough to take risks. These women were fighting for their husbands, their sons, their fathers. Was there anything worse that could happen to them? Was it a true civil society in this jail's yard? Too early, perhaps it was just its beginning. Quite simply, years of terror and of falsity hadn't managed to eradicate human impulses. My uniform aroused interest. It wasn't Russian, but when it had became evident that I was a soyuznik (ally) and that Dad was in jail, I at once became one of them. The women knew everything and willingly shared information gained with great torment: if you have no news about your dad, that meant the investigation was ongoing and you would not learn anything here because "they" don't give information during an investigation. It would be better to go to the prosecutor's office. Indeed, Dad had allegedly been sent on a business trip to a nearby town and had disappeared. That was all. There had not been a written warrant for his arrest, nor had he been arrested in front of witnesses. This was the Russian way. I learned the same thing at the window as I had been told by the women. I immediately went to the prosecutor's office and was received by the deputy prosecutor for special cases, that is, the political ones. It was a tough conversation. He didn't admit to knowing anything about Dad's fate. At one point he deigned me with a tale of a case then pursued by prosecutors: a peasant woman had collected a bit of food to sell in a city. At that time in Russia, one was not allowed to simply buy a ticket at a railroad station; one had to have a special permission and she had no chance to get it, so she arranged with the engineer to be transported in the engine car for payment in kind. The engineer and his helper killed her on the way, hacked her up, threw the body to the furnace and split the food. You see, he said, it's a horrible war, people become animals, so how could I know what happened to your father? I went back to Baranovka.

The end of my leave was drawing near. I didn't want to go back without news of Dad, so I decided to try once more. I knew the NKVD's addresses and I had some idea, although not entirely, what to expect. I can't say I wasn't afraid. Anyone who had to deal with the NKVD would have been scared. The NKVD respected no laws but I was surrounded by a sort of aura; ranienyj frontowik (a wounded front-line soldier), that protected me from the worst. A year, two years after the war, when the NKVD was in its element, nothing could have shielded you. I started with the prosecutors. They told me to see the NKVD. I was immediately received by a major; a very high rank for that institution. He told me that despite the ongoing investigation, I would be able to meet with Dad because they were going to make an exception for me . . . here he couldn't stop his praise for my "great valor." Then he explained that the conversation would take place in front of him, only in Russian, and with time restrictions, I believe about half an hour; I don't recall exactly. He brought in Dad, who right away burst into tears. This was the most important part of the dialogue; a disaster. I told him about Mom, Grandma, our family. We talked about women in Baranovka and about Chaim and Mania Segal's children. We probably said more with our eyes than with words. I was trying to be very careful. For instance, I was afraid to mention Uncle Bernard. When the visit ended, Dad was escorted out and I was told that the department's head would speak with me. A second later a colonel walked in and introduced himself as Ivanov. There are as many of those in Russia as Kovalskis in Poland. He was a big guy with a red face and a uniform that was cracking; clearly he didn't lack for food. This visibly separated him from the pale, malnourished, ordinary people. He looked somewhat like a Jew, but it was hard to tell. There are many Semitic-looking ethnicities in Russia. He started on the same topic as the major had, that I had been spilling my blood at the front and here some people plot against the Soviet Union. At one point he started talking in Yiddish, and rather well.

Those little Jews (in Yiddish *Yidelech*), he said, don't appreciate that the Soviet Union had saved their lives. *Yidelech* sounded particularly contemptuous in his mouth. I tried to say something, that my dad had always loved the Soviet Union and Comrade Stalin in particular. This was a commonly accepted expression, but it made no impression. At one point he said something that for many years I couldn't understand: "We don't judge people for old sins." That could have meant only the Bund. If not that, then what? Dad, who didn't like to talk about prison, explained this to me after his return. The bigger the case, the more people arrested and sentenced, the greater the recognition for the NKVD officers would be and the higher their promotions and medals. It started with the Bund, perhaps with Dad and Chaim Babic's denunciation, although that's not sure, but there were so few Bund members among the "nine." How can you sentence someone like an owner of a cheese or a coal wholesale business for belonging to the Bund? Yet there were such men among the arrested. They had probably concluded that it would be better to "create" a group involved in an anti-Soviet propaganda. And that's what they did. I left Colonel "Ivanov" with a heavy heart.

But it wasn't the end of my surprises for the day. One more still awaited me. Before leaving the building, I was sitting in a small, poorly lit room. I was filling out some form or other (my arrival and departure time and similar idiocies) when the door opened and two young girls walked in. One was wearing glasses and an NKVD uniform; the other, taller and much prettier, a dress. The first one addressed me from the start as Volodia, as if she had known me for years. She couldn't shut up and was about to throw her arms around my neck. I looked at the other one and . . . I was struck dumb. If the ground didn't swallow me then it never will. This second one was Lidka, my Lidka. At first I was scared by the idea that all this had been set up and that I had to be very careful because many eyes were looking at this scene through cracks in the wall. And then by another: when I asked friends in Baranovka about Lidka, they all told me that she had left for the city and then they would look away, without mentioning what she was doing, where she was working, etc. Nobody wanted to say that she was working in the same place where Dad was jailed. I felt uncomfortable. Lidka and I almost didn't talk, but the one in uniform kept blabbing. The girls invited me home for dinner. They were sharing a room and quickly put together a meal. In the middle of the dinner the lights went out. That happened often and there was a paraffin oil lamp ready, just in case. We talked only about great victories and about my "heroism." But not a word about what interested us most: Dad's fate, how Lidka had joined the NKVD, whether she still felt something for me. Lidka sat herself as far as possible from me, with the chaperon between us. I spent a polite amount of time there after dinner and then went to the hotel for military personnel, where I was staying. The hotel was near a railroad station and was very shabby. There was only one room for low-ranking people like me. Next day I left for Baranovka. I never saw Lidka again.

More than a year later, in the summer of 1946, I unexpectedly received several letters from her; I still have them. I don't know how she found my address in Lodz. Perhaps through the NKVD? She wrote straightforwardly that she would like to join me in Poland which seemed odd. At the time Russian citizens needed a special permit to travel to Poland and to marry a foreigner. She also sent me her picture with a sentimental and a rather pretentious inscription: "As a souvenir of the past, with hope for the future"; she probably found this sentence in some old album. Well, I didn't answer her, for by then I was with Felusia.

It was April, leave was over and it was time to go back. In my papers it said that on my way back I was supposed to stop at the Polish embassy in Moscow to get a referral to a new unit. That was my first stay in Moscow. And a miracle happened: I met Lutka, Michał, and Ilonka, the entire family, in the street in front of the embassy. Finally a truly happy event: people close to me and who had no intention to immigrate, like Uncle Bernard. In Moscow, for the first time, I played chess with Michał as an equal. All three of them lived in a "hotel" by the railroad station in Ulyanovsk. It was cleaner and warmer than mine, but here too they put many beds in each room. I quickly understood that things were not as good as they should have been between Lutka and Michał. These problems resulted in their divorce some years later, very painful.

I got a referral to the 1st Army headquarters in Włochy, a small town west of Warsaw. I was going to Poland. As soon as the train stopped at the Lublin station, it was clear that something extraordinary had happened. People on the platforms were dancing and singing "Poland has not perished yet."[37] Germany's unconditional capitulation was announced through loudspeakers.

It was May 1945. The nightmare was over. Over? Mom had been murdered. Dad was in jail. What kind of end was it?

---

[37] Tr: Poland has not perished yet (Jeszcze Polska nie zginęła): Polish national anthem.

Figure 12 With Felusia winter of 1945/46 a few months after we met.

PART III

After the War

Traveling from Lublin, I reached Praga; trains were not continuing any further across the Vistula. There was one pontoon bridge built by military sappers. Some small trucks were parked on the shore; they were called, I don't know why, "Canadas." As soon as there were enough passengers or, as we used to say then, noggins, the drivers would announce that for a small fee they would take "Canada to Warsaw." There was no city. Building stumps and a sea of rubble, that was all. People walked on little paths formed among the ruins in the middle of what once used to be a road. The Jewish district, a ghetto in the time of the Germans, was even more pulverized. I found Leszno Street, the east-west route, but I was not able to pinpoint our house on Karmelicka Street, third from Leszno Street. I spent several hours walking in my city. Was it still a city? One could see trucks and horse carts taking away the rubble. Two kinds of notices stood out. On nearly every building there were pieces of wood fastened between bricks with writings, left by Russian sappers: "min nyet."[1] And in Polish, left by relatives looking for each other. These were tragic and many. "Dear Stasieniek, I'm at mom's"; who was that "Stasieniek"? A husband, perhaps a son, and where was mom? Only the author knew, and Stasieniek. Was he alive? God only knew. Hard to believe, but people made homes in many places among the rubble. It was May, and rather warm. There were food stalls. Prostitutes came out in the evenings.

I don't recall how I reached Włochy, a small town over a dozen kilometers west of Warsaw. I found a place where a number of militaries were hanging around and it turned out that the 1st Army headquarters where I was supposed

---

[1] Tr: Min nyet (Russian): no land mines.

to report had some time ago moved west, and only the Political Education Administration had been left in Włochy. I didn't quite know what to do. My leave permit was ending and I didn't come under their jurisdiction. They had no idea what to do with me, either. Finally, I was told that their main commander, a colonel, would speak with me. What I'm going to tell now is strange: neither one of us could have known that this short conversation would have a crucial influence on my entire life. Immediately after entering his room and reporting to him, I realized who my interlocutor was: before the war, Wictor Grosz had been a well known communist activist and was a relative of Michał. I had met him couple of times at Lutka's and Michał's in Miedzeszyn. At that time I was a boy so he couldn't have remembered me, and now, with my Dad in the NKVD jail, I wasn't eager to renew this rather questionable acquaintance. Obviously, he didn't remember my name. He was to the point, said that he could send me to my unit, which was in Germany, but the war was over and there was nothing for me to do over there. During the conversation it came out that I had a high school diploma and wanted to continue my education, go to the university. Grosz said then that they were organizing a school for officers specializing in political education. They were in need of front line officers like me—with battle experience and knowledge of infantry weaponry; I could work there teaching how to shoot. Most of the courses there would be of political nature, so I wouldn't have too much work associated with my teaching and would have time to study. The school was being created in Lodz; the city had not been damaged and a university would start operating there. I agreed right away; it was precisely what I wished for. And Lodz, this I couldn't know, was the home of brothers Zygmunt and Oskar Strawczyński, where in a few weeks their niece Felusia would come to stay. Lodz meant a university, where couple of months later I began my chemistry studies! To think that, if I had arrived at that town near Warsaw just a bit earlier, when the army headquarters still had been there, I would have ended up in Germany. The head office had no possibility to send me to Lodz, they wouldn't think of it. Most probably I would have been referred to my old unit and that would be that.

So, I ended up in Lodz. I spent almost five years there and in hindsight I see that it was the most significant, and yet the most difficult to describe, part of my life. I met Felusia; we started a family, and we stayed together for over sixty years, until the end. I chose my profession in Lodz and I finished my undergraduate studies. During those years, somehow I had to accept the loss of my family and all of my pre-war community, and this wasn't—isn't—easy. It was then that I, or rather Felusia and I, met people who have remained our faithful friends for the rest of our lives. Finally, I belonged to several different communities there. In the army and, in particular, in my school, there were many communists, but during the initial postwar years, there were also a number of officers who had returned from German camps and who hadn't been dealt with; I associated with both. I spent time as well with what remained of Polish Jews from all backgrounds; from the bourgeois to the few Bund members still left alive. It seems that these postwar years between 1945 and 1950 had greatly shaped your dad.

So, in the first half of May 1945, Mister Lieutenant—people still were using this term, although they were supposed to call me "Citizen Lieutenant"— with all his belongings held in a green military bag, reported to the unit located at November 11 Street. (Later the street was renamed Stalingrad's Defenders' Street, and now is again November 11.) One can gain rough knowledge of the last 300 years of Polish history following the name changes of Warsaw's main square: it was Saski Square in the eighteenth century, later Tsar Alexander First Square, Piłsudski Square, Hitlers-Platz, Victory Square, and now again Piłsudski Square. What's next? (It's a terrible question, but since there have been so many changes, how can a logical mind reject the possibility of extrapolation?) And, what was most important in those days, the military right away provided me with a roof above my head and nourishment. The former was an order for taking up a room with a family living at 34 Mielczarskiego Street, within a couple of minutes walking distance from the barracks, the latter—dinners at the military canteen (disgusting) or rations. A ten-day portion consisted of "rąbanka" (pork, more bones and fat than meat), some canned fish or other canned stuff, rusks, and 200 cigarettes or tobacco, and paper for rolling the cigarettes. I was also receiving a bit of money, ridiculously little. At first, I ate at the canteen. Later, Felusia would prepare something with my ration. My room, or rather, my tiny room, was located in a nice, front side apartment, on the third floor. There was almost no furniture in this place, just a bed, a small table, and perhaps two chairs. For the first time, I lived in an apartment with a bathroom that had a gas heater; one could heat up water for a bath. The problem was that, because of breakdowns, usually there was no water and the bathtub served as a water tank, so the bathroom was of little use. My relationship with the landlords—Władek and Stasia, with their two little children and the wife's younger sister Irena, was correct, but we didn't become friends. I didn't use the kitchen. Władek was a truck driver. Later on, I learned by chance that Jews, whom the Germans had banished to the ghetto, had lived there before the war. I don't know how my landlords became the apartment's owners; we never talked about it. I lived in the little room on Mielczarskiego Street for about a year; in the summer of 1946, after the murder of Fiszka, who was then living with me, I permanently moved in with Felusia to the apartment—now a family legend—on 31 Piotrkowska Street. Long before the move, it had already become my second home.

I quickly understood that my school duties wouldn't be particularly laborious. Each week I had no more than four or five lectures about infantry weaponry that I knew by heart, and once or twice, I had to take my pupils, by truck or street car, to a park called Zdrowie,[2] where we had an allotted piece of the woods and of a clearing for our outdoor training. The cadets were organized into companies and battalions led by front line officers; during the first post-war years, even the school's commander was once a pre-war front line officer. Since I was teaching, I had no commanding duties. Most of the time was spent pounding all kinds of pseudo Marxist-Leninist wisdom, mixed in some false "democratic" gravy with our beloved comrade Stalin, Poland's liberator, into our students' heads. Those cadets were poorly educated boys of "good," working class or peasant origins, for whom any military school—political or not—meant an unparalleled advancement. There was a slogan placed at the barracks' main entrance:

> Nie matura lecz chęć szczera zrobi z ciebie oficera.
> Not a high school diploma but a desire true will make an officer out of you.

Sometimes someone would add underneath:

> Nie pomogę szczere chęci, z gówna bata nie ukręcisz.
> Good intentions won't help a bit. You can't make a whip out of shit.

This inscription would be erased immediately, only to reappear after a while.

It was a strange army and a strange Poland. The authentic (?) PPS had existed until 1948, and Stanisław Mikołajczyk's independent peasant party lasted until 1947. After that, the communists took over everything, even the smallest, public organizations. (In the middle of the 1960s, before emigrating, we joked in the lab that the only free elections in Poland were the elections of the President of the Polish Society of Biochemists. We were wrong. The party candidate won even in this case!) Officially, there were no political parties in the army and my school even had a chaplain, and the cadets sang beautifully "God who protects Poland" or "Rota"[3] at the morning assembly. Essentially, people already knew, although many didn't wish to know, that all this was hypocrisy, since the "politicals," that is, communists and their party, the PPR, were in power. One

---

[2] Tr: Zdrowie (Polish): health.
[3] Tr: Rota (The Oath): an early twentieth century Polish epic poem and celebratory anthem.

day in 1946, or perhaps 1947, at the training in Zdrowie, a certain ensign sat next to me and without any overture told me that a "secret" political organization called PPR was active at the school and that I would be a good match for it. Clearly, they knew nothing about my dad, the counter-revolutionary. I didn't tell him about Dad and somehow wriggled out of this. What I did later shows how stupid and confused I was at that time. The editorial office of *Robotnik*,[4] for many years a famous PPS newspaper, was located in Lodz, and one of its editors—his name was, if I'm not mistaken, Jan Dąbrowski—had learned about me from another of this publication's co-workers, a Bund member. I met Dąbrowski and later we got together a couple of times in an elegant, for those days, restaurant, Tivoli, on Narutowicza Street, near Piotrkowska Street. In the summer, tables were placed in a small garden. I liked these encounters because the man was interesting. There would also be a good dinner with vodka, which I couldn't normally afford. I told Jan about the "secret" PPR organization and offered to set up a similar one for PPS. He had a good laugh and told me not to dare; it was enough that Dad was still in jail. I found out from him about the situation in PPS and in the country. "The communists"—he said—"are taking over everything; the rest is nonsense and window dressing. Soon PPS and '*Robotnik*' will cease to exist." (Indeed, in 1948, the political parties, as they called them, "merged together" and the Polish United Workers' Party was formed.) "The then prime minister"—he continued—"a PPS member Osóbka-Morawski is a weakling, and the only tough man in the party's leadership, the deputy minister of security Wachowicz is being ignored; he carries no weight in the department because it's the communists who rule, and hence, has decided to resign. There already are people from the party's leadership who are getting ready to leave the country. There is also another group;" (he named among others Cyrankiewicz,[5]) "who believe in a dialogue with the communists—for good careers of course." He knew well what he was talking about. He also made me understand that he had talked with Wachowicz about my dad and that nothing could be done. Later, I lost sight of Jan.

The only person at school with whom I had a friendly relationship was Captain Józef Smela, also a teacher of infantry weaponry. Much older than I, he was a pre-war professional officer, fought in 1939, was wounded, captured, and spent the war in Germany in an Oflag. He got married before the war but

---

4 Tr: Robotnik (Polish): The Worker.
5 Tr: Józef Cyrankiewicz (1911–1989): Polish socialist and communist politician, Polish prime minister (1947–1952 and 1954–1970), and president of Poland (1970–1972).

had no children. I talked with him a lot; he was a pleasant, intelligent man. I found out that he came from a village at the feet of the Carpathian Mountains, the younger of two brothers. Their farm was too small to be divided. The older brother had taken it and so he had to make a choice: to join the priesthood or the army. Since he had no calling for the former—that became obvious soon after we met—his father "paid him off" by sending him to high school and, because he was smart, he got accepted to a military academy. After the war he came back to Poland and to his wife and was sent to our school. He was good looking, his uniform fit him perfectly, his shoes were shiny, and he knew how to behave and generally was liked and respected. He took to the army like a fish to water. Here he was in his element. He certainly was a better teacher and role model for the cadets than I. Unfortunately, he didn't stay long in the military. He was kicked out around 1948, when great numbers of pre-war officers were gotten rid of. I saw him from time to time; he was very depressed. When we were serving together, Józef organized, for some reason or other, a ball with an orchestra in a beautiful hall for the Lodz garrison officers. He was an outstanding dancer and was instrumental in making Felusia queen of the ball. She has never forgotten it.

At first, I was very unhappy in Lodz. I was clinging to people and before meeting Felusia and our friends, I was totally alone. After years of wandering through Russia, I settled in a normal city, but having lost my parents, family, and friends, I felt forlorn and lonely. One thing was for certain; I had to study. The military was not a long-term solution. Studies at any university were free. It seemed like fairy tale. After all, I was looking at the world through the eyes of that boy, whose parents had been so happy, in 1936, to be able to afford an inexpensive high school for their son. Higher education had been outside our boldest dreams. I wasn't aware that after World War II, in the more developed countries, universities had ceased to be the realm of only the very wealthy. My attempts to apply to the university began immediately. For this, I needed a high school diploma. My plan was to start the semester in the fall of 1945. I was 21, I had "lost" three years, after high school, fighting the war, and I didn't want to waste any more time. In the course of my first visit to the school board, I was told that my Russian diploma hadn't much impressed the paper pushers; they decreed that I would take regular exams of all the obligatory subjects in Polish, just without the necessity of going to school (matura externa). I believed that this wasn't right, that they should at least give me credits for my science courses. The exams were to take place shortly. I went again to the school board and succeeded in seeing the board's head, who wasn't any more agreeable than his functionaries. During our conversation, suddenly, a short man walked in. Seeing him, the official jumped up from his chair, and with an exaggerated respect, addressed him as "Sir Minister." Later, I learned that he was the deputy minister for education. It looked like an unexpected visit. Again, I presented my arguments and both men—probably in order to get rid of me as soon as possible—agreed that I should only take exams in Polish language, Polish history, and Polish geography. Geography was the worst—one had to remember all of the Vistula's left-bank and right-bank tributaries, various Wieprzs, Bzuras, and other such unnecessary facts that burden one's memory (since it's not infinite). What to do? I crammed, and perhaps not an hour after the exam, all those names evaporated from my head.

In the summer of 1945, I was accepted to study at the Department of Mathematics and Natural Sciences, majoring in chemistry. Classes were beginning October 1. It was done! I would be the first in my immediate family to study at a university. I was very proud.

Before leaving Lublin, Uncle Bernard had left me some addresses where I could find him or get news about him after my return from Russia. One of these addresses was in Lodz. This is how I found Marek Edelman[6] and later met his wife, Ala Margolis, and her mother, Anna, a well known pediatrician, and their friends. Before the war, most of them were young Bund members. They fought in the Warsaw ghetto, in the resistance, in the Warsaw Ghetto Uprising, and they were the few who escaped certain death. Now they all lived in Lodz. Marek was the only one that I knew from before the war. He was a friend of Janek's cousin; we had gone to the same CYSHO school before the war started. Being among these people, so dear to me, for a long time I felt embarrassed that I hadn't been in Poland during the war. I felt the same (a complex?) toward Felusia. Those feelings wouldn't leave me for a long time, decades. They had all lived through unimaginable hell. They were different, and there was a sort of wall between us. From their vantage point, my war troubles amounted to nothing. They never talked, not ever, about their war experiences. They simply couldn't. These became our circles of friends, both in Poland and in the United States, following our departure.

After a while, Uncle Bernard surfaced in Lodz. He stayed for a short time and left almost immediately—escaped—to the west. He feared commu-

---

6 Tr: Marek Edelman (1919–2009): Jewish-Polish political activist and cardiologist. A Bund youth leader, he co-founded in 1942 the underground Jewish Combat Organization (Żydowska Organizajca Bojowa), and was one of three sub-commanders and later the commander of the Warsaw Ghetto Uprising. Edelman was the last surviving leader of the Uprising.

nists. Felusia never got to meet him—she arrived at Lodz literally a couple of days after he left. Before leaving, he took me to 31 Piotrkowska Street— it was fate!—to meet Hanka Fryszdorf. He didn't know the Strawczyński brothers with whom Felusia was soon to dwell, but he knew Hanka, and she already lived on Piotrkowska. Both brothers had participated in the Treblinka uprising of 1943 and became separated during their escape. Oskar joined a resistance unit made mainly of the Ghetto Uprising fighters. There he met Hanka and her husband. Hanka's husband had been killed before the birth of their son. In a Warsaw basement, during the uprising in September of 1944, Bernard acted as the midwife during this birth. Later, he wrote about an idea that struck him during the delivery: to immediately strangle the newborn. A mother without a baby would have had a better chance of surviving. You press a finger against the baby's throat and it's over. But he couldn't do it; they both lived. I had also known Hanka from before the war; for a while she worked for my mom. I also knew her from the Bund community. At the CYSHO school on 36 Krochmalna Street, she had also been Janek and Marek's classmate. Later, Hanka would become one of our closest friends and was one of the noblest people I had met in my entire life.

And that's how I found myself at 31 Piotrkowska Street. Frankly speaking, I liked both brothers from the very start. Before I try to describe the kind of home it was—not an easy task—I will depict the apartment. It was located in the front part of the building, on the third floor. From the hallway, one entered a large front hall. On the right were doors to two big, nice rooms, overlooking Piotrowska Street. These were the brothers' rooms, and later the couples': Oskar and Celinka's and Zygmunt and Maryla's. On the left, there was a small room that Felusia occupied after her arrival. Your dad used to be a frequent guest at all hours of day and night. And further on was an entrance to the very important, large dining room that was the epicenter of all social and other kinds of life's experiences. A long passage led from the dining room to the kitchen; on the left there was a bathroom and a small room called "the staff room," since in the past it was where the maid used to live. Hanka and her baby lived there; it was convenient, located between the bathroom and the kitchen. In the kitchen there was an entrance to a separate hallway, which led to the backyard, so the lady and the gentleman of the house who were using the main hallway wouldn't, God forbid, run into the servants and suppliers of milk, bread, etc. The apartment was typical of the rich upper middle class of the end of the nineteenth and beginning of the twentieth centuries, and it was not remarkable. But for us, at that time, it was the height of luxury and chic.

I am not able to name all those who passed through our dining room during the year and a half when 31 Piotrkowska Street was operating (Spring 1945–Fall 1946). Passing through meant: they ate, drank, slept—mainly on the floor—how else, how would one get so many beds and blankets—until they found either relatives or a better place under the sun. This was a warm and a welcoming home created by decent people. Felusia came back to Lodz with four young girls with whom she had survived several camps. One of them found her brother—a revolting rogue, he took in his sister, but didn't let the other girls even spend the night—so the sisters, Rosa and Marylka, with Helka, lived on Piotrkowska until they found a better place. Helka stayed longer, until she was married. One evening, I arrived—as I usually did—on Piotrkovka Street and heard somebody playing the violin, a musician had come back from a camp in Germany and was flaunting his talent. A total stranger, no idea where he came from, anchored himself in the dining room. Abramek (I don't recall his last name), the son of Felusia's grandparents' friends, lived in the dining room for some time. After him, there was the brothers' cousin, who came from Russia, also named Oskar (at that time he was called Oskarek or "little Oskar") and he, too, lived in the dining room. As I recall, initially, Abramek and Oskarek shared the large single bedroom. Oskarek didn't stay long: he moved to a hostel for Jewish youth run by the Central Committee of Polish Jewry; many solitary, orphaned young people lived there. It was a good organization, useful and timely. Almost all of the youth supported by this organization went to school and graduated from universities.

I know an expression, in Yiddish, not in Polish, which could roughly illustrate the atmosphere on Piotrkowska Street during the initial post-war period: *hefkie pietruszkie*, completely impossible to translate, because the literal translation "care-free parsley" makes no sense whatsoever. It was as if nothing existed beyond the present moment, neither the world nor the future, it was a sort of—not at all Jewish—recklessness. There was lots of vodka; dishes got washed when there was not a single clean plate left. This was the response of people who had lost their families in Treblinka, who had witnessed the annihilation of countless victims and had faced their own death every day and every hour. Piotrkowska Street lasted only a year and a half, but life there had such intensity that it left a mark on all of us. And one more thing; both brothers had strong family feelings: it was with their help that, years later, Oskarek with his family, and eventually we, emigrated from Poland to Canada.

At first, Zygmunt worked at some administrative office and Oskar managed a metalwork factory. Oskar inherited this profession from his father, who had been a real expert. After a short while, Zygmunt came to the conclusion that office work was not for him and joined his brother. While Oskar was in charge of production, Zygmunt took care of the rest. The business prospered beautifully. Most of Zygmunt's problems had to do with getting raw materials, mainly tin, since selling the merchandise wasn't difficult. Production wasn't very complicated and after six years of war, poverty, and all kinds of shortages, pipes, buckets, watering cans, and cake pans were selling like hotcakes in little villages and in the city. Had the brothers continued the business for several more years, they would have undoubtedly become rich. Or perhaps not; in a few short years the communist authorities would kill such "burgeoning capitalism." The process was as follows: after paying legal taxes, the owner had to shell out a so called surtax, an absurdly high, totally disproportional amount that exceeded his means. Such policy assumed that the owner was a priori a class enemy and a thief; the surtax being an expression of a higher, revolutionary justice. That is how all private trade as well as small business were ruined in Poland.

Your mom, a graduate of the Lodz ghetto, of Auschwitz, of terrifying transports in cattle cars, of work and death camps, came back to Lodz in the early summer. The last camp was Theresienstadt in today's Czechoslovakia, where Russians had liberated and saved her, literally a day or two before the gas chamber. Oskar, the more emotional of the two brothers, fainted upon seeing his niece. And I had been, sort of, waiting for her on Piotrkowska Street. Her beautiful, thick, curly hair was barely growing back, but she was already a striking beauty. She was lovely and charming, and despite all the tragedies she had experienced, her joy of life was undiminished. How else could it have been: she was young, the summer was beautiful, and the world was her oyster. It didn't take long before we became a couple, and it has remained so.

In the fall of 1945, Fiszka Najman turned up in Lodz. He had managed to leave the army even though only the married and not the single men were routinely demobilized. We "captured" an additional bed and Fiszka moved into my room on Mielczarskiego Street. He quickly enrolled in the Department of Social Sciences at the university and began part time work in some sort of business in Lodz. He was also active in the Bund organization that was being launched. Another close friend of mine, Awrem (Arkadiusz) Kahan, also a Bund activist, was studying economics in Lodz. After immigrating to United States, Awrem received his PhD at the University of Chicago and became an eminent economist. At that time in Lodz—and in Poland in general—there weren't many Jews. Mainly there were those who had survived in Poland and had disclosed their Jewish identity (many individuals didn't discard their "Aryan" identity acquired during the war), or those like myself, who came back with the army. The hope was that the Jewish population would grow significantly after the return of Polish citizens who had been sent to Russia in 1940, because many Jewish Holocaust survivors would be among them. This is why both Bund and other Jewish political organizations began forming local chapters.

University studies were going well for me. I tried my best to attend as many lectures as I could and participate in various chemistry and physics labs. It wasn't always possible; the army had its demands. I worked a lot. In principle I was allowed to study, everybody at school knew this, and my fellow lecturers tried to help. However, my situation was still ambiguous and some of my superiors were not happy with my studies. I was expected to participate in front line officers' "betterment" exercises and sit for various exams. One day I was taking an exam on the "rules of prison staff"—to this day I am uncertain whether I actually knew what that was (is?). I perused the wisdoms' manual and my "interior mechanism" concluded that there wasn't anything interesting and that I would somehow manage. Indeed, initially things went well; the examiners were two or three of my co-workers who knew full well that I wasn't interested in the topic. They sat behind a table in the exam room, facing the door, while I was facing them, with the door behind me. At one point I drew the following question: "How high should horses' troughs be placed in military stables?" I didn't have a clue but after deep reflection I came to the conclusion that this should depend on the horse: if the horse is tall, its trough would go high and if it's short, then lower, and that's what I said. Looking at the examiners' expressions I understood that something was amiss, and a second later I heard the commandant's stentorian voice: "Lieutenant, you treat your military service as a steppingstone to a scientific career." I, a first or perhaps a second year chemistry student, and a scientific career, what nonsense! That's how this army was, or perhaps every army is like that? He had entered the room quietly; my examiners saw him but I didn't. As it turned out, I really did deserve to flunk, because I didn't know the correct answer; in the military all horses have a standard height (and, most likely, intelligence) so the trough's positioning at a particular height makes a lot of sense. If I'm not mistaken, this was the only exam I failed in my life.

Nothing good was turning up from Russia. Sometimes I would get a short letter from Dad where he would say that he was fine, feeling well, and that he didn't need anything. Later there were questions about me and that was all. Letters from other, "free" friends from Baranovka were similar, for fear of censorship. Six months after the war ended, in the fall of 1945, there still was no mention of the return of Poles taken to Russia, and it was anyone's guess if that might happen. Few individual people were coming back, mostly young ones like "little" Oskar, but a mass repatriation hadn't started. At the end of 1945, I made the decision to visit Dad in jail and to go to Baranovka during my school break. This wasn't difficult for active duty officers because the border with Russia hadn't been closed yet. There were still many in the military that traveled home during furlough. I reached Baranovka without any complications. After all, I had officer's papers in two languages, my name was Vladimir Mikhailovich, and I spoke fluent Russian without any accent. Once there, I found a real tragedy. All the prisoners' wives and children were helping each other as best as they could and somehow they were managing, but "somehow" signified both hunger and freezing cold. Baranovka winters were bitter. Mania Segal walked her two children to school every day: little Józio to primary and Vyera to her nursery school, where the children would get a warm meal.

Several days later, travelling on the beaten path, I reached Ulyanovsk and continued to the fenced yard of the building on the corner of Tolstoy and Marx Streets, and to the familiar window with the boor in it. Many other prisoners' wives and daughters had come with me; all the men were jailed. I was granted a visit right away, while they were turned down. The aura of the wounded warrior was still working well. We were of course, accompanied by an NKVD officer, the very same one as in the spring, and our conversation was conducted strictly in Russian. No other language was allowed. The atmosphere was bad. It had been a year since his arrest and Dad looked worse than during the last visit. I told him about Felusia and gave him a photo of her with me. He was moved. The NKVD officer, all smiles, said "khrasivaya dievushka"—"pretty girl." Years later, Dad recalled that, as soon as the door had closed behind me, the officer took the photo and tore it into shreds. In answer to my question about his future, Dad said that the investigation was ongoing and that according to law, their "law," no information could be disclosed. I left depressed, powerless. I accomplished nothing. This time neither colonel "Ivanov" nor Lidka made an appearance. Good. I didn't miss them.

First train transports from Russia began to arrive in the spring of 1946. This was the start of mass repatriation of people deported to Russia in 1940. The returning Jews were generally sent to Lower Silesia, where they were set up mostly in empty, formerly German towns and cities. Substantial Jewish clusters formed then in Wałbrzych near Wrocław, in Dzierżoniów and in other, smaller localities. We learned that our transport from Baranovka would travel to Wrocław through Koluszki; the train would not stop in Lodz. Somehow I arranged for a military truck and together with Fiszka we drove to Koluszki. Our encounter was very painful. There were only women and children, not one single male. For them, as for me, the war was not over. We had to decide quickly what to do, because the train was leaving shortly. Several families chose to go to Lower Silesia, others to Upper Silesia to towns not destroyed where they had lived before the war. We took Mania Segal with Chaim Babic's children to Lodz—essentially, we had come here for them. I had an "apartment" for Mania and the children, where they lived for the next four years. It was a strange place, practically located in the same area as the barracks. From the barracks' gate, one entered a large room on the first floor; there was a kitchen in the corner and a sink with running cold water. This was not the main gate, rather the secondary one, but nevertheless guards stood there 24 hours a day and protected the children of the horrific "enemies of the people!" This bizarre situation was likely only possible in Poland out of the entire communist block. The room used to serve for storage, where I and other teachers kept models and other aids for our classes with the cadets. The co-workers agreed to move the display units somewhere else and the battalion's commander, Captain (later major) Szwedyk, agreed to house Mrs. Segal and the children there. Decent people helped each other. Together with Fiszka, we prepared the room as well as we could, put in some necessary furniture, and that was it. And the soldiers ended up liking the old woman dressed like a peasant who talked to them simply and who took care of two small children, although it was obvious that she couldn't have been their mother. But the children called her Mom and treated her as such until the end of her life. She had not been childless; she had two children of her own. For me this living arrangement was very convenient, because I went to the barracks almost every day and often was able to see all three of them. Money was a problem; neither Fiszka nor I had a penny to our name, but members of the American Bund helped. American dollars were worth a lot in post-war Poland, and the apartment, water, and electricity cost close to nothing; the Lodz' Polish Jews Committee helped as well. These were, after all, two total orphans. Around 1950, it came to light that Józio and Vyera were not Mania's first "children." This was a surprise; she never talked about it. Paweł, an orphan for whom she had cared before the war, was a well known Zionist activist. At that time he led a youth group called Ha-shomer ha-tzair (Young Guard, a leftist organization preparing Jewish youth of the Diaspora for work on farms, particularly Israeli kibbutzim). There were numerous such youth groups in Poland; in the late 1940s they left for Israel, mostly illegally, or rather half-legally. Before his departure, Paweł took Mania and both children to Lodz, where his group lived, and later to Israel. That was what Mania wanted. There wasn't a better solution. Her friends in Israel and in the US chipped in and bought her an apartment in Tel Aviv. By the late 1950s, Paweł was a highly-placed official in the Israeli defense ministry. We met Chaim Babic's children again after many years—they weren't children any more—during my and Felusia's first trip from the US to Israel in 1969. They were waiting for us at the airport. Mania wasn't there; she had left us during the 1960s. If she saw our reunion from above, and I hope she did, she would have been very proud. Vyera became a teacher and Józio managed an ice cream factory, likely a good business in Israel. We saw "the children" several more times, but with the passage of time our contact ceased. One more odd thing happened. After Mania and the children moved to Paweł's place in Lodz, I received a letter from the military housing office asking if I wanted to give back the apartment. I had no idea it had been "classified" as mine. I answered that I didn't wish to give it back and was able to place another family there, a widow of a Bund member and their children, who had no place to go. Chaim, a friend of Dad's, had died in exile in Russia; I don't remember the circumstances. My military, or rather its housing authorities, apparently hadn't realized that the tenants changed. Or perhaps they did but couldn't care less who lived in the storage room.

I will go back now to the times in Lodz right after the war. Rumors of anti-Semitic incidents had been heard from the very beginning, that is, from the moment the war was over and the few Jews still alive began returning from camps and various hiding places. We didn't feel it as much in Lodz, a major city. But Felusia and her four friends had experienced disturbing and even dangerous encounters with the mob, surprised that so many "little Jewesses" were left alive and loudly expressing its displeasure at several railroad stations, on their way from Thereisenstadt to Lodz. The worst one happened at the Częstochowa station. The girls were easily identifiable, not so much by their appearance—three had "good," Aryan-looking faces—but by their camp rags and shaved heads. It was summer of 1945, the beginning of a new regime, before it was possible to declare them collectively—as it was the case with the Jews—responsible for "Judeocommunism"—the belief that the communist government was controlled by Jews, especially in the security sector. Reports about attacks on trains, especially south of Lodz, began to arrive with regularity. Trains were being stopped by armed gangs who dragged out two kinds of passengers; those in uniforms and those with Semitic features. If there were any doubts about the latter, they used a method that had been validated by the Gestapo and the szmalcowniks:[7] drop your pants, you filthy Jew. For us it was a continuation of our tragedy. An average Pole with a good, straight nose, and who was not in uniform, wasn't affected by any of this. People were afraid to ride the trains. Generally, killings took place right there on the spot, by the railroad tracks. Who were these criminals? They called themselves an underground liberation movement fighting for Poland. Mostly, they were savage militias of the fascist-like NSZ,[8] a splinter of NDK. Their brute anti-Semitism, poisoned by blind hatred, their total lack of respect for human life, which was a result, to a large extent, of almost six years of a wicked war, and all that could be most evil in a human being, led to these events, and Jews were murdered. Even *Naród*,[9] the paper of the "sound" rightist Labor Party,[10] wrote in September 1942, during the height of mass murders: "Let us not force ourselves to grieve the demise of an entire people, who had frankly, never been close to our hearts." Oy, these were cold hearts. And in May 1943, while the Germans were quelling the Warsaw Ghetto Uprising and ultimately ending it, *Szaniec*,[11] a paper of the ONR,[12] wrote: "Germans annihilate Jews better than anyone else, particularly when compared with us." Well, they regretted their inability to equal Germans in this endeavor. Killers. There is, as always, the other side to every coin. Among our friends, before emigration, was Iga Przybylska-Wolf[13] and her family. Iga's parents had been teachers. Zdzisław Przybylski, a Piłsudski legionnaire, his wife Jadwiga, and Iga, then a teenager, hid Jews in Warsaw during the occupation. For this they were awarded the Yad

---

[7] Tr: Szmalcownik (Polish): a Pole who, during World War II, denounced Jews to the Germans for money, or who extracted money from Jews in hiding in exchange for not betraying them.

[8] Tr: Narodowe Siły Zbrojne or NSZ: National Armed Forces, an anti-Soviet and anti-Nazi, extreme right-wing, and anti-Semitic paramilitary organization, part of Polish resistance during World War II. NSZ fought against the Nazi occupation, as well as against pro-Soviet resistance movements.

[9] Tr: Naród (Polish): The Nation.

[10] Tr: Stronnictwo Pracy: Labor Party, Polish Christian Democratic party, active from 1937 until 1946. During World War II, it was part of the Polish government in exile.

[11] Tr: Szaniec (Polish): Barricade.

[12] Tr: Obóz Narodowo-Radykalny or ONR: National Radical Camp, Polish extreme-right, anti-communist, anti-Semitic and nationalist party, formed in 1934 by youth radicals, dissolved in 1944.

[13] Au: Iga was a nurse during the uprising in which her younger sister Wanda was killed; see W. Przybylska, J. Przybylska-Wolf, *Dzienniki z czasów wojny* (Warszawa: Wydawnictwo Serwus, 2009).

Vashem Medal of Honor and a tree was planted in the Forest of the Righteous in Jerusalem.[14] Since Poland was the only country in Europe where the entire family would be killed on the spot for helping Jews, this was great heroism, greater than great. Such bravery is true of a few only. In the face of such risk one has no right to expect great courage from "the everyman"; that's not what I mean. The point is that, between the attitudes of *Naród* and *Szaniec* (and these are only two examples, I could offer many more, even some papers of the underground government's civilian administration weren't much better), there is an entire spectrum of decent and noble people's attitudes. But these were not common during the war. Unfortunately, even in today's Poland there are communities, marginal I hope, that continue to glorify these murderers; both bring shame to Poland and to Poles (I have already mentioned the notorious anti-Semitic media consortium from Toruń). I'm not going to dwell upon this. These are well known facts, but my blood boils when I think about it.

Information about killings of Jews, perhaps even more terrifying from those at railroad stations and not dressed in any "ideology" of fighting for freedom, was endlessly arriving from provincial towns. Everyone knew of incidents when individual Jews, returning to their villages and small towns where they lived before the war, and where they were now either looking for relatives or trying to regain their houses and belongings—were murdered without pity. There is evidence that about fifteen hundred innocent people died this way. Such was the situation at the beginning of 1946 that the Bund in Lodz decided to orga-nize self-defense units. A good buddy of mine, Awrem Kahan, an exceptionally nice and smart man, got in touch with me and asked me to teach them how to use weapons. Because of his suggestions, several times at Bund premises I met with a group of over a dozen young, and not so young, men. A couple of times I took them to Zdrowie park to practice shooting. I was familiar with the school's schedule, I knew when no one would be there and when we could practice shooting the same targets as the "political" cadets I had been teaching. The Bund "army" had hand weapons, revolvers, given to them in secret by, if I'm not mistaken, local police, aghast at the attacks against Jews. Awrem and the then head of Lodz's Bund thought that revolvers were not sufficient, that their fighters should have better equipment, such as automatic weapons or machine guns. Not able to get them from the police, they came to me. At the cadet school there was a repair shop for guns. Refurbished weapons were given back

---

[14] Au: *Dzieje Żydow w Polsce 1944–1968: teksty źródłowe*, oprac. A. Cała i H. Datner-Śpiewak (Warszawa: Zydowski Instytut Historyczny, 1997).

to the units, but those not suitable for repair would be classified "for trash" and become scrap metal. The classification was made by the repair shop's supervisor and cosigned by, I think, two officers. The supervisor happened to be a young Jew, a non-commissioned officer, a crafty fellow who proved very willing to "arrange" something, but he wanted money. We set it up in such a way that we would sign the "for trash" certificates and the weapons would be funneled to Bund instead of the scrap yard. There was no problem taking the weaponry out of the barracks: we simply needed to wait for a rainy day when we wore enormous canvas capes, called, from Russian, coats-palatkas. One could have hidden a cannon under this covering, and the guards at the barracks' gate never stopped officers. These were not major thefts: a couple of automatics and one machine gun. I don't recall our "army" being called upon to fight any battles, but they felt safer. A long time later, in the 1970s in New York, I would at times see my "pupils" from the Lodz self-defense school at the yearly reunions commemorating the Bund's creation.

During several post-war years, Lodz was Poland's true cultural capital. Warsaw had been completely destroyed and many eminent actors, musicians, and writers who had survived gathered in Lodz, which was untouched by warfare. Felusia and I never missed a theater play, opera, or concert. The city's military headquarters had several free tickets for every performance—I don't know the origins of this odd custom—and as I had good buddies there we could attend shows for free. Given our financial circumstances, despite the tickets' low cost, this was significant. Looking back, we saw spectacular shows starring the giants of Polish theater, among them Aleksander Zelwerowicz and Jacek Woszczerowicz in Fredro's *Revenge*, or in modern plays by Jean Giraudoux, and Irena Eichlerówna in Shaw's plays. For the first time in our lives we attended a cabaret, where the king was Ludwik Sempoliński, a comedian of rare talent. As Warsaw began to rebuild, these people, who constituted the elite of Polish culture, migrated to the capital; by the late 1940s it was a true exodus. Aleksander Zelwerowicz together with his daughter, also an actress, had saved many Jews in their apartment in downtown Warsaw. One of those who had found shelter in their home was Leon Fajner, the Bund's head in occupied Poland. They were both awarded the Yad Vashem certificate of honor, a memorial stone, and a tree in the Forest of the Righteous in Jerusalem.

On June 24, 1946, another tragedy hit us like a bolt of lightening: Fiszka was murdered in our apartment. I will start with the facts. I was returning to the apartment on Mielczarskiego Street in the afternoon when, in the hallway, I ran into Z., a young Bund member. He was screaming in Yiddish, completely hysterical, that Fiszka had been murdered. Together we ran to the apartment. The front door as well as the doors to our room and to the bathroom were wide open. The landlords were absent; the door leading from the hallway to their part of the apartment was closed. Fiszka's body was in the bathroom, hanging at the waist over the edge of the tub, his head submerged in water. The tub, as it often happened, was filled with water. In pants, shirt, and high boots he seemed to be supporting himself. There was a sink to the left of the tub and it looked as if he had shaved before dying, because his shaving tools were there. He had been shot once in the back of the head and the bullet came out above his right eye. This is clearly visible on a photo I still have. He was killed by professionals. This is how the NKVD was killing its prisoners and the way they killed Polish officers in Katyń. The Gestapo killed this way as well. There was a lot of blood on the bathroom floor and in the bathtub. Perhaps after the shooting they had thrown the body into the tub with the head in the water so he would not have a chance to survive; in case he had not been killed by the bullet. Our room wasn't especially messy. I saw that the military uniforms were missing, but the civilian clothes, of which we didn't have many, hadn't been stolen. Two revolvers were missing; the one belonging to him and my spare, because at that time I usually carried one on me. A pair of Fiszka's gold or perhaps gold-plated cufflinks sat in an open box on the table; an ostentatious statement that the murder had ideological justification. The police arrived; they questioned us, and the landlords, and took the body. The Bund's leadership in Warsaw pushed the central authorities to lead a vigorous investigation. In Lodz we even tried to bribe some "higher ups" in the police department, but it led nowhere. I think that, in those years, the skills of the police and their investigative techniques were very primitive. The perpetrators were never caught. Or perhaps they were looking for me and Fiszka happened to be in the apartment? Who knows? In any case, Felusia insisted that I leave my room on Mielczarskiego Street and move in with her on Piotrkowska Street. Fiszka was buried with military honors in the Lodz Jewish cemetery; a huge crowd of people attended the funeral. Any day now, he was to leave for Sweden; his girlfriend had gone there shortly before and they were going to settle in the US. That is what happened to Fiszka's life. He was an intelligent, wise man; he loved to learn. He was naturally active, drawn to working for the public good and possessed the necessary for it altruism; he was a worthy person. Together we had endured Russia, including Siberia, and army service. I have never had a closer friend.

This death shook up our community. An ordinary Jew, not some known personality, is no longer safe in his own house and dies murdered in plain sight in the then biggest Polish city. Was it rational to stay in this country, to start a family, to raise children? The Strawczyńskis, following their sister's and her husband's repatriation from Russia, couldn't stop thinking about it; Fiszka was the brothers' and Felusia's dear friend. And then a new disaster struck, this time a murder on a large scale. Less than two weeks after Fiszka's assassination, on July 4, 1946, the Kielce pogrom took place. It was neither the first nor the only pogrom in post-war Poland, but the scale of this attack hadn't been seen for years. More than forty Jews were killed in a savage, bestial way; scores more were wounded. The reason for the pogrom was a hateful falsehood dating back to Middle Ages, a so-called ritual killing. A boy, allegedly kidnapped and killed by Jews who supposedly needed his blood, was found safe and sound several days later; many of us died. There is significant evidence linking the Polish secret police and the NKVD to the pogrom.[15] This means that the secret service caused the boy's temporary disappearance and spread the rumors that he had been taken by Jews. This is quite plausible. In June 1946, there was a referendum whose results were grossly falsified by the communists. Western diplomats objected and foreign press cried foul that the communists were cheating. The pogroms would divert the west's attention from dishonesty at the polls and would hold the Polish right wing responsible for the pogrom; a cunning and very likely alternative. What's more, some in the west might think: "Perhaps it's best that the communists take over and keep these people in line, if they are capable of killing the remains of their Jews a year after the Holocaust." I believe that the best synthesis on this subject was published in the 1970s in *Kultura*, in the form of an ongoing discussion of the underlying causes of Kielce: it's hard to say what really happened. If in fact the NKVD and the secret police were involved, that meant provocation. Whatever happened, the heart of the matter is that the spark caught fire on "parched land." That's the gist of it. No more, no less. But there is more, even though it is obvious. My bitter remarks concern the mob and not the enlightened and noble Poles among whom I thrived throughout my entire life, people with whom I associated.

According to Jewish Committees' and the Polish Red Cross' registration lists, after the Jewish repatriation from Russia, there were about 300,000 Jews in Poland. This was the summer of 1946. Barely a year later, about 50,000 remained. This was no longer emigration; it was an escape. Kielce became a turning point in Polish Jewry's post-war history. Was anti-Semitism the sole cause of the escape? It was a direct incentive, but other "isms" existed as well.

---

[15] Au: Michał Chęciński, *Poland* (New York: Kartz-Cohl Publishing, 1982).

Polish Jews who had spent the war in Russia had no illusions about Soviet communism. And there was one more aspect. The possibility of creating a Jewish homeland on the British mandate's territory in Palestine—Israel did not yet exist—was a powerful magnet. To finish once and for all with the Diaspora—could there be anything more attractive than Zionism after the Holocaust? The chances for creating an authentic Jewish community—Yishuv—in Poland after the war had ceased to exist.

After the Kielce incident, Felusia's uncles had no illusions—we must get us out of here. Business was business, but staying made no sense. Even their sister and her husband, who had had communist inclinations before the war, were ready to embark on the unknown. Celinka, who was in advanced stages of pregnancy with Leo, told Oskar that she wouldn't have a baby in Poland. Celinka lived through very trying times both during the occupation and immediately after the war. She had been hiding in a small provincial village and almost lost her life multiple times. Oskar and Celinka left for the west in the late summer, in order to be abroad before the birth. They found refuge in occupied Germany, where millions of *dips* (displaced persons) from all European countries lived at the time; their little boy was born in September. Zygmunt and his family stayed in Lodz because they had a "problem." The uncles' "problem" had to do with your mom. True, she was with Włodek, but there had been no wedding, and who was he, anyway—a mere student at the start of his education, a low-ranking officer, earning just pennies. Could be a decent boy but you never know, right? How can one leave one's niece with this guy? Several months earlier, Zygmunt had found a great match for her: a good acquaintance of his, a serious fellow (they were the same age), a lawyer, wealthy, attracted to her (no wonder); who could have wished for more? But the girl was unwise: she didn't want him, she preferred her officer; girls were silly. She didn't understand that the time of *hefkie pietruszkie* would soon be over and that one had to think about *parnose*. The officer had problems as well. I was seriously considering immigration with Felusia and her family. I think that after Kielce they would have allowed a discharge from the military without difficulty (desertion was not an option). Two reasons were keeping me here: the possibility of continuing my education in Poland and Dad still in a Soviet gulag. Leaving for the west with the aim of going to the States, Canada, Australia, or perhaps Palestine would have been then, for me, a complete break up with my dad. It was an extremely difficult decision, which I was unable to make. Finally I decided to go one more time to Ulyanovsk, see how things were, and then make up my mind. Zygmunt and the rest of the family stayed in Lodz, waiting for my return. Theirs was an extraordinary loyalty, more than that, since the western borders could have been sealed at any time and the family would have been separated. And the brothers were unusually close.

This time the trip to Russia proved to be more complicated than before. The eastern border hadn't been sealed, but people were saying (yes, "people were saying," nothing was "for certain" in those times) that one needed to have a pre-war Soviet location indicated on the military ID as one's birthplace. Without this they wouldn't let anyone in (that's how it was commonly said—"they": our rulers, invisible but omnipotent, some "they" who made decisions for us and in our name; one heard this at every step). I was afraid to leave with a document where my true birthplace was indicated; this would have been risky. What would I do if they sent me back from the border? I got help from a human resources officer, an acquaintance. He changed my birthplace from Warsaw to Kharkov, Ukraine. I don't know why he picked Kharkov. After my return he gave me back my old ID, and destroyed the one with Kharkov. It turned out that the border control was rather lenient.

There was one more problem, very serious: money needed to pay for the trip and to leave with Dad. Here Zygmunt again proved invaluable. He introduced me to a jeweler whom he had known before the war. An elderly gentleman with a substantial belly, amiable and jovial, he had a store in the Grand Hotel on Piotrkowska Street; at that time it was the most elegant hotel in the entire city. The entrance was both from the street and from the hotel lobby, just like at the legendary Pierre Hotel on Fifth Avenue in New York, unbelievable. The two men had determined that I should take with me as many silk stockings as possible; apparently they were priceless in Moscow. This proved to be true. And in Lodz a year after the war there were countless small manufactures making all kinds of stockings and socks. Zygmunt and the jeweler paid for the purchase, and Felusia sewed nearly all the stockings inside my military coat. I looked incredibly fat. Then the jeweler gave me a letter in Yiddish and an address in Moscow where I was supposed to report with my stockings. The addressee, also a jeweler who, after the revolution, was hiding from view in some cooperative and, at least officially, was repairing watches, had been our Lodz jeweler's friend. They had done business together before the Russian revolution, and had kept in touch during the last war in Russia, where the Lodz jeweler and his family had survived. The Moscow stocking prices were more or less known, and the enterprise was supposed to bring enough money to cover all my expenses in Russia as well as repay, and then some, the two investors; preferably in diamonds. Diamonds were much cheaper in Russia than in Poland. Russian rubles and Polish zlotys were not exchangeable. I understand that in hindsight this, Lord have mercy, financial operation seems complicated, hard to understand and, what's more, absurd; I can't help it, such were the times and I wanted to give Dad as much money as possible. Before my departure I was instructed on how to evaluate diamonds and given a small magnifying glass, which one put in one's eye, like a monocle. Friendship aside, our Lodz jeweler obviously wanted me to appraise the gems I would bring from Russia as well as I possibly could. I met his family then, a super nice son, an engineer, older than I, and his younger sister, my age, also nice. Zygmunt was learning jeweler's skills with me. Without him, the entire venture wouldn't have been possible.

I went on my way at the end of August or at the beginning of September. It was my third trip to see Dad in prison. I couldn't have suspected then that Dad wouldn't return to Poland for another ten years, and that for many years there would be no news of him, not a thing. And the investigation into his release had been ongoing for almost two years.

There were still hotels (or rather hostels) for the military operating near the bigger railroad stations and, having found a place in a common room for lower rank officers, I went to see the jeweler. I didn't know Moscow well and the apartment, as the address indicated, was rather far from the city center. It was located in an area of single wooden houses, villas, most probably for the wealthy before the revolution. Now these houses were in pitiful disrepair, most likely divided inside into apartments for multiple families, so-called comunalkas (communal dwellings). Most often, there was one room for the entire family and one bathroom for everyone; sheer torture. I arrived in the evening and, after showing the letter of introduction, I was very warmly welcomed. The elderly couple was living, as I had guessed, in one room, so extremely cluttered that it was difficult to move; furniture was everywhere. It was the same in many comunalkas. I unloaded the stockings and breathed a sigh of relief; the merchandise was accepted enthusiastically. It turned out that the deal would be unexpectedly successful; there's nothing like free trade between nations. We agreed that I would get a down payment in cash and immediately leave to see Dad, and that the final settlement would take place after my return. The jeweler went somewhere to get the money, and I had a conversation with the hostess. She could have been my grandmother. They had lost their son in the war; the daughter-in-law was trying to come to Moscow with her children and move in with the in-laws in their room. To get to Moscow and to register to live there was very difficult; one needed a special permit and the dash to the capital was great: people desired to live here rather than in provincial towns at all costs. In general, shops in Moscow were better equipped, the cultural life—richer, and universities—outstanding. With time, they would have a possibility to find a better apartment. It could take few years. It was a new normal, that is, tragic post-war Russian reality. Everyday life before the war hadn't been much better. The jeweler came back; I took the money, ran back to the station, and continued to Ulyanovsk. Nothing had changed at the corner of Marx and Tolstoy streets and I was immediately granted a visit with Dad. But Dad wasn't the same: he seemed downcast, broken. He didn't seem like my dad; the engaging smile had faded from his face. He said that he understood that he had erred against the Soviet Union; he had thought it over a lot in prison. All kinds of nonsense. What can I say, the conversation didn't make sense, it couldn't. They had probably taught him "how to love freedom." Or perhaps he was just pretending; I don't know. Present at the conversation was another NKVD officer of lower rank. The last two times it had been the same major; now it was a lieutenant, I believe. I gave Dad my photos with Felusia and copies of Mom's, Grandma's, and all of our pre-war pictures, sent to Lodz by the family from Argentina. I told him that I had money, sweaters, and other warm clothes for him. The officer provided me with information where I could leave it all, and that the investigation was over but the trial hadn't taken place and there was no sentence. In general, a trial consisted of a decision of a "troika," that is, a representative of the party committee, of the NKVD and of the prosecutor's office. The sentence was read to the accused in jail and that was the entire "trial"; there was no appeal. A judge, a defender, proofs, witnesses, appeals—those were bourgeois superstitions. This was standard procedure in the case of political prisoners. It was September 1946; nine years had yet to pass until October 1955—when Stalin would die and the mass terror would lessen—until news from Dad would arrive, and a month later I would manage to go to Siberia and see him.

In Ulyanovsk I learned that Chaim Babic[16] and all other "conspirators" had been sent, after the end of the investigation, to an interim prison near Ulyanovsk, from where they were going to be dispatched to labor camps. I was pondering whether I should go there and see Chaim: for two years he had heard nothing of his children. Such a meeting wouldn't be simple. Seeking news of close relatives, asking for visits, sending packages—yes, that was common, it didn't arouse suspicions—but to travel from one prison to the next to see not only one's father but friends, that didn't look good, this could hide a counterrev-

---

[16] Au: Ch. Babic, *Fin Krochmalna biz Kolyme* (Tel Aviv: Isreal-Buch, 1985).

olutionary conspiracy. Paranoia? Yes, true, but that how it was. Finally I decided to go. Probably, had I been older and had a family, I wouldn't have done it. From the "regulars" in the NKVD yard behind the fence, I learned how to get there. From the nearest railroad station you had to walk for hours to get to the prison. But this was Russia, and one had to find a way to live, so people were finding solutions to everything (or, let's say, to almost everything): there was a sharp turn near the prison and an uphill railway embankment where trains were moving slowly and one could jump out. Before the war I used to jump out of the last street car wagon at the Wilson Square in Żoliborz near my high school, but I had never jumped out of a train. What to do, one has to try everything during one's life. I made an appointment with the people who were traveling to the same place, mostly peasant women, wives, mothers. They knew on which days you got to see prisoners. We left together and the train really slowed down at one point. The jumping method was as follows: first, one had to throw down the sack with food and one's things, and immediately after one had to jump out on the right foot, but backward, that is, in the direction contrary to the train's movement and in such a way that the back of the heel would hit the ground; in the same manner as jumping from a street car before. The others jumped out and so did I; it went pretty well. The prison was nearby, in a clearing made in a beautiful forest of tall trees, in a wasteland.

I was sitting in the visitors' room when Chaim was brought in. He staggered, weak-kneed, so very shocked he was to see me. It seemed that he was going to faint. A moment before, he was called to see the warden without a word of explanation. In such cases, the prisoner expects the worst. He couldn't have imagined that it would be my visit. We talked for as long as was permitted; I gave him news of his children, of Mania Segal, of his friends. I left him all the clothes and money I could, and it was time to say goodbye. We were very sad. In his memoirs, written in Yiddish and published a long time afterward in Israel, where he settled, Chaim gave a touching description of that meeting. The next time we saw each other, years later, in Israel, he was waiting for us at the Tel Aviv airport. During the following years, I saw him several times in New York at Bund celebrations and meetings. He died in the late 1980s. He was a fascinating man, self-taught; a carpenter. He was a true Bund Socialist; intelligent and well read. I doubt there are many like him anymore. Physically strong, he survived in the worst Soviet camps in the far north. A dear friend; I liked Chaim and his wife Rywka very much.

Visits were over and the entire motley crowd that had traveled with me assembled in front of the prison gates and chose to go back to Ulyanovsk the same way we had arrived here, that is, to jump onto the train at the very point where we had jumped off. I didn't want to do it; I was afraid and preferred to walk. To jump off a moving train is one thing, but to jump on is a lot more dangerous. The way led through the forest, along the railroad tracks. It became dark and I was overwhelmed by sleep. Using my sack as a pillow and my military coat as blanket, I slept for several hours under a tree. Wild animals did not devour me. On my way back, I stopped for a day in Moscow, collected two diamonds—one for each of my investors—and immediately set out for Lodz. The jeweler and Zygmunt were very pleased with the Moscow deal and both paid me a rare complement: with you, they said, we could "sell ice to Eskimos." Thank God we never tried. There was however a small problem with the jeweler; he had picked me for his son in law and made me understand, without any unnecessary subtlety, that as a dowry she would get, among other things, a five carat diamond of the best quality and of great value. Well, it was too late and it wasn't an option.

I had gone to see Dad to figure out what to do next: emigrate or not—the eternal Jewish dilemma—and I returned none the wiser. I hadn't even learned what sentence he received. In the end, Felusia and I stayed in Lodz. Dad's imprisonment undoubtedly influenced this course of events. This was the period following Churchill's famous speech about the "iron curtain" befalling on Europe from the Baltic to Adriatic seas. Division of the anti-Nazi coalition into two enemy blocs was quickly becoming a reality. I rationalized that to keep in touch with Dad I had to stay in the Eastern bloc. University studies, immensely important to me, were also keeping me in Lodz. Finally, by nature your dad is a rather indecisive man: I worry about the future, particularly the totally unknown one, and that as well, without a doubt, played a big part. And so it was done. When we left Poland, exactly twenty-one years later, I had a secure and excellent job waiting for me in the United States. And, frankly, Felusia was not too eager to leave Poland even in the fall of 1967.

Soon after my return from Russia, on October 1st 1946, we were married. Zygmunt arranged both the ceremony and the reception, such as they were. He wasn't able to do much for his beloved niece, but he did what he could. The wedding ceremony took place at the registrar's office, not so proper without a rabbi, but still better than nothing. And since our union endured throughout our entire lives, not so bad after all. Uncle Zygmunt and Helka, with whom Felusia had survived the Lodz ghetto and the death camps, acted as our witnesses. The reception, grand for those times, was held in the dining room on 31 Piotrkowska Street. Very few of the guests are still alive today. Soon afterward, Zygmunt with Maryla and little Krysia packed their belongings in knapsacks—

this is not a metaphor—and left. It was a very sad good bye; we did not see them again until the 1960s in Canada.

We upgraded after their departure: we moved from the little room with a window overlooking the courtyard to Zygmunt's large, front room with a balcony looking out on Piotrowska Street. Strangers now occupied the other three rooms. The apartment on Piotrkowska Street lost its lovely familial identity. It became an ordinary Soviet comunalka for four families. At the entrance, a code under each strange name appeared; how many times to push the buzzer for each family. The dining room became a thoroughfare, a sort of hall that everybody used to reach the communal kitchen, bathroom, and lavatory. After a time, when each of the four families, as if programmed, had a child at the same time, the dining room finally found its calling: lines were hung across and lengthwise to dry diapers. Including yours, Karusia. In order to cross the dining room one had to duck one's head. The diapers, made of linen or flannel, were washed in a tub and it was customary to boil them after washing. Because we only had one big pot, I claimed that we cooked diapers one day and soup another day, in the same pot. Felusia felt that it was slander; perhaps she was right. After being washed, the diapers were ironed. This was a world without washing machines, clothes dryers, or refrigerators.

The day after our wedding and one day too late, your grandma Lutka with Michał and Ilonka arrived in Lodz. It was such great joy: dear close people and my only link to the past. They settled in Lodz and we saw them often; these were people dearest to us; that is how my mother's friendship with Lutka from almost half a century ago survived. When Karusia was born in August 1948, Michał, who was working near our apartment, would stop by almost every day after work to assist Felusia in giving the baby a bath; he adored that ritual. In the fall of 1948, they left for Sweden. From there they were supposed to go to the States. When leaving Poland, Lutka and Michał left us their apartment on Bandurskiego Street, which was much more modern than ours on Piotrkowska, and we would have two rooms; for us it was a major advancement. But problems continued because this apartment was also a comunalka: Sabina, Michał's cousin, her boyfriend (her husband had died in the ghetto), and her daughter were living there. There was also a small dog, adored by Sabina; its name was Fly. The daughter was very nice, so was the boyfriend, Wacław Matysiak, a veterinary doctor who had rescued the family during the war. But Sabina treated us like intruders. She was furious, hoping to have the entire apartment to herself. She made our lives a misery, especially Felusia's, who spent more time at home than I did. One day your mom, while holding Karusia, was cooking something in the common kitchen, which was, because of its function, the main battlefield. Sabina, holding the dog, said to her boyfriend: "There isn't a child in this world whose eyes are more beautiful than my Fly's." Your mom, who wasn't very resilient, fled the kitchen and began to avoid the cousin like a plague. One day, Sabina told us that she would sue us since we had occupied the apartment illegally and that I would go to jail, but that she, in respect for my parents, whom she had known before the war, would be the first one to bring me food parcels to prison. The woman wasn't altogether sane. According to Felusia, I responded that I would be the first to bring flowers to her grave. Those were the charms of life in a comunalka. Soon Sabina and her daughter left for Israel, the boyfriend moved to their room and gave his room to a friend. These were the times when the smallest piece of roof over one's head was worth its weight in gold. Life with two bachelors became more tolerable, and we lived with them until we moved to Rembertów. There the army gave me our first independent apartment. You both remember Rembertów.

Karusia's arrival in our world was a great event, a true miracle—our first child! And so much more: you were the first child among our contemporaries in Lodz. The Holocaust, although never mentioned, weighted heavily on us day and night. This first post-Holocaust child transformed the situation: we were finally a normal family. Perhaps the sun would shine on us now!

Although the hospital where Karusia was born enjoyed a good reputation, the doctors didn't tell us, perhaps themselves not having noticed, that the baby's feet turned almost 180 degrees inward. Dr. Anna Margolis, Ala's mother, an excellent, experienced pediatrician (she also had a wonderful history of helping people during the war; her "card" was full), saw it when she came to the hospital with Ala and Marek Edelman to see Felusia, almost immediately after the birth. The next day, Anna Margolis returned to the hospital with a friend, a pediatric surgeon, and both women physicians performed the necessary bloodless intervention. The opinion was that the sooner it was done, the better. For many years Karusia wore special aluminum braces taped to her legs that didn't allow her feet to turn inward. The braces had to be replaced as you grew. Once you started walking, you had to wear special laced up orthopedic shoes, made to measure by a cobbler; no pretty shoes or sandals were allowed. The shoes made it look as though the right shoe was on the left foot and the left one on the right. During their walks, strangers would constantly point to Felusia the incorrectly placed shoes and poor Felusia had to explain that she wasn't a ditzy mother and wasn't neglecting her child. Our little girl was four when doctors finally decided

Figure 13 Laboratory of the Organic Chemistry Dept. (Masters candidates), University of Lodz, Summer, 1949. First on the left is the author.

that the special shoes were no longer needed. No trace of the birth anomaly remained. We owe a lot to Dr. Margolis.

More and more of our friends were leaving Poland. First Lutka and her family, and afterward other dear friends and almost all of the Bund members left. We were more and more isolated. Our circle in Lodz was changing and some friendships were falling apart. Of the four girls with whom Felusia returned from Theresenstadt, one married a confirmed and primitive communist. One day we had a party in our apartment; I don't recall the reason, there were lots of such libations attended by many friends. Many toasts, nothing more than pretexts for drinking, were raised. The exception was the third one, drunk in silence, symbolically, for the absent ones. Unexpectedly, this jackass raises his third glass to comrade Stalin's health. It was revolting; such a thing was possible at some public, official banquet, but not in a private home, and especially not in mine. But these were different times, and the guy worked for the police. Silence fell, except for Marek Edelman, who, sitting next to me and at the opposite side of the table from the nitwit, said in Yiddish: fine, let him live, as long as your dad comes back.

Earlier, shortly after her relatives left, Felusia went back to school, a special high school for adults. I graduated in January 1949 with a Masters' degree in organic chemistry and, instead of beginning my doctoral studies as I had intended, I was kept in the military and transferred from Lodz to Rembertów.

Konstantin Rokossovsky, a soviet marshal of Polish origin, one of the true vic-
tors of the war against Germany, had become, at the onset of the Stalinist terror
period in the winter of 1949–50, Poland's defense minister. The parliament,
that is to say, the fake communist parliament, had adopted a law—apparently
at his request—by virtue of which the army could draft any university graduate
for an unspecified length of time. This happened to me, and when I objected
and presented my masters' thesis promoter Professor Anna Chrząszczewska's
laudatory letter, I was told that I was exactly what they needed, especially with
my front-line experience. I continued to protest and went as far as Warsaw, to
the army's human resources department, to plead my case. I was received by
a colonel, no longer young, who stank of vodka in the middle of the day, and
who, instead of wasting his breath, simply showed me Cracow's regional military
court's decision sentencing a physician, who had refused the draft, to three years
of prison. That was convincing. The army's upper echelon was then composed
mainly of "insiders," mostly pre-war communists. My doctoral studies had to be
postponed; I have always regretted that. Possibly I had made a mistake. Perhaps
if I had told them that I was a son of the "peoples' enemy" they wouldn't have
kept me in the military. I hadn't done it, so I don't know what the result would
have been. Or maybe that colonel knew about Dad; this cannot be ruled out.
A few years later I discovered that "they" did know, but considered me an
"expert" (which I wasn't); you can't trust him and he has to be watched closely,
but on the other hand it would be a sin not to use the guy to build "socialism";
especially if he seems smart.

Letters from Dad stopped coming. His fellow prisoners' families with
whom I stayed in touch weren't getting any news from their relatives, either.
An idea that this couldn't be a coincidence, that the prisoners' writing privileges
had been taken away, started to germinate. After a while we learned that before
the war, during the mass Stalinist purges, this had been a "practice" widely
used in the case of "counterrevolutionaries"; evidently it was applied again. I
began then to regularly write requests concerning Dad to Soviet authorities.
I wrote letters by hand, four copies of each, using carbon paper. Typewriters
were available in offices only; such dangerous instruments weren't sold to the
public: they could have been used to make and distribute hostile propaganda!
The request's original copy was addressed to Comrade Stalin, the remaining
copies—to Soviet Union's president Mikhail Kalinin (a puppet of little importance), to the minister of interior Beria (a very important Stalin's confidante,
a truly omnipotent NKVD commander, also a Georgian), and to the Gulag's
commandant; the latter's name wasn't publicly known. At first I would send

these requests twice a year; later—once. I didn't accomplish anything—infinite amounts of such appeals must have existed—and I never received a response. Years later, however, I learned that my letters were not completely useless. When he was finally let out of exile, at the end of 1955, the local Siberian NKVD chief presented him with a thick bundle of my letters—all those years worth! This is how Dad learned where we lived, and was able to get in touch immediately. Without those appeals, he would have had to look for us everywhere on God's green earth. And this wouldn't have been easy, from some tiny forsaken village, somewhere at the back of beyond, in the far away Siberia. It is all very strange: there must have been some sort of order at the NKVD, "their" special kind of order.

In January 1950, I began working as a lecturer at the School for Officers of the Technical Corps (Kurs Oficerów Służby Technicznej or KOST), read, Chemical Corps, in Rembertów, on the outskirts of Warsaw. The capital "T" was a smokescreen for Chemical. This is how I ended up in the Polish army's Chemical Equipment Company and worked there for six years. The beginnings were particularly hard, because we were not given an apartment. I moved into a small hotel room, and Felusia stayed in Lodz with Karusia. I went to see them as often as I could, taking the train to Lodz almost every Sunday, changing trains in Warsaw, and continuing from a different station. Two-day weekends had not yet been invented. In the spring, I managed to acquire and furnish a one-bedroom apartment next to my lab; Felusia and you, Karusia, finally joined me in Rembertów. We were there until late fall. Felusia called that place a gardener's shed. Indeed, the military camp was like a park. Karusia would play on the lawn near the house—just like in the countryside. The apartment was primitive and not winterized. When the cold weather arrived, they went back to Lodz and I to the awful hotel room and weekly commutes to Lodz. It was not until 1951 that the military finally set us up in an apartment block on the camp grounds and we left Lodz for good. Our first non-communal apartment was spacious, with three large rooms, a sizeable kitchen with a recess for a bed, and a bathroom. The Bandurskiego Street apartment was modern; the one in Rembertów lacked both central heating and gas. We used coal in tiled stoves and in the kitchen stove, like before the war on Karmelicka Street. There also was a small coal furnace for heating bath water in the bathroom. In the winter we would heat two rooms, the children's and ours, the third one was, as Felusia used to call it, a fridge; the hallway, the bathroom and the toilet were cold as well. Rembertów marks the end of our comunalkas; this was the main thing, we could breathe. Nobody told us ever again that some retriever's eyes were prettier than our little daughter's.

I had a lot of work because in addition to teaching I worked in a laboratory. Soon, Edmund (Mundzio) Kuczys, a good friend from the university, joined me. We had been in the same year of chemistry studies in Lodz and knew each other well. Mundzio was pleasant and amusing, and working together proved cheerful and fun. Too bad he didn't stay long in Rembertów; he moved to Cracow for family reasons, if I'm not mistaken. We taught both general and organic chemistry, focusing on explosives and toxic gases—all of it important for military training. Our students were, in general, young officers, some with war experience, who were being prepared by the military for work in the Chemical Equipment Corps. There were no proper textbooks, so I wrote a manual based on my lectures. At first our laboratory didn't have a particular niche. We did what we were told, such as identifying a component of napalm that was sent to us by Korea. The Korean War had just begun. A bit of something like brown gel stuck to a piece of twig—that was napalm. I don't doubt that samples of napalm, which was then a new igniting agent, had been sent not only to our lab. It turned out that the essential component of napalm is aluminum (Al) in the form of fatty acids suspended in naphtha or gasoline; I don't recall the details. I suspect that my course book and the napalm—nothing major, to tell the truth—made my bosses consider me an expert. A tad later I became a co-author (there were three or four of us) of the Chemical Equipment Corps' basic textbook. In part it was a translation from Russian, and in part, our own work. The textbook was properly published, in hardcover, but without our names—clearly those were military rules. But the authors received substantial honoraria. This was the first time your dad made such a large (by then standards) amount of money, in his life. We decided, your mom and I, to buy new furniture; a dining set. All we had then were pieces leftover from Piotrkowska Street, and several nice bookcases left by Grandma Lutka. This was the first complete set, not some jumble, all shiny and very elegant. There was not much choice then, one bought what one found, and even that with difficulty. We put it in the "cold room," and a few days after the purchase Felusia woke up in the middle of the night, frightened, and ran screaming to the "cold room" to check if the furniture was still there. She dreamt that thieves had stolen our new acquisition. That's how important an event it was.

There had already been, before the war, a School of Infantry on the Rembertów army base, and the tradition continued after the war. It was a huge unit; by comparison, our KOST was like a mouse next to an elephant. This school provided us with all kinds of facilities, for example a library, a hotel, an officers' mess, a pre-school, a cinema, etc. The KOST cadre consisted of about ten officers, all of them young and in general very congenial, so our relations were friendly. They all drank a bit too much, especially the bachelors. Only the school's commander didn't drink. Colonel, and later, as the head of the Chemical Equipment Corps, Brigadier General, Leonard Szymański was much older than the rest of us. A well educated man, he was experienced, extraordinarily hard working, and, in hindsight, exceptional. He understood that the Chemical Equipment Corps should have its own research facility and, without a doubt, his was the initiative to create there the first (after the war) proper scientific institution. We became close then, he and I, and spent many an evening in conversation, especially when Felusia and the baby still lived in Lodz. A Pole, he spoke almost proper Polish, with a Lvov accent. His father was a railway worker who had been evacuated, during World War I, from Białystok to the East and found himself and his family "beyond the cordon" as they used to say, that is, in Soviet Russia. After graduating from a polytechnic institute and a school of chemistry, Leonard served in the Red Army, while his brother was apparently in the Air Force. In the late 1930s, his brother was jailed during one of the many purges of the Red Army's cadre; purges that affected Poles particularly hard (Rokossovsky ended up in a prison in Siberia), and Leonard literally slept on his coat, expecting at any moment a nighttime visit from the NKVD. His wife, an ethnic Russian, told me that a travel bag filled with warm underwear and dry biscuits was always packed for him. Despite all this, Szymański was a dedicated party member who referred to Stalin solemnly as "khoziain," that is to say, boss. Everything that descended from above was sacred; they sure taught him "how to love freedom." But one shouldn't be surprised: he had lived through so much, had seen mass terror, executions, and deportations; those scenes are difficult to forget. Once, while talking about his brother, I told him about Dad. He was reserved and made me understand that this was not news to him. Military Information, or the army's secret service, hadn't been asleep. In Poland, Szymański wore a Polish general's uniform, but when he vacationed in Russia, where he had an adult daughter, he wore the uniform of the Red Army general. Before long, Szymański became the head of the Chemical Equipment Corps and picked me to head up a task force to create and build a new scientific institute in Rembertów. The decision to pick me was difficult and in those days required a degree of moral courage. I was, after all, a potential enemy of the state because, as we well know, "the apple doesn't fall far from the tree," and Dad had been sentenced in Russia for anti-Soviet activities. Besides, let's be frank, I lacked the necessary experience to assume this post. I made up for this by consulting with many competent people, such as Anna Chrząszczewska, who suggested hiring Prof. Andrzej Orszagh, her pre-war student, as a scientific consultant. Andrzej spent many subsequent years in Rembertów and remained connected with the institute until the end of his life; a man of great knowledge and modesty, dedicated to the institute, and altogether splendid. I believe that the institute's rich tradition of scientific mentors was born and solidified with Andrzej's appointment. To make sure that all modern technical conveniences available in those days were included in the new building, I visited new laboratories being built in Warsaw.

Figure 14 With Felusia, in 1952.

I worked closely with architects, engineers, and suppliers, supervising every aspect of construction. The building, situated in the middle of the base, grew in leaps and bounds. I also took care of carefully selecting both the military and the civilian faculty and staff. It appears that I hired many exceedingly talented young people. (I learned this in the late 1990s, when I visited Rembertów during the Polish Republic's 3rd Chemical Convention; I had been totally cut off from the Institute during my many years in America.) During the initial phases of the Institute's growth, I made a great effort to create a science library and, relatively quickly, journals and textbooks collected on the shelves. I even got a hold of Beilstein,[17] the then accepted "bible" of organic chemistry.

---

[17] Tr: The *Beilstein Handbook of Organic Chemistry*, named after the Russian chemist Friedrich Beilstein, is a collection of information on organic compounds. The first edition was published in 1881 in St. Petersburg and the subsequent three editions in Germany. They cover data from the beginning of the field of organic chemistry (early nineteenth century) until 1918. Due to the rapid growth of this field, instead of issuing new editions of the Handbook, supplements to the fourth edition were published until 1979. Today, the *Beilstein Journal of Organic Chemistry* continues to publish research articles on all aspects of the subject.

From the perspective of over 50 years and the Internet, Beilstein is obviously stale and out of date. But in a quarter of century, today's Internet will no longer be what it is today; that's how the world turns.

After 1953, scientific research at the Institute began in earnest and the time had come to transform our small Preparatory Group into the Scientific Research Center for Chemical Equipment; it seemed that I would direct this institution. But it turned out not to be that simple. Szymański told me plainly that, yes, he would like that, but a person in this position—in military parlance the commander of an independent unit—must belong to the Party. The position was reserved for a party member; ergo, if I wanted it, I had to join the PZPR.[18] This situation dragged on for some time. I argued that, because of my dad, I shouldn't be a Party member, but if I'm qualified and had worked my tail off to create this institution, why not? In a way, I deserved this position. Their answer was simple and entirely convincing: "Lenin wrote" they said, "that a son is not responsible for his father's sins but that all people are replaceable." This Lenin of theirs was not only a saint, he was also a total genius: everything could have been justified with a quotation from his "opus." Had they wanted to throw me out on my ass, they would have found an appropriate Lenin quotation.

One day Szymański—he knew what he was doing, he was not a fool—began to ponder aloud who could be nominated instead of me. I knew these people and I would be lying if I said that I didn't take it personally. At home, with Felusia, we discussed these matters. We said that, of course, the regime was awful, that Dad and so many others were imprisoned for doing nothing, but that on the other hand . . . because there's always the other hand, and because one likes to justify oneself to others and, what's more important, to oneself. After all, we rationalized, isn't education, even higher education, free here? And health care, isn't that free as well? And what about vacations for workers? In addition, my pay would go up and there would be a car with a driver at our disposal. In short, the virgin succumbed. I didn't realize it then, but now I think that ambition played a major role, too.

But here is how my Party story progressed. After October 1956 (Gomułka came back to power in October 1956, the terror-filled Stalinist era ended and, for a short time, maybe a year or two, the atmosphere in the country radically changed), I left the Army without registering in my new job, as I was supposed

---

[18] Tr: Polska Zjednoczona Partia Robotnicza or PZPR (Polish United Worker's Party) was the Polish communist party.

to, as a member of the General Party Organization (the thing was called POP, Podstawowa Organizacja Partyjna). I thought that it would be the end of the Party and me; I was naive. After a while, over the phone, someone from the party apparatus reminded me "comrade, you should get in touch with the POP." When I clarified, in the most courteous of ways and without any preconceived notions, that nothing was further from my mind, I was summoned for a talk. I found myself, for the first and last time in my life, no more and no less, in the PZPR Central Committee behemoth of a building (currently, irony of ironies, the stock exchange) in the section reserved for minorities. There, I talked with a man whom I remembered from my Lodz years as a military "ideological" colonel. It was an exceptionally unpleasant conversation. They didn't like to lose a soul once they had caught one. But these were different times. Right after October, one no longer dreaded the sheer mention of the Central Committee, and I did not relent. And that was the end of my connection with the Party; a virgin cannot be seduced twice.

I'm going back to the 1950s, in Rembertów. I was very involved in the Institute's development and worked hard and long. It took literally five minutes to walk home from the lab (just like many years later in Manhattan, from our apartment to the Department of Biochemistry at NYU medical school). I wasn't wasting time commuting to work and found this arrangement very convenient. Felusia was working at the base as well, first in administration, and later in the library. We made close friendships with several families. This was one side of the coin, but there was another. Life in Poland was getting, in many respects, uglier and uglier. There had been real poverty right after the war: people literally had nothing to eat. In the years 1946–47 this changed. I cannot say that there was food galore, but the improvement was noticeable. In the 1950s, when the authorities proceeded to build "socialism" in earnest, poverty returned to cities and villages. Almost all the food was rationed: there were "vouchers" for meat, cold cuts, sugar, flour, butter; everything. Only bread was cheap and available without coupons. There was a saying: in Poland one can live well on only one zloty a day: once you paid half a zloty for a kilogram of bread, you still had another half left for *Trybuna Ludu*[19] which contained everything else one could need (*Trybuna Ludu* was the communist party newspaper).[20] At the base, one could exchange some of the "vouchers" for cooked

---

[19] Tr: Trybuna Ludu (Polish): People's Tribune.
[20] Au: A title stolen from Mickiewicz, who, in 1848, during the Spring of Nations, had published a paper called "Peoples Tribune" in Paris. It was financed by one of the Branickis, called the Red Count among the immigrants.

meals from the officers' mess; that's what we did from time to time because it was convenient, although dinners from the officers' mess in general were much less tasty than home cooked.

At one point, the leadership had determined that all the officers should educate themselves in the tenets of Marxism-Leninism. A committee made of political officers was formed. They talked with each of us and thus determined the level at which we would start our "education." There were three levels: two here in Rembertów for regiments and for divisions, and a third, highest, the "university" of Marxism-Leninism, in Warsaw. Although I qualified for the highest level, I was sent, before the start of classes, to the Central Political Council for an additional evaluation. After a short conversation, my examiner concluded that I didn't need the "university"; I blessed him silently. There would be no waste of time. My pre-war Marxism, without Leninism, learned in the Bund youth organization, proved useful. And by the way: all that institutionalization and stress stole any rationale for an otherwise noble initiative of self-education.

One day, during the winter, Karusia was playing with other children in the snow in front of our house, while we were watching her through the window. You were around five. The camp was a very safe place, the guards stood by the gate 24 hours a day. I realized then that an officer was leaning over you. Nothing odd; you were a beautiful child. A moment later we both realized that it was Comrade Zweig, the head of the Information Section, drawn not by the little girl's loveliness but by her red nylon snowsuit, undoubtedly foreign since you couldn't get those in Poland. And any contact with other countries, particularly receiving anything from there was not acceptable. We were all afraid of Zweig. Such was the atmosphere on the base. We didn't have to wait long for what happened next. Felusia was summoned for a "conversation." I suppose they sent for her, rather than for me, because the letters and parcels from the Uncles who settled in Canada were generally addressed to her. Zweig asked her with whom we were maintaining relationships abroad, and Felusia told him about her family left alive after the Holocaust. She offered to let him read their letters to see that they didn't contain any "spying." He declined, probably because he read them before we did. The Strawczyńskis had very distinct handwriting. He left us alone.

In the early 1950s, newspapers endlessly covered trials of so-called traitors and spies: pre-war generals and high-ranking officers. On the base no one talked about this out loud. Morover, those purged from the military were not generals but ordinary officers, many of them our friends, for whom military service was both a calling and their only profession. The theory of "potential enemies" was a manifestation of advanced class consciousness, only the "weaklings" among the intelligentsia were uncertain. The decision to get rid of pre-war officers certainly had been made somewhere high up, perhaps even in Moscow. This decision had a very Jewish face in Rembertów; I already mentioned Zweig and comrade colonel Knoll, School of Infantry deputy commander for political matters. I hardly knew the former and talked only a couple of times with the latter, a dull dimwit. Both were considered the most important people on the base. The dismissal also affected our neighbors and friends the Zielińskis, an exceptionally warm couple with three children, all girls, a bit older than Karusia. It went without saying that when Felusia left for the hospital to give birth to Dzidzia, Karusia stayed with them; in those days a post-natal hospital stay lasted about a week.

Nothing could be done about certain things, as I discovered in the case of other "potential enemies." Soon after the war, the Bolsheviks unleashed a propaganda campaign against "cosmopolitans." This seemingly innocent and even positive term was allegedly hiding a terrible meaning: cosmopolitans were people devoid of any patriotic feelings, had no idea about the meaning of fatherland, and, above all, were unable to love the Soviet fatherland: in brief, enemies of the people. And who was it hiding under that epithet? Yes, of course, who else but we, Jews? The person who excelled in this shameful nonsense was Zhdanov,[21] a close associate of Stalin. There was no doubt as to who was pulling the strings. This was no joke. Members of the Moscow Anti-Fascist Committee were murdered first. A bit later it was reported that Solomon Mikhoels, the famous director and manager of the Yiddish theater, mysteriously died in a car crash when in fact he was killed in an ambush. Finally, in the summer of 1952, a court-ordered mass murder of the most prominent representatives of Jewish literature in Russia was committed: more than a dozen poets and writers were shot in one day. At the end of his life Stalin "uncovered," just in time, a physicians' plot: they were apparently planning to murder him and other "great" Bolsheviks. All the names published in the newspaper (there were more than a dozen of them) sounded Jewish; get it? He "uncovered" but didn't kill them, because the poor thing died (March 1953). Khrushchev[22] freed them after his death with the exception of one or two who hadn't withstood the torture and died. No big thing, just a couple of old Jews. And how was it with us, at the Chemical Equipment Corps?

---

[21] Tr: Andrei Alexandrovich Zhdanov (1896–1971): Soviet politician, one of major architects of the Great Terror, personally responsible for hundreds of executions.

[22] Tr: Nikita Sergeyevich Khrushchev (1894–1971): leader of Soviet Union during the Cold War, First Secretary of the Russian communist party from 1953 to 1964, and prime minister, 1958–1964.

The rule was that every person of importance was creatively expanding Marxism-Leninism in his realm by observing what those above and more important than he were doing and replicating it, that is, by sacking the appropriate people. . . . This is how Captain Gabriel Tencer was selected for discharge. No longer young, he had studied chemistry before the war and had become a very good specialist. He worked for Szymański in Warsaw, not in my Institute, but I knew him well, since we often collaborated. I asked Szymański why he was discharging Tencer. One couldn't fault him for anything, so was it, perhaps, his ugly origin? This very even-tempered man got indignant or perhaps was just pretending, and gave me the following lesson in ideology: as long as the war had been going on, German fascism was the main enemy. For obvious reasons, Jews were on "our" side and thus were not subject to class criteria. Now, with American imperialism being the main enemy, the party has decided to apply the same criteria to Jews as to everyone else, and Tencer was born in a bourgeois family. Simple? Everything had to have theoretical foundations. True, the Tencers were rather wealthy before the war, so what? Potential enemies, collective responsibility; I had no doubt that what I had heard constituted the doctrine's official interpretation (Lenin had said that . . .), since Szymański was a member of POP, the meeting place of the soviet generals' elite that was in control of the military. At the same time, he was the same man whom I had easily convinced that a unit like mine, where almost all the officers were university graduates, didn't need a political officer; in general they were not very sophisticated. Isn't this odd? Thanks to Szymański, that position had been cancelled and I got rid of my deputy for political matters; I wouldn't have been able to do it myself (after leaving the military I learned from one of my colleagues that, after a while, the "political" position was reinstated: what goes around, comes around).

There wasn't a hospital at the base, so for Dzidzia's delivery we drove Felusia to Warsaw, to the military hospital on Koszykowa Street. It so happened that Felusia made the decision to go to the hospital somewhat late and the delivery almost happened in the car. We, and especially the officer who drove, were besides ourselves; he drove the vehicle as if competing in a car race. We got there on time; later, in the course of her life, Dzidzia would also do everything on time. As a child Dzidzia was often sick, but not Karusia. Adventures were had with both, because both of you preferred your ways from an early age. In the summer of 1951, when Felusia was pregnant with Dzidzia, we spent our summer vacation in Międzyzdroje at the Baltic seaside—the military had vacation houses in beautiful locations on the coast and in the mountains.

Figure 15 Elimination round prior to team 1952 county of Warsaw tournaments. I won and our team won the regionals.

We were sitting together on the beach, Felusia was tanning, the baby, in a straw hat with a huge brim, was playing in the sand, and I was playing bridge. Suddenly loud shouting erupted: the child was gone, and the hat was floating in the sea! My bridge partners and I jumped up like a shot and we got her out of the water. She didn't even cry, but I got yelled at by your mom. One summer day, Dzidzia, not yet three, who was playing with other children on the lawn, in front of our house at the base, suddenly disappeared. This was serious because it lasted for some time, and the two of us almost lost our minds. There was a big commotion; virtually the entire base was looking for Dzidzia. Finally, our good acquaintance Captain Czarnecki brought her back, asleep in his arms. The little girl went to see the world and travelled as far as the officers' mess, a good half a kilometer if not more away from home; the poor thing got tired, crept under a table, and went to sleep. That's where Czarnecki found her. His wife worked as the head of camp's pre-school; both were extremely nice, warm people.

The Rembertów base had its advantages, especially for the children. Here they felt as though they were on vacation, but in fact, it was a small town full of gossip, where everyone knew everything about everybody or at least they believed they knew. We longed for the anonymity of large city dwellers, where nobody would poke his nose into our affairs. Felusia, especially, felt this; I appreciated not having to commute to work. Getting here from Warsaw wasn't easy and took a lot of time: streetcar to the railroad station, electric train to Rembertów and about three kilometers *per pedes* from the station to the Institute, all together much more than an hour one way. Friends who were visiting us at the base had to register at the gate and get passes; this wasn't very pleasant. And our Sunday visits to friends in Warsaw were, albeit infrequent, complicated expeditions. Dzidzia was too little to march to the station and had to be carried almost the entire way. In early 1956, Chemical Equipment Corps received a few, not many, apartments in Warsaw. They were, of course, at the boss's disposal. But Felusia was able to sway Szymański; perhaps he had a class-unrelated fondness for her, I don't know. She also persuaded me to move, although I had my objections: commuting. Szymański sent his right-hand man to deal with her and not with me. There was talk that he was the "eminence grise"[23] of the secret service ("officer for special matters"); he took your mom around Warsaw and showed her all the options. That's when your mom chose the apartment where we stayed for nearly twelve years, until emigration. If I remember correctly I was allowed to approve Mom's choice. We didn't realize how important this move would be because we didn't suspect that I would soon leave the military. Had we stayed in our base apartment, there's no way I would have gotten such a nice apartment in Warsaw after my demobilization. Sheer luck. Mom was our relocation's *spiritus movens*.[24]

It was end of September 1955. The four of us were sitting at home in Rembertów eating dinner when the mailman rang the door bell—it wasn't his usual time—and brought me a summons to report the next day at seven PM at the Central Post Office in Warsaw on Nowogrodzka Street for a phone conversation with someone from Krasnoyarski Kray in Siberia. The name of whoever summoned me wasn't indicated. This could have only been my dad; we had no one in Krasnoyarski Kray. In those times making international calls from a private apartment was impossible; you had to do it at a post office. We were both shaken; first news after nearly ten years. I kept writing to the sovereigns of the Soviet world because not writing was not an option; my writing had become a sort of ritual. I wasn't very hopeful, although I knew that several people connected with his case had come back, and Dad was the oldest among them. The next day I talked to him from the post office cabin. I learned that for many years he hadn't been in prison but in exile. NKVD had removed the ban of communicating with the world just now because, in accordance with Supreme Soviet's

---

[23] Tr: Eminence grise (French): a person who wields power and influence unofficially or behind the scenes.
[24] Tr: Spiritus movens (Latin): driving force.

decree, he had been released from exile and so he went to a post office and arranged a call to me. We exchanged addresses; I understood that Dad couldn't come to Poland from that place. He didn't have his Polish citizenship that had been taken away—who in the middle of Siberia would waste their time taking care of such silly things as a citizenship—man, you got freed from exile, be happy and leave us alone. After all, it's been known since the times of the tsars that:

Kuritza nye ptitza
Polsha nye zagranitza

A chicken is not a bird
Poland is not a foreign country

At that time, three years after Stalin's death, political prisoners were being freed in droves. I decided to go to see Dad and right away began preparations for the trip. Szymański was very concerned by my news and proved immensely helpful. Thanks to him I quickly received the Russian visa, and not only the visa. For a small amount of Polish money I got quite a few rubles, some coupons for a good hotel—food included—and train tickets. It was all a fake exchange, the zloty/ruble relation had been fixed from above since free markets didn't exist, and I got the same benefits as soviet militaries serving in the Polish army, people like him, when they were going on vacation to Russia. This time it was I who was privileged. He also gave me a very valuable piece of advice: he said, wear your military uniform with all the ribbons showing prominently under a warm jacket without any military insignia; when you need to, open it, and instantly you are lieutenant colonel, a war hero, wounded in a battle as indicated by the ribbons, and this can be useful. He hit the jackpot.

To get to Moscow I took the Soviet Berlin-Moscow train, quite comfortable. The passengers were solely occupation forces officers from East Germany. Starting in the early morning, they would drink beer and eat hot sausages and in the evening they drank vodka. In Moscow I stayed at the Hotel National in the city center, and from the start I began to arrange to take Dad with me back to Warsaw. It all ended in total failure. Office workers were polite, but there were hundreds of requirements to be taken care of and I left each office more and more bitter and anxious. We still have my letter from Moscow to Felusia where I wrote about these things. It was January 1956; Dad didn't return to Poland for another nine months, not until September. Several days later I took the Trans-Siberian Express, so much more comfortable than the cattle car in which we had been taken to Siberia in 1940. Plane travel wasn't used much yet. I sent Dad a telegram because he wanted to meet me at the Kansk station, a railway stop located at the trans-Siberian thoroughfare about 200 kilometers east from Krasnoyarsk, a major city, the capital of central Siberia. From Kansk we were supposed to travel together north to his village. The train arrived at Kansk in the middle of the night. It was very cold. There were only a few people on the platform. I recognized Dad's silhouette. We looked at each other, we hugged, we couldn't speak, and before long the chill forced us inside to the buffet. It was warm, light, and noisy. Lots of people: they were eating, drinking, and talking loudly. A military patrol was going around: an officer, possibly a lieutenant, and two privates. We sat down, ordered our food, drank vodka, and talked; we had so much to tell. We hadn't seen each other for almost ten years. He didn't know much about the Holocaust. I told him about Mom, about Grandma and our family, about Felusia and the children, about everything. Afterward he talked. He survived prison thanks to his transfer, after two years, to office work. He felt that hard labor in the forest, without enough food and in temperatures reaching -30 or -40 degrees Celsius would finish him off. There were no other companions from their common court case with him. Our old Kurenyevo was, as he put it, a nice guesthouse compared with prison, or rather with the labor camp. He felt more at ease once in exile in a small kulak village—we knew those from our first deportation to Siberia. After prison, this was freedom. But why hadn't he tried to get in touch with me, when he was exiled? He had been afraid to risk it since for such an attempt people were sent back to prison. And he didn't have my address, so what was he supposed to do? I asked him about the investigation that took such a long time. He talked about it reluctantly. In principle, "they" had planned everything ahead of time and all they wanted was for the prisoner to sign every page of his statement that contained incredible nonsense. What sabotage assignments were you getting from Erlich and from Alter? The very same NKVD had murdered Erlich and Alter in December 1941 (see page 176, footnote 29). Dad and others were supposed to be getting those "assignments" several years later. I asked him about torture. In his village, they occasionally showed war movies depicting Gestapo tortures and he said that he didn't have systematic beatings, but it had been easy to get hit from time to time. It was enough to be sitting for hours on end in a windowless room, on a high stool with legs dangling in the air, with a strong lamp shining in your face and the interrogating officers taking turns; finally, you signed everything that was in the statement. The worst, he said, were confrontations with other accused from the same case; he didn't want to talk about it. Given what he had lived through, he looked exceptionally well. He still had his thick, black mane of hair with just a bit of gray, a healthy complexion, keen eye, and energetic gestures. Dad was then 55 or 56. Only his teeth were in bad shape. We did something about it after his return to Warsaw.

A long trip awaited us the next day. We had to travel 80 kilometers north, to a large village called Aban, an administrative center. A sled from his kolkhoz, the village Krutovka, was supposed to wait for us there. To Aban we would get by truck because, despite the existence of some sort of a road, there was no public transportation. This world's movers and shakers traveled by car, an official car, since there weren't any private ones, and little people—by truck, hitchhiking. Drivers gave rides for a small fee. Because of snow and ice driving was tough; one had to put chains on tires.

There was a lot of traffic, because the road connected the railroad station with the basin of the Angara, a powerful Siberian river, and that basin (Angara flows into the Yenisei) was, at that time, one of the biggest islands of the Gulag Archipelago; it was known for gold and iron ore mines. Dad had been jailed nearby, his camp dealt with cutting trees, like in Kurenyevo. This was seemingly better that slavery in the mines. After his release from camp in late 1949, just when I finished my chemistry studies, Krutovka was assigned as his place of exile. I suggested a few hours of sleep in a hotel before the trip. Dad sniffed at it, he was afraid to walk to the hotel at night. He said that together with political prisoners, regular criminals were freed as well—a result of disorder or perhaps of bribery: "there are loads of those here and they could rob us or murder us." He added that, in his opinion, people here at the station had nosed out that I was a foreigner and might have money. And Russian bandits were ruthless: to kill a man was as easy as to drink a glass of water. Dad had seen them in prison and was careful. But Dad also told me many times that, on the other hand, he had seldom enjoyed such great company as he had in prison: lots of interesting, intelligent men, many of them with higher education; such were Soviet prisons in those times. The lieutenant with his squad was constantly leaving and coming back to the warm station buffet, and I decided to ask him to accompany us to the hotel. I told him who I was, showed him my ID, opened the jacket, and after carefully checking my documents, he saluted smartly and announced that he was at the disposal of the allied army officer. Szymański knew his Russia. On the way to the hotel we passed an enormous prison. High walls with barbed wire on top, guard towers with sentries, a well lit, empty strip of land outside the wall, and powerful moveable spotlights—all that created a terrifying and grim impression, especially at night, a symbol of Soviet power. Your Marshal

Rokossovsky had been jailed here in Kansk—said our ally, the lieutenant. The hotel turned out to be a guesthouse, and I was familiar with those. There were twenty to thirty beds in our room, only a few of them taken. It was cold. The toilet was outside, in the iciness; sheer luxury. We got comfortable on two side-by-side beds and . . . "the bomb exploded": "Włodek, I have to tell you something. I have a son a month younger than your younger daughter." I was speechless. I expected anything but that. And then he began to talk. We didn't sleep at all that night. He had been placed in a small kolkhoz among so called kulaks and their descendants, exiled to central Russia at the end of the 1920s. Here he was told by the NKVD—you will end your life and don't expect anything different. He was the sole deportee in the village. When he said that he was a Jew, the locals laughed and didn't believe him: all Jews have two horns on their foreheads! He became an accountant at the kolkhoz. It was a very important job; he performed it perfectly and was greatly respected; he felt revitalized. He was assigned an apartment room at the house of a widow whose husband had died in the war. Maximovna, as she was generally called (it wasn't her name but her father's, a so-called patronymic, an expression of both respect and age) was a grandmother with several married daughters living in Krutovka. They didn't expect that she could get pregnant, but when she did, there was no way out. Anyway, Dad said, he wanted that child. "I didn't believe I would ever get out of here. It was different in Kurenyevo, the war still raged, we were many, all from Poland, and we had no doubt this was a temporary situation, that we would go back home after the war. Here there was no hope." And here I was, listening and thinking that nothing good could come of this.

The following day we bought some gifts so as not to arrive at Maximovna and Vasya's[25] empty-handed. Vasily, that was my little half-brother's name. A gift from a guest, especially from a foreign visitor, was important in Russia and in particular in Russian villages. Kansk was the only place where one could buy something; there was nothing further north. Unfortunately, this "something" was nothing in particular. We then walked along the road until a truck stopped beside us. The three of us shook terribly in the cab. Around us: the forest or snowy desert. After several hours of travel, we passed only a few settlements. We got out in Aban; here the kolkhoz sled was waiting. It was snowing and getting dark; days are short in Siberia in January. So Dad decided to spend the night in Aban. He knew this place well. The NKVD office, where he had to report during all the years of his exile, every ten days at first, later less often, was located

---

[25] Tr: Vasya: diminutive of Vasily.

here. A few weeks earlier, during one of his visits, he had been read a ruling of his discharge from exile in this office and had been given my requests addressed to Stalin and to others. His kolkhoz had a rented room in Aban where people on kolkhoz business from Krutovka could stay. There was an agency for agricultural and tractor-related matters in Aban, as well as other offices, a post office, a high school, a movie theater, a club: in short, high life, and also a small factory, of furniture I believe. There was no electricity in Krutovka, but here—yes. The rented room was in a cabin belonging to a widow, whose husband had died in the war. Russia continued to be a tragic country of war widows; there were millions of them. Two young women also lived in that cabin; they were renting a bed—that's right, a bed, not a room—separated from the main cabin by a curtain. They worked different shifts at the furniture factory so one bed was enough, although sometimes they slept in it together. I observed them: young and pretty, to say they were thin would be understatement, they were emaciated and their pale, almost translucent complexion couldn't be missed; surely they didn't have enough to eat. They came from nearby villages and would have had more food in their kolkhozes, but preferred to live in Aban, in the big world. Dad told me that the owner was an NKVD informer, but since everybody knew, it wasn't a problem. I realized later that this was NKVD country—the Gulag Archipelago—and everyone there was in one way or another working for NKVD: if "they" asked about something or, rather, about someone, you couldn't refuse to answer. It wasn't so bad in big cities. In the morning we went to Krutovka. It took an hour, perhaps a bit longer, by sled. Dad had crisscrossed this route many times, first on foot and later, after gaining his position at the kolkhoz, by horse cart, by sled in the winter, and sometimes, on horseback.

Vasya was a smiling, four-year old happy boy, the spitting image of your grandfather Misha, but with a rounder face. His mother was slim, likely very pretty once, with a typically Slavic but by now much ravaged face. Dad was older, but looked younger than she did. She had an engaging smile, gray eyes, and a piercing look; I liked her. The entire village came through the living quarters that first evening—such a sensation, Misha's son had arrived! I stayed about a week in the village. My notes from that visit have weathered through; I wrote my thoughts down in a Moscow hotel on the way back to Warsaw. The village, just like Kurenyevo, was situated at the edge of the taiga. Dad warned me not to venture too far into the forest. The village consisted of about forty houses, half as many as in Kurenyevo. There was a tiny shop open a few hours a day. It only offered vodka, which nobody would buy since it was too expensive, and anyway all of them made moonshine, some canned fish, a sort of shrimp, good but inaccessible because of the price; hard candy for children, shoelaces, shoe polish, and other trifles. The most important article was salt.[26] From time to time, most essential merchandise was delivered to the store. Each family had its own cow, pigs, fowl, and an allotment near the house where they grew all that was possible to grow in the Siberian climate. The forest gave them mushrooms, berries, and wood for heating. After a yearly tally, the kolkhoz gave them a bit of money and grain. This yearly calculation was a great event whose hero, a very positive one, was my dad. It had to be approved by a higher office in Aban. They also baked their own bread; a self-sufficient economy in the middle of the twentieth century. The kolkhoz was very small and poor, but on paper, as Dad would say, all looked perfect; just like in "*Trybuna Ludu*." In the village everybody was either a relation or a close friend and people, especially, it seems, women, shared their work and their worldly possessions. During my stay, for example, Maximovna made bread. She made so much that relatives and acquaintances came to her for fresh, remarkably tasty bread. Families shared moonshine, meat, and sausages after someone killed their pig. In Kurenyevo all the houses were identical but here, just like in a normal village, there was no cookie-cutter method. Almost every dwelling had its "banya," or bath. Once a week they would heat up its stove, and carry the water back and forth or one could splash cold water on the hot stove and create a steam bath, or a sauna. The bath was first used by the women, then by the men. A couple of days before my arrival, a little lamb was born at Maximovna's. It was too cold to leave it with its mother in the barn, so the lamb was placed in the house's vestibule. During my stay the temperature plunged, the vestibule got too cold, and the lamb was moved to the room where everybody slept; no harm could come to it. From the day of my arrival, every evening we were invited to visit various families. Menus were the same everywhere: moonshine and kvass[27] to drink, and food: salted mushrooms, sauerkraut and pickles, bread, soup with chunks of meat, pelmeni, that is, fabulous little meat ravioli, sometimes even cold cuts. Everything homemade, nothing bought with money: genuine communism. Marx called it primordial; it was followed by slavery, feudalism, etc. The dishes reminded me a bit of Baranovka in 1941, but then it had been war time and we had much less food. I couldn't drink the

---

[26] Au: Some historians insist that the high price of salt was the main reason for the eighteenth-century French Revolution. The king, who had monopoly over salt sales, imposed enormous taxes and this income provided a basis for the country's budget. People, especially the poor, were furious. Bolsheviks averted this mistake: salt has always been cheap in Russia!

[27] Tr: Kvass: a fermented beverage made from black or rye bread.

moonshine, wasn't able to swallow it. The hosts noticed it and a store-bought "kazyonka," regular vodka, appeared on the table, just for me. (The old Russian word *kazna* signifies treasury, and in Russia the country's treasury has had sole control over vodka's sales from time immemorial. *Kazyonka*, a diminutive of kazna and a word of feminine gender, has an affectionate sound to a person who knows Russian.) Every meal was like a ceremonial ritual. They ate slowly, with poise and solemnity, clearing their throats. Soup, usually the main dish, stood on the table in one big bowl, from which everyone ate with their own spoons. Men kept their spoons in the top parts of their shoes or felt boots, women somewhere in their skirts. No one tried to pick pieces of meat from the soup. For breakfast we ate scrambled eggs from a communal bowl; there was also bread, milk, and the fabulous Russian "kisloye moloko"—neither yogurt nor buttermilk but a very special dish that has to be prepared slowly, not inside but on top of a peasant stove; I remembered it from Baranovka. During those visits I realized that Dad was very popular and well liked. Despite that, he wasn't one of them. He could harness a horse to a sled, but couldn't kill and butcher a pig, so how could he have been one of them? Rather, he was sort of a prince consort. Vasya, adored by his older stepsisters, was the apple of the entire village's eye, and Maximovna enjoyed particular respect. She seemed smart and reserved. Hers was the village's "first family." Saturday, there was a "vyecherinka"[28] at the kolkhoz club, in a large room in a one-floor building, where the office of the kolkhoz's head and Dad's office were both located. From time to time they showed movies here: the gear was brought by the technician who showed the film. This time, the entire village turned out to see the visitor from another planet. Young people danced to accordion music, the older ones sat on chairs lining the walls. The accordion is an authentic Russian folk instrument. Even in the most God-forsaken village there is always someone who knows how and likes to play the accordion. And I like Russian folk music and songs. I'm embarrassed to say, I like them more than all those American screamers.

My visit was coming to its end, it was time to go back home; I had never before left Felusia with the children for such a long time. Dad told me that he wanted to accompany me to Krasnoyarsk. Maximovna looked at me and said that if Misha leaves, he will never come back to Krutovka. This time he came back. She was smart, but not aware that Poland was not Russia, that one had to have proper papers to travel, etc. What can I say?—most probably Maximovna, just like the majority of older people in Krutovka, was in principle a case of

---

[28] Tr: Vyecherinka (Russian): an evening of amusement.

secondary illiteracy. After his release from exile, Dad had the status of a kolkhoz member and hence didn't own a document allowing him to travel throughout Russia and to change his place of residency without a special permit. At that time, people from the kolkhozes, unlike city dwellers, didn't have such a domestic passport and were not so differerent from the serfs, liberated from serfdom by Tsar Alexander's II decree of 1861.

The road to Krasnoyarsk through Aban and Kansk—by three vehicles: sled, truck, and train, took an entire day. In Krasnoyarsk, Dad realized that for the first time since 1939 he was visiting a major city. We went to a large grocery store for supplies. So well stocked, it was like night and day compared with Krutovka's little shop. Dad couldn't stop staring. There were several separate sections: sugar and confectionery, fresh and canned meats, breads, etc., and a salesman in each of them. One had to stand in one queue to see the salesman, order the goods from him, take a receipt, line up in another queue for the cash register, pay, and then go back to the original section with a stamped receipt to get the goods, and there stand in yet another queue. And it was so in each section— that's business the socialist way. I suggested that we buy first what we wanted by going from one section to the next, take all our receipts and pay them all at once at the register, and then go and pick up the wares. At first Dad agreed, it made sense, but then he couldn't keep his eyes off the confectionary department and said that, if we take the time to shop in other sections, they may run out of sugar. I learned then that sugar was "delivered" to Krutovka only twice a year: on May 1 and on November 7, the anniversary of the revolution. I felt my eyes tearing up. They destroyed my dad's life. We went to get the sugar. That's how things were ten years after the victorious war. The vanquished Germany had already implemented the Marshall plan and the world was admiring Adenauer's and Erhard's[29] economic miracles.

Before we said goodbye I gave Dad all I had: underwear, clothes. I went back literally with one shirt and one pair of pants, whatever I happened to be wearing. Leaving Poland, I knew that the situation in Siberia would be bad, but I was not able to imagine how bad it would be in reality. We discussed in detail what had to be done in various departments, both Polish and Soviet, so he could come to Poland as soon as possible. Dad went east to Kansk, and I west to Moscow. As luck would have it, West Germany's chancellor, Konrad Adenauer, "der Alte," the old man, as he was called in Germany, was then in Moscow for an

---

[29] Tr: Ludwig Erhard (1897–1977): German politician, Chancellor of West Germany 1963–1966, author of reforms that led to the economic recovery of post-war Germany.

official visit. The main goal of the Moscow talks was the return to Germany of thousands of war prisoners left in Russia, who were still cutting trees in Siberia or were working in the mines, and "der Alte" achieved it (your dad wouldn't have minded if he had failed). There was never any mention of how much and in what way he paid for it, but he was an exceedingly crafty man. Once, to ingratiate himself to Khrushchev, he maintained that his ancestors had been related to Frederick Engels; what could be better than that? Newspapers widely publicized this kinship. It made me furious: they were letting fascist murderers go but were keeping my dad who wouldn't hurt a fly? Where in this world is yosher?[30] I had an outburst in the prosecutor's office, where I had been trying to take care of some bits but it accomplished nothing. It was late January 1956 now, and one could sense in Moscow that changes were coming. In both railroad and subway stations, and in other public places, there were many people whose clothes and behavior made them different from "solid" masses. Some would lie down on the station floor, one heard well known prison songs, and the police didn't react. These were recently released political prisoners still wearing their prison rags, probably on their way home: the result of Khrushchev's policy. Or perhaps they were stopping in Moscow to present the "tsar" with their complaints and grievances? This was an eternal Russian custom, because the tsar in Moscow was good and only the regional petty chieftains were governing poorly and tormenting us, the simple folk. The fact that the police weren't reacting, that they weren't chasing them out of the stations or locking them in jail, was unprecedented. Moscow should have been squeaky clean and neat, because homeless tramps dressed in rags and beggars didn't exist in "socialism"; as long as the leader of nations was alive, such was the way. A month later, in February, Khrushchev gave his famous speech condemning Stalin's crimes at the twentieth congress of the Soviet communist party. Ilya Ehrenburg[31] had just published his book *The Thaw*. Its title was significant, because it defined a period of great hopes after Stalin's death. Indeed, the mass terror had lessened, but hope for lasting and significant changes did not materialize. They couldn't have: it's clear now, but wasn't then.

From my letters to Felusia—I believe we kept them all—it seems that I was gone for about three weeks. As it happens, this was an exceptionally bad period for both Karusia and Dzidzia. Felusia was working and taking care of two children would have been too difficult. Karusia went to school, so we figured that

---

[30] Au: Justice (Yiddish, Hebrew).
[31] Tr: Ilya Ehrenburg (1981–1967): Russian writer, journalist, and translator.

to make Felusia's situation easier during the time of my absence, Dzidzia would stay in a sanatorium in the nearby Otwock. We made sure that the children received excellent care and food and we believed that she would be happy there. But our four-year-old child was convinced that she would remain there forever. We didn't understand her, and she was unable to explain it to us. When saying goodbye, the poor thing kept repeating that she "will be good"; she held on to us and it was hard to tear her away. A similar scene occurred when Felusia came to visit her during my absence. Our little girl was so miserable in Otwock that she wept the entire time. This was one of your life's first events that you remember well. It took many years before it got clarified. I recall it from time to time with Felusia, and we cannot forgive ourselves for hurting our child. Karusia, too, had experienced an unpleasant incident that could have ended badly. One evening when Felusia went to see the neighbors, the electric wires began to smolder. A neighbor passing by smelled the stench and started shouting. Felusia ran back immediately, grabbed the child, and fled the apartment. The fire didn't get beyond the kitchen alcove and the neighbors extinguished it quickly. There was more commotion than fire, but the situation had been dangerous. The family myth proclaims that the seven year old Karusia hid in the safest place possible: under her bed. When I returned, the kitchen was newly painted and squeaky clean; only the smell of something burning hung in the air for some time.

The year that began with Khrushchev's speech was important for the entire "communist bloc." The changes that had taken place in Russia spread to other countries and influenced our family's fate. Things loosened up and, when they did, the idea that had never totally left me, that military service was not my true calling, came back. The decision to leave the army was essential and, in contrast to everything thus far in my life, it was my own; "they" didn't make it for me. Felusia supported me bravely, although she was aware that our life, at least initially, would be more difficult than it had been until now. I will try to summarize the events that occurred in Poland that made my discharge possible.

In February 1956, still during the twentieth party congress, Bolesław Bierut,[32] the Little Polish Stalin, died in Moscow. Not much was known about him except that he was "primus inter pares"[33] among Poland's owners. His successors didn't seem to be as rigid as he was. In June of that year, workers at Cegielski, a large railroad car factory in Poznań, went on strike. This was

---

[32] Tr: Bolesław Bierut (born Bolesław Biernacki, 1892–1956): Polish communist leader, hard-line Stalinist, President of Poland from 1945 to his death.
[33] Tr: Primus inter pares (Latin): first among equals.

the first harbinger: a spontaneous outburst against poverty-level wages, against callous dictatorship, and despicable deceit. The strike was quashed more ruthlessly than during the worst tsars' reigns. The "socialist" government ordered the police to shoot the workers. Its prime minister Józef Cyrankiewicz, a former PPS member, said that "they" wouldn't hesitate, that they would "chop off the hands of enemies of socialism." I hated that traitor more than the authentic communists (he was a careerist, but, to be truthful, he had been a prisoner in Auschwitz and, according to witnesses, his behavior there had been irreproachable). The turmoil spread through Poland and to the other bloc countries. In September, a government that refused to obey Russia was elected in Hungary. That government, composed mainly of revisionists, that is, former communists, was disenchanted with Stalinism. The Russian army suppressed the Hungarian resistance ruthlessly and cruelly. But this wasn't the first time in Russian history. A century earlier, in 1848, Nicolas I, the policeman of Europe and the same one who crushed the November Uprising, dispatched his soldiers to deal with the Hungarian Spring of Nations in the same cruel manner. Bolsheviks continued the tsars' imperial policies. There was no uprising in Poland thanks to Gomułka, who re-assumed power after several years in Stalin's prison and was trusted by the people; this was the Polish October with a capital "O." One had to admit that there were many changes. The new chief took power away from the worst Stalinists; among them many Jews. The persistent pressure on farmers to form collectives that would surely make them happy, stopped. The shameful and disgusting anti-church policy changed. Gomułka even knew how to oppose Russia (or perhaps he was only pretending—both he and they—that he was able to do it, in order to bamboozle Poles?) Was it a sovereign Poland? "Le Monde's" correspondent in Poland asserted that if free elections had been held in 1956, Gomułka would have won them. It's possible, although there were many doubters from the very start. Students habitually attached pieces of paper with notices such as: "I will exchange the textbook for Grotowski's physics course for Filipowicz's biochemistry book" etc. on the left side of the Warsaw University's gate on Krakowskie Przedmieście (I saw, recently, in the same spot, elegant glass cases with various ads). Soon after October, while going to the university, I noticed a bigger than usual crowd in front of the notices. Someone had written, on a large piece of paper in huge letters: "I will exchange the newly regained Independence for a better geographical location!" Well said, no need for more or for less. And one more joke that, in its own way, helps to bring back the atmosphere of those times. How did the various nations behave after October? Hungarians behaved like the Poles (because they rebelled); Poles—like the Czechs (changes happened but peacefully, without an uprising); Czechs—like pigs (nothing happened there); and the Jews? Well, the Jews behaved like the Cossacks! Why? Because they jumped the most. It meant that, among the party's reformers, who were to a great extent the engine behind the October changes, were many Jews, many eloquent Jews: journalists, writers. So, we were, as always, on both sides of the barricade: among the party's "tough guys" and among the "Cossacks." Unfortunately, it was the Stalinists rather than the Cossacks who were kept in peoples' memory; too bad. No doubt, before the war there were people, Poles and Jews, drawn to communism by their feelings about human misery and injustice; I knew such people. They possessed a sort of intransigence; perhaps this was a particular aspect of their minds that led them to a deep belief or, even more, a certainty that "they" and only "they" held the recipe for human happiness. This produced a feeling of superiority, for example in relation to social democrats, and led to fanaticism. I believe that herein lies the seed of later crimes committed after they gained power. Because such a recipe doesn't exist; it's a fantasy. How could people not devoid of critical intelligence remain communists after the Moscow trials of the 1930s? I will never understand. Perhaps it's a "mind set."

After October, significant changes were introduced in the military. Soviet officers, mostly generals, including Rokossovsky, were sent back to Russia. The army's reorganization and reduction was ordered; until October the military had been too swollen for the needs of a medium-size nation that, in any case, was under the Soviet nuclear umbrella (just as it is now, along with the rest of Europe, under the American one). Szymański was bitter. "Here, I'm a Russian," he told me, "and there, I will be a Pole." He wasn't wrong; neither he nor other "pops" were welcomed warmly by the grateful motherland. On the contrary, the Red Army's leadership didn't trust them. Poland, even a "socialist" Poland, was much closer to the corrupt West than communism's homeland; they could have been "spoilt." Most of them chose civilian life and early retirement; others received low-ranking positions in far-away garrisons. Before his departure to Russia, I told Szymański about my intention to leave the military. He emphatically disagreed with it and assured me that I had a big army career ahead of me (in fact, two of my successors did advance greatly later on and achieved the rank of general). It's hard to say what kind of career it would have been—because it didn't happen—but it's not difficult to guess that ten years later, after the Israeli Six-Day War of 1967, they would have kicked me out without mercy, just as they kicked out all the Jews, no exceptions, accompanied by revolting anti-Semitic persecution. I would have been over 40 years old by then; too late to begin a research career in biochemistry. Even in 1956 I considered myself too old for it. And so, the story from twenty years before was repeated in the years 1967–68 in the military: then, the potential enemies and victims of collective responsibility were pre-war officers; now—it was us.

To tell the truth, it wasn't easy to leave Rembertów. I left behind a big chunk of my life. The Rembertów Institute had been my first serious job after graduation. Later on I never had an opportunity to create anything like this, *ex nihilo.* . . .[34] Felusia recalls that once in my presence she complained to Szymański that I was working too much, that everything fell on her shoulders, that there were two children at home. He answered: "you see, it's his third child, the youngest, so he needs to devote most of his time to it." The last time I came across Szymański, indirectly, happened before I left Poland. He was already retired and living in Moscow. I kept in touch with some colleagues from Rembertów and in the fall of 1967, when we knew we would be going to the US, one of them was in Moscow, where he saw Szymański and brought a message from him: he wished me and my family good luck, but if by chance we were to meet somewhere he wouldn't shake my hand! Leaving for the west was still, in his eyes, a betrayal.

My youngest child kept growing and was transformed, in the 1970s, into a research Institute (Military Institute of Chemistry and Radiometry). Many years later, already in the Third Republic, I learned that almost all of the colleagues I had hired worked in Rembertów for many decades and played an important role in the Institute's development and success. In the fall of 1994, the Institute's leadership and my colleagues from the 1950s organized a meeting with me, the first after all those years. For me it was a deep and moving experience. I was particularly gratified that all of my colleagues and coworkers from forty years ago, many retired, attended that meeting. Some years later, on the occasion of a full anniversary of the end of the Second World War, the national defense minister nominated me, by the Parliament's decree, to the rank of full colonel.

Now back to Rembertów, immediately after October 1956, before my demobilization. One day, out of the blue, a young lieutenant came to see me; I had known him by sight and was aware of his work for Zweig, in Information. He sat in my office and, a grown man, began to sob; he was so shaken. He was my guardian angel, led to me by his guilty conscience. He decided to quit Information and came to tell me his story. A son of a poor family, he had been recruited to the Information School. In Rembertów, he was "taking care" of my

---

[34] Tr: Ex nihilo (Latin): from nothing.

Figure 16 With Dad after his return from Siberia, September, 1956.

unit and especially of me, because of my counterrevolutionary Dad and relatives in Canada, and it was me he chose as his confessor. He was told that foreign intelligence showed special interest in my unit because it was scientific and important. He had, that is, he recruited, a team of informers, he told me who they were—this wasn't allowed under any circumstances. Among them were several members of the administration and of the technical crew, but none of the science staff. One episode in his story has stayed in my mind. It had been reported that I went to Praga to attend a synagogue. (There has been no synagogue in Praga since the war or now.) And this wasn't acceptable, it absolutely had to be straightened out, it could lead to inappropriate contacts and, who knows, to treason. One day I left the base for Warsaw—I had a permit to drive an official car and usually didn't need a driver—with an Information car following me. I was going with Felusia to the Różycki Market on Targowa Street in Praga, open for many generations (and still existing!), to buy some fresh vegetables, sour cream, a freshly slaughtered and plucked chicken, and other victuals. The Party had won the "battle for commerce" (that was its name then)—this battle's commander in chief was Hilary Minc (yes, yes, a Jew as well)—and such merchandise had long ago disappeared from the shelves of state-run shops. It's hard not to laugh imagining the Rembertów Information searching for a synagogue among all the stalls and vendors known for their crude language! Or perhaps they used the opportunity to buy a bit of healthy, fresh food? This would have been the smartest move. Sounds funny, but it's nauseating, isn't it? I lost sight of my guardian angel.

The initial period after my discharge was difficult. My entire life had changed. I couldn't find a job that suited me. Felusia remembers that I didn't sleep well at night. She believed in me, but apparently I like to worry, even in advance. We were already living in Warsaw and she hadn't yet started working.

Financially we were so-so, because I had received some money, a so-called end payment from the military (most of it was used to buy a piano for Karusia; Dzidzia showed no enthusiasm for piano playing). Just before October, Dad came and moved in with us. It was such great joy, the girls finally had a real grandfather, but not for long. After years of prison and Krutovka, Warsaw was an incredible jolt for him. He kept going to the Polytechnic Institute, where students were rallying almost constantly, asking for "good" socialism, and he couldn't believe his eyes. One day he came back from the Polytechnic Institute and said that it would all end badly because the Bolsheviks—he always called "them" Bolsheviks—were too close and we have got to flee them. He was afraid: they had taught him how to "love freedom." He couldn't get Maximovna and Vasya out of his head. There was no good solution. To go back there after all he had suffered? Krutovka and Warsaw were two shockingly different worlds, like night and day. He considered the possibility of bringing them to Poland and then leaving for the west. That was unrealistic. Dad had a Soviet passport and they weren't married. And was it reasonable to rip Maximovna from her community? Would she be willing to leave? In the end, the only thing he was able to do was to send alimony payments for Maximovna and the youngster. I don't know how Dad arranged that. He found some pre-war pals in Warsaw, not just from Bund but communists as well, and they helped him. It came to light then that the human resources employee who, ten years earlier, had changed my birth place from Warsaw to Kharkov when I was going to visit Dad, knew him and was aware of his being in Russia but never divulged it; what a small world. Dad told me that this man had slept in our Karmelicka Street apartment before May 1. The Blue Police usually locked up suspected members of the communist party for several days so they wouldn't brawl during the May 1 PPS and Bund marches, so they did not to sleep in their own apartments. Before the war there were internal fractions in Bund, just like in any social democracy. Dad was a leftist: he belonged to the "zweiers" (two's); the "eins" (one's) were the right and constituted the majority. From the perspective of years, the differences between "ones" and "twos" were rather subtle. Neither could stand the Zionists or the communists and the core issue was: whom one should loathe more. People from both factions were proponents of Jewish autonomy and the development of Jewish national culture in Yiddish, as well as democracy, respect for individual rights—in short, all good things. The world will be beautiful, there will be no wars, people will be happy, and life will be prosperous. Exactly like in Beethoven's Ninth Symphony, when the chorus sings Schiller's poem "Ode to Joy": "All men will be brothers"; right. I'm sitting now, writing, and I think that this old man who has adopted an easy cynical manner is totally different from that young, and possibly better one, who hasn't existed for a long time. I'm sure there are—or rather were—many who think the same.

After taking care of alimony, Dad didn't stay long in Warsaw. The Israeli consul stamped his Soviet passport with a visa and in the spring of 1957, Dad left for Israel. He spent several years there, then moved to the US and settled in New York City. In August 1962, he suffered a sudden heart attack and then a second one, nine days later, in the hospital. They weren't able to save him. Dad was sixty-one or sixty-two years old; Vasya was ten. In his last letter of July 15, a month before his death, Dad sent money to be forwarded to Krutovka (we have all his letters). I arrived in New York in January 1963. Dad had known about my PhD and that I was to begin a yearlong postdoc in the Department of Biochemistry at NYU. He was proud and happy that we would soon see each other. I placed a tombstone on his grave on the first anniversary of his death. Old Bund friends attended, there were speeches, and they sang the Bund anthem; that's all. As long as we lived in New York, Felusia and I visited his grave once a year. No one will visit it again. Dad was buried in the Jewish cemetery Beth-El in New Jersey, in the part of the cemetery belonging to the once famous workers' organization Arbeter Ring. At the Cedar Park cemetery adjacent to Beth-El, there are the graves of Bolek and Ania Ellenbogen, Hanka Fryszdorf, and other dear friends who fought in the ghetto, in the resistance, and in the Warsaw Uprising; all magnificent people. Recently I read that according to the beliefs of a certain African tribe a person dies twice: the first time when the physical death occurs, a death that is not final since his image is kept alive in the memories and minds of those who knew him. He dies the second and final time when all those who knew and remembered him are no longer living.

After October, I worked at the Antibiotics Institute. The work was interesting but not what I liked, because it had to do with technological solutions rather than with bench research. The pay was miserable and, in order to help the family's financial situation, I supplemented it by working in the evening on contracts called "work on commission"; these were simply services. At first I worked for the Institute of Experimental Biology of the Polish Academy of Sciences. After learning about my syntheses, David Shugar, then an associate professor at the Polish Academy of Sciences' Institute of Biochemistry and Biophysics, asked me to do similar work for him. The Institute didn't yet have its own quarters and individual departments were scattered throughout the city. Shugar's department was located in the building of the State Institute of Hygiene on Chocimska Street. Since my Antibiotics Institute was situated in the same building, it was a convenient arrangement and I immediately accepted the additional work on commission. Such were the humble beginnings of the crucially important period, to me, of working for Shugar. I would spend an entire day working at my regular job on the second floor, and in the afternoon I would go down to the basement, where Sugar's laboratories were located, and I would earn a bit of extra money. I stuck with the antibiotics as long as I had to, to pay the bills. On my way from the second floor to the basement I would stop—or not—for a bite at the canteen. The canteen was particularly unpleasant, so most often I didn't go there. A potato, contrary to its nature, black rather than white, sitting on a plate with a piece of fried fat rolled in breadcrumbs pretended to be the main dish. Before walking in one would frequently smell rancid grease; such were cafeterias in those days (perhaps not all: Experimental Biology had a better one). In official Orwellian-like newspeak, they were called "mass feeding facilities"; it sounds like something for cattle, not for people.

After a short while in Shugar's department, I metamorphosed from a laborer of "works on commission" to a doctoral candidate. I felt that I had found my place. At that time—the second half of the 1950s—Shugar was truly an ideal mentor. Extraordinarily talented, exceptionally hard-working, and ambitious, he was exceedingly well read in his subject. In my opinion, he was the only one in Poland who understood the research needed in the area of then a young but burgeoning science of molecular biology. It wasn't by accident that he assembled a group of loyal people. Many lasting friendships developed between us at that time. We were aware that our work was not too distant from the questions asked by the world's academic elite. This was neither commonplace nor easy in Poland. Our labs were primitive, located in a basement whose red brick walls were not covered with plaster. Compared to American equipment, ours was not worth mentioning, and we had to laboriously prepare chemical reagents, so easily accessible in the west. Basement or not, thanks to Shugar, we had what was most important: enthusiasm and a difficult to define, divine spark, that is, talent. I reflect on the years spent on Chocimska Street with deep emotion. If only I had found such a place when I was younger! Several years after my PhD, I received my habilitation.[35]

---

[35] Tr: Habilitation, which does not exist in the US, is the highest academic qualification a scholar can achieve in many countries in Europe, and is mandatory for more advanced teaching staff at universities and at numerous research institutions. Some years after obtaining a PhD, the candidate writes a professorial thesis (or habilitation thesis) based on independent scholarship and without a faculty supervisor's guidance. It is reviewed by and

Figure 17 Author squatting, surrounded by friends and colleagues from the Institute of Biochemistry and Biophysics (PAN), just before emigration to the US, fall 1967, Warsaw.

During that time, the Shugars were stricken with the worst tragedy that can happen to parents: their only child, the eighteen-year-old Basia, died of cancer; she suffered greatly before her death. They were no longer young people.

Shugar's interests in nucleic acids were wide-ranging and diversified; all of us worked on a different aspect of his research. This was possible because our young field, shortly after James Watson and Francis Crick's historic discovery of DNA structure (1953), was at the threshold of its turbulent development and hadn't been as sub-specialized as it became later on. Shugar was already known abroad and was helping his collaborators in various ways; for example, he would receive enzymes as gifts, necessary for our research but inaccessible in Poland. He would also secure year-long postdoctoral fellowship abroad for his students. The apprenticeship in his lab had a profound impact on each of our paths.

My life's next chapter was the trip to the United States, in January 1963, for a year-long fellowship in Dr. Severo Ochoa's Deparment of Biochemistry at New York University School of Medicine. I waited a year for permission to go

---

defended before an academic committee. The level of scholarship of such thesis is higher than that of a PhD dissertation.

abroad. Finally I got a passport—just me—you and your mom had to stay in Warsaw as hostages. It was simply barbaric. In every letter, Karusia counted the days until my return. Your mom managed very well without me. Many of my peers did their postdocs in foreign countries, mostly one year long, but without exception all had to leave their families behind. In "socialism" this method was widely accepted and nobody dared to request to take their families along, since this would eliminate any possibility of their leave. Such leaves, even at the expense of separation from one's family, were almost unheard of in other countries of the "democratic bloc" or in Russia. Poland, it seems, was still the best barrack in the "camp." And a trip to the west was important for many reasons. It offered experience of great magnitude in conducting research, in general, at a good scientific center in America.

And, of course, the pay was incomparable with Polish wages. After a year of (very frugal!) life, one could bring back a good car, the greatest dream and an impossible achievement in Polish circumstances. Our first car was a Peugeot 404, the only car I ever truly took excellent care of. It wasn't like that with the subsequent ones: they brought neither joy nor satisfaction. They were a simple necessity, and why rejoice about a thing so easy to acquire?

After Poland and Russia, everything in New York amounted to a revelation: from the medical school labs to the architecture and highways (the multileveled, as if touching the sky junctions between the roads, left an enormous impression on me!), and the unending row of skyscrapers on Park Avenue, to two daily newspapers: the *Times* and, more to the right, the *Herald Tribune*. At first almost everything looked positive; it took a while before my sight sharpened and I lost my naiveté.

Severo Ochoa's department was a true Tower of Babel: one from Japan, another from China, a Dutchman, two Swiss, a German, an Indian, a Hungarian (a refugee from the 1956 revolution), a Chilean, several Spaniards (Dr. Ochoa was born in Asturias), and me. A decidedly smaller fraction of Americans: just a couple faculty members. The entire fraternity hung onto his every word, and Ochoa, then three years following his Nobel Prize and a member of many science academies, among them the American, Soviet, and Polish, as well as president of the International Biochemistry Society, reined over this tribe. He deserved to be king; his head was filled with pure diamonds. A talented experimenter, whatever he touched produced important results; he knew what to do and how to do it. He had been publishing since he was in his twenties and kept working until his late eighties, remaining for over sixty years at the center of attention; an uncommon phenomenon. He was a member of a small group of eminent scientists

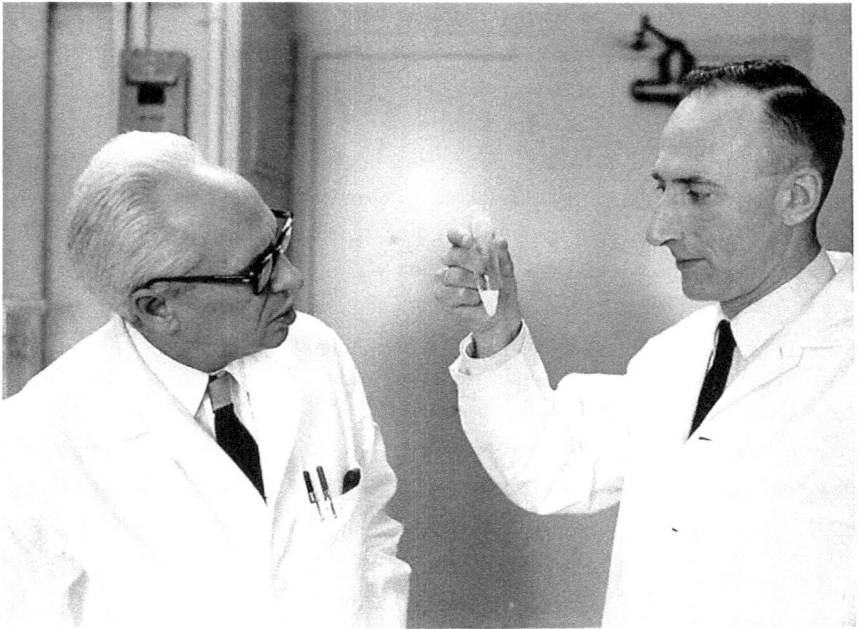

Figure 18 With Dr. Severo Ochoa, New York, 1969.

who built a bridge between the classic metabolic biochemistry of the first half of the twentieth century, and the contemporary molecular biology of today.

No longer young, he worked six and a half days a week: Saturday was a regular workday, Sunday mornings were dedicated to administrative duties and letter writing (afternoons were most often devoted to the opera). He liked to paraphrase the well known Pasteur's saying: "Good luck accompanies the well prepared mind," with an additional part: ". . . and the hard working fellow." His enthusiasm and passion were contagious because they were totally sincere. In addition, God gave him an endearing appearance. Tall, slim, with a mane of white hair on a head resting on a long neck, he looked like a cardinal from an El Greco painting, only dressed in a jacket and a shirt with a tie. Easily approachable, smiling, he was the opposite of the crazy, absentminded genius' stereotype. Age-wise, he was of my parents' generation. His marriage yielded no children. Although informal, friendly, and accessible, not one of us found the courage to address him by his first name, as was customary in America. The exception was a trusted technician, Morton S., who had been working with him for a very long time, even before, as it was said, Ochoa became "Ochoa." And he became

"Ochoa" not, as it often happens, as a result of one great discovery, but rather because of his enormous contribution to metabolism and molecular biology research.

I arrived in New York with a particular hypothesis and, after a rather general conversation, I received approval for everything. A separate space, a small laboratory, and a technician were assigned to me. The department's administrator was told to provide all the supplies I needed, without the necessity of asking each time for the boss's consent. My coworkers enlightened me that the latter was a gesture of trust; no doubt I owed it to what I had published in Warsaw with Shugar.

For the first few months I lived on campus, on the top floor of the dormitory where guest rooms were located. I worked 24/7, almost without leaving the building. There was no need for it thanks to a cafeteria on the ground floor: a better version of a canteen, nothing spectacular but still far from that at the Hygiene Institute. There was even a men's hair salon (but not women's).

The beginning was hard. Ochoa left for Europe for a period of time, and I was struggling with my experiments, which were progressing extremely slowly, like molasses or worse. After his return, during one of his regular "rounds," which he did around six or seven in the afternoon, Ochoa sat on a stool next to me and began with his usual question: how is it going? And I had to fess up. As soon as I finished, he began thinking aloud and in just a few sentences showed me where and what kind of an error I had made. I had gone up a blind alley without realizing it; that's the worst thing. Without his analysis I would have lost precious time. I realized then how little I knew or understood. That was depressing and painful, although I didn't hear a single harsh word.

In principle, my work with Shugar had prepared me quite well for the research in the mechanics of protein biosynthesis *in vitro,* which I began in New York. The problem was that I came to molecular biology from organic chemistry, and my knowledge of bacteriology and virology, absolutely required in my new field, was simply miserable.

Ochoa's department was a very vibrant—and filled with great anticipation—intellectual center. Every day at about four thirty PM, we would go to the departmental library for coffee. In fact this "coffee break" was a pretext for a never-ending exchange of views about our team's results and plans, about other labs working on similar subjects (including the competition), or about minutia of the latest publications in our field. Basically, we were being continuously tested by Ochoa as well as by each other, since there were many know-it-alls among us. It took the assassination of the President of the US—I was in New York when John F. Kennedy was murdered—for the conversation in the biochemistry library to forsake the problems of DNA-RNA-protein.

Two kinds of weekly seminars took place here: on Saturday afternoons, the internal discussion, where one group after another presented its findings and received both advice and critique, and the external, Wednesday afternoon seminars, where invited guests from outside presented their work. The topics on Wednesday mostly concerned research outside of our field, because Ochoa believed that one shouldn't overdo "marinating in one's own sauce." The Wednesday seminars were well known in the city and the crème de la crème of New York biochemistry establishment attended them; an invitation to give a lecture there was considered an honor. After the talk and the discussion, we had a customary dinner at the Irish restaurant Limerick, just around the corner from the medical school. It wasn't very elegant, but it was comfortable, with big drinks, good food, and wonderful bread. It was only here and only after a few drinks that one could allow oneself to talk about something other than the "holy" topics. On very special occasions, we would go to the elegant French restaurant Mon Paris, also near the school. The owner, the cook, and the waiters, all French from the mainland, treated Ochoa with great respect not for who he was—I doubt they knew it—but because he addressed them with impeccable French, that is, he was a civilized human being. He spoke German perfectly as well, because as a young man he had spent several years in Berlin at the then excellent biochemistry institute with the two of that era's giants: Otto Warburg (Nobel Prize in 1931) and Otto Meyerhof (Nobel Prize in 1922). He considered Meyerhof his mentor. The Nazis completely decimated that institute (and many others). In my opinion, the Germans have not yet succeeded in making up for the devastation perpetrated by Hitlerism in the sciences; the center of scientific gravity left Germany for good. Clearly, it's easier to rebuild cities and industry, even literature, than science; it is a delicate flower.

It's noteworthy that Ochoa left a specific mark even on the lectures given to first year medical students (120–150 people). And it was our, as we used to say, "daily bread." During the first semester, these took place every day, and year after year, Ochoa appeared at nine AM in the auditorium to hear the lecture! This was unique, but since he was doing it we had no choice but to attend them as well. As a result, every lecture was flawless and perfectly prepared and not a routine, humdrum class. Mostly, we sat in the back row of the lecture hall and exited en masse together. On our way back to the department, Ochoa would make pithy

Figure 19 The famous coffee break in the library of the Department of Biochemistry, NYU Medical School in the 1980s. Author, philosophizing, while colleague Dr. Bill Robinson does not look convinced.

comments, but only if no one else was listening. Typically, they were positive, sometimes—sharp, some became the departmental folklore, for example "Joe, talk to the students, not to me" or "Bob, appeal to your listeners' innate intellectual curiosity rather than to their patience." He lectured a lot himself and never hesitated to inform the first year students of the latest published research if he considered it important enough. To entrust one of us with a series of lectures that were part of the course (usually five, six, or more out of over sixty) was a significant event that could lead to a permanent position. Every Wednesday morning, instead of an hour-long lecture, we conducted two hour seminars with groups of 20–25 students. It was mainly a review and a reinforcement of the knowledge of the material covered in lectures and was conducted in the form of questions, answers, and discussions. This was his idea, but we were executing it; these conferences were liked by the students. We taught well, I believe, and had a lot of satisfaction. It wasn't easy, this earning of our daily bread. In the spring semester there were no longer medical students taking biochemistry; we conducted only specialized seminars and classes for PhD candidates. This was less burdensome.

In early spring, after about half a year, it turned out that my efforts in the lab hadn't been fruitless. There was still much to be done, but both Ochoa and my smart-alecky colleagues right away understood that it was an important contribution—nothing extraordinary or revolutionary, but a "contribution" nevertheless—to the problem of protein biosynthesis that was the passion of our group. Our department was at the forefront of this research and my findings came about at the right moment; so, as it happens in America, the news spread fast among friends and competitors. From the fall of 1963 until the end of my stay in the US, I was often invited to participate in seminars and conferences. This gave me much satisfaction, allowed me to visit the country a bit, and—not unimportant—the honoraria paid for at least half of the Peugeot! Several times

Figure 20 In my office at NYU next to my laboratory. Experiments, publications, grants, lectures, seminars, deadlines, etc.—not an easy life, but I wouldn't exchange it for any other.

in my life I accomplished fine work and climbed—but for a short time only—to the peak, but not once did I manage to stay there. Before my departure in January 1964, Ochoa assured me that I could count on a permanent job (tenured position) in his department at NYU, if I was ever allowed to return. This was the greatest achievement of my year-long trip to the US.

Shortly after my arrival in America, I contacted our friends from the post-war Lodz community who immigrated in 1946–48. Many ended up in the States and settled in New York. These were particularly moving and emotional reunions: we found each other again and felt as if our long separation had never happened. I also met some of my parents' friends from the Bund, whom I knew as a child before the war. They escaped to the US at the beginning of the war, in 1939–40, via Vilnius, then the capital of the puppet Lithuanian Republic, and not yet formally part of Russia. In New York they published *Unzer tsayt*, a monthly periodical in Yiddish, published until 2006, and printed some important works, among them the Bund's history. They also tried to restart the Bund, but that was doomed to fail from the very start. Intelligent, super honest people, they couldn't achieve it, since post-war America wasn't pre-war Poland. A Jewish working class didn't exist in the US anymore, the possibilities of social progress were huge, and Yiddish had been completely eliminated due to advancing cultural integration. The creation of Israel took over the imagination of world's Jewry to such an extent that no place was left for non-Zionist social movements; this is understandable. Marxism, even in its most decent version, fits America like the proverbial square peg fits a round hole. In any case, American Jews' (today 5.2 million, under 2 percent of the total population; 5.8 million forty years ago) aspirations went in a different direction. Education, from time immemorial a typical Jewish objective, became easily accessible after the war and led to social integration and to success, in the areas of both social position and wealth. In a country known for its—often unhealthy—fascination with money, the latter was exceptionally important. What is the difference between the ILGWU[36] (no longer existing, in its time a powerful New York trade union of Jewish tailors) and the AMA (American Medical Association)? One generation. This is the heart of the matter. Integration led to a situation which Jews in the Weimar Republic (600 thousand, one percent of Germany's population) defined as a reversed social pyramid: in a natural diagram, established for centuries, the pyramid's base consisted of laborers and peasants (farmers); artisans and small traders occupied the higher level; above them were free professions, journalists; and on

---

[36] Tr: International Ladies' Garment Workers' Union.

the top: financiers and scholars. Unfortunately, it was so in the past and after "seven fat years" it never ended well for us, neither in fifteenth-century Spain nor in twentieth-century Germany. Where and when will the next tragedy happen? The answer is not simple. In any case, predicting the future isn't a wise pursuit, and is best left to fortune tellers. But one theme keeps coming back, as if inevitable: the collective Jewish responsibility.[37] It's like a never-interrupted chain of all kinds of persecutions, harassments, exiles, deprivation of rights, crimes sanctioned by law, pogroms, and, from time to time, murders on gigantic scale, that is, genocides. It's odd, but the phrase "from time to time" could be more or less determined as occurring every 250–300 years. The Holocaust of 1939–45 was unique and cannot be compared to any past events. However, Bohdan Khmelnytsky[38] and his Cossacks, who in the years 1648–54 killed all the Jews in the major part of southeastern Europe, didn't have such technical and organizational means as Hitler's Germany. Neither did the Western Europeans, who, from 1348 to 1352 during the "Black Death," murdered their Jewish neighbors for allegedly poisoning wells, nor the Teutonic Knights, who during the first and the second crusades (1095–1148) destroyed the flourishing Jewish communities in the Rhine Valley and murdered its inhabitants. Well, if we are undertaking a long and dangerous journey to the Holy Land to kill the infidel Muslims there and have papal dispensation for that purpose, wouldn't it be right to first kill other infidels who are nearby, close at hand? It's rational. And after conquering Palestine, they obliterated the remaining Jewish villages, which had existed there for centuries. Mass Jewish exiles in the Middle Ages took place every hundred years as well: England in 1290, France at the end of the fourteenth century, and the most famous: Spain, 1492. I will not argue that such a cyclical "pattern" has a deeper meaning.[39] Most probably it's a random oddity. Or perhaps our mind is inclined to look for (alleged?) systems and superimpose them on true events. However, our Latin teacher at the Limanowski school taught us: *Historia magistra vitae*,[40] and our school was an excellent one.

---

[37] Au: Heinrich Graetz, *Historia Żydow*, trans. Stanisław Shenhak (Warsaw: Judaica, 929), t.1–9 (of course Graetz is old-fashioned and antiquated, but I like him).

[38] Tr: Bohdan Khmelnytsky (1595–1657): leader of the Zaphorozhian Cossaks, organizer of a rebellion against Polish rule in Ukraine that led to the transfer of Eastern Ukrainian territories from Polish to Russian control.

[39] Au: See N. Paumgarten, "The Secret Cycle, *The New Yorker*, 10.12.2009.

[40] Tr: Historia est magistra vitae (Latin): an expression from Cicero's *De Oratore*: "History is life's teacher." It conveys the idea that the study of past should serve as a lesson for the future. The author omitted "est" in the text.

When in the summer of 1963 I knew that my year in New York would be fruitful, since I had obtained good research results, I took a vacation and went to Florida with a few friends from the department, although there was still a lot of work to do before publication. I didn't feel at ease in Miami Beach: it was too hot and, for me, the place was vulgar, starting with its architecture and ending with the "entertainment." After two or three days I decided to go back to New York by bus, on the way stopping in several cities. I wanted to see for myself how the black population was faring in the South. I first visited Savannah, Georgia, then Charleston, South Carolina, and Richmond, capital of Virginia and, during the Civil War, capital of the South. In each of these cities I would board a bus headed downtown and ride until the last stop. All the black people who entered the bus immediately moved to the back: the front of the bus was for whites only. It seemed so everyday that this didn't cause the slightest protest or even distaste in either of these groups. It had been like this for a long time, everybody was used to it, that's all. I felt ashamed, worse than in Miami Beach. And this was the year of mass protests, the year of Martin Luther King, Jr. and his famous "March on Washington." Looking thorough the bus window in all three cities, one had the impression that each had been built according to a plan, although it hadn't been so: downtown there were skyscrapers, mostly office buildings, parking lots, garages, and gas stations everywhere, malls and couple of movie theaters (there are only a few cities in the US where people live "in the city," like in Europe, rather than in the suburbs), a bit farther, poor black ghetto districts and, at the end of the bus route the white suburbs, mainly for the middle class: beautiful, well cared-for houses, spectacular, colorful plants, flowers, well cut grass, all picture perfect. Lawns, flowers, nicely kept houses: all that thanks to the blacks' and Latinos' cheap labor, thanks to illegal immigrants, paid the lowest wages possible.

On the main square of the town: a monument of a Confederate soldier with a bouquet of fresh flowers underneath. I had the impression that the war had not yet became history here, that it happened yesterday and not a hundred years ago at the time of our January Uprising or when the serfs gained freedom in Russia and that it was not won by the North. Had much changed since 1963? Without any doubt. Has much remained the same? Yes. And one more thing: at that time I wasn't aware that the problem of black emancipation was extremely complicated and that, with the exception of some of its aspects, many of them of legal nature, did not depend solely on whites. But it depends on a complete eradication of racism among whites, which is not simple. It's not without cause that the great American writer Toni Morrison, a Nobel Prize winner, wrote that, in the United States, the indigenous anti-Negro racism in some incomprehensible way replaces the European anti-Semitism (up to some point?). One needs Freud to explain this.

Finally the time to go back was coming closer. I longed for home, for Felusia and the children, I had enough of loneliness in New York. What kept me going was the great amount of work and the feverish pace before my departure. I was writing articles, applying for grants to buy equipment, which later on allowed me to continue my research in Warsaw, and preparing a paper for a conference in Denver, which was going to take place in January 1964, literally a day before my departure. Of course, I was also busy shopping for my three ladies and our home. Compared to New York, "socialist" Poland was a sea of hopeless drabness: for example a stereo radio with separate speakers, record player, and tape recorder, as well as the albums I brought, became a sensation in Warsaw. I was no longer living then in university housing but renting a room in someone's apartment in Gramercy Park, within ten minutes' walking distance from work. The area was great, the apartment—so-so. I was able to afford a better, private place, but I preferred to save money. I had no idea whether or when an opportunity of earning more in one year than in many, or perhaps during an entire lifetime, in "socialism" would happen again. My landlord was a young painter, practicing solely geometric abstraction, different from Mark Rothko's. I met him by chance through mutual friends. He was unable to pay rent for the entire apartment which included his studio, and that's how I ended up there. My room was nice, rather big because the building was old; my window looked out on a small park. Coming back from work, even late at night, to this empty room was the worst. Solitude was unbearable after all the years with Felusia and the girls. The entire apartment, including the hallway by the front door was filled with my landlord's paintings. One had to squeeze between them and the wall to get to the rooms or to the kitchen. He wasn't well known then. But in the 1970s he became an acknowledged painter and had an individual exhibit in one of the better known—and most exclusive—New York galleries on Madison Avenue. Strange, because all his paintings were done in a similar manner: concentric, multicolored circles on a light or brown background. I'm not sure whether the proverbial *ars longa* (as in, *vita brevis*)[41] was supposed to look like that, or whether this was a passing fad and snobbery. I asked him once why the circles were so colorful and in various shades so that some paintings seemed to have a joyful color scheme and others a sad one, but all had monotonous backgrounds.

---

[41] Tr: Ars longa vita brevis (Latin): Art is long, life is short, or: Art survives the artist.

He answered that he had two girlfriends, one white and one black, and the background was the skin color of either one or the other. Well, he was an artist, God bless him. He was nice. It was good to drink vodka together.

What was left now were only few receptions, saying goodbye to friends and colleagues, a conversation with Ochoa, and finally—I was going home. I spent a few days in Paris and in Holland, where I gave several lectures, picked up the Peugeot in Amsterdam, and continued by car. I had a clever idea to spend the night in a small Dutch town near the German border, leave early in the morning and cross the whole of Germany—the "bad" West and the "good" East—in one go and spend the next night in Poland. Disturbing, this, but I couldn't stand the sound of their language. Was it collective responsibility? I think so, but this was an exception, reasonable I believe. We didn't pass this on to our children. Later, after immigrating to the States, Felusia and I, we travelled through Europe in every direction, but never through Germany. Taboo? No, we just didn't feel like it. We have never bought anything made in Germany either (except for some albums for my classical music collection). I did get, from time to time, invitations to conferences and meetings in Germany, but I would always send my coworkers. Perhaps this was not right; too bad, that is how it was.

And finally a great delight, "home sweet home"; I don't know a better saying. I was happy. It was January 1964. For the first and last time I had left my family for an entire year, but there was no other way. Brave Felusia, she worked and took care of the children, and the girls grew up. Both of them went to a Żoliborz school, which in a sense had been continuing the traditions of my own school from before the war, minus Bolesław Limanowski as its patron; clearly one of the creators of the Polish Socialist Party was not considered "socialist" enough. During meetings with teachers, which we attended diligently, I understood that the school had many, but not all, truly good educators. The girls were getting good grades. In my absence they lived through another international crisis that happened in Berlin or somewhere else, between two camps, one marching toward the "glorious future," the other—the imperialist one. The first reaction in Poland, so well taught by its war experiences, was to buy, in grocery stores, everything one could keep for a longer time; total panic. Since Mom was at work, the girls called her, were told where to find the money (it was stashed on a closet shelf under the underwear, of course), and ran to join the long queue in front of a store to buy flour, pasta, sugar. In normal, non-critical times they both liked to buy bread or a long baguette and eat the ends on their way home. They still like those ends even now, and so do I. Because we were both working, meals were not always prepared, so they would be given money to eat in the school cafeteria. The cafeteria lunches were disgusting, just like mine at work, so both would buy pastries for two zloty in a private store. Those pastries were pretty tasty and a good metsiye[42] in Poland. But what was it, eating pastries instead of lunch? Lunch should be hot and nutritious, so mother was not happy when the truth came out and the daughters were punished, but not too severely. Since the mid-1950s, we had at home a small, black and white TV: tiny screen, with the back sticking out, heavy, but we owned one! There was only one channel, stupid of course, but sometimes showing good movies like those directed by Vittorio de Sica (in my opinion, *The Bicycle Thief* is one of best films ever), and I even remember the sex symbol Brigitte Bardot. This "movie theater" was placed in the living room and in the evening its reflection was visible in the window. Coming back late from the theater or from visiting friends, we would know that our dear daughters were watching TV instead of sleeping soundly. They would jump into their beds and pretend to be asleep the moment we entered the apartment. We would kiss them, pretending not to realize that they were awake. Sometimes, however, they would smile while "asleep." Dzidzia had an odd habit: when leaving for summer camp she wanted to get news from home as soon as possible. She would make sure to witness me posting a card addressed to her! "These were the fun and games of those times."

We didn't have too many friends in Poland then, but they were all close and dear. These were the good years. We met often, went to the theatre and to the movies, and sometimes spent summer vacations together. During many decades as immigrants, we have never recreated such a group nor had such friends. Evidently one has to build long lasting, deep friendships in one's youth. These were our children's "aunts" and "uncles." You didn't have real ones. I am so moved when today their children, some of them already grandparents, address us as Auntie and Uncle. We were scattered around the world after 1968: Israel, the US, Canada, Sweden, Denmark, and some stayed in Poland. . . . Sure, we all did well, were able to adapt to new circumstances, to settle down, to learn new languages, to take care of our children, and it appears that our grandchildren will not do poorly either. But is it right, to reach middle age and to have to leave behind everything one has built and start anew? Such is Jewish fate. On the other hand (again that other hand, one can never avoid it) there are always those who would love to immigrate to the west, Jews and non-Jews.

The Peugeot proved very useful. We saw half of Poland, took a long trip to Yugoslavia, and visited Czechoslovakia and Hungary on the way. It was very

---

[42] Tr: Metsiye (Yiddish): a find, a bargain, a really good buy.

beautiful and interesting for the two of us, but auto trips with parents ceased to be a great attraction for our teenagers.

Sightseeing was not the only aim of our trips. We wanted you to see all the places where your mother had endured great ordeals. We went to Auschwitz, where in July 1944 the entire family had been sent from the Lodz ghetto. After leaving the cattle cars, the men and the women were immediately separated on the railway platform. When the next day Felusia asked a man in a striped camp uniform where her father and younger brother Lolek had been taken, he silently pointed at a chimney and the black smoke visible at a distance. Soon the same happened to her mother and her little sister Gutka. There had been yet another "selection" where young women your mother's age were chosen for inhumanly grueling work and a life of slavery and starvation in death camps. Mom didn't want to leave her mother and sister, she was holding tight to them. She was beaten and pushed to the right, to live; these were the Germans, *Ordnung muss sein*.[43] This is how she ended up in a camp/factory in Chemnitz in Saxony. For many decades she didn't want to (or couldn't?) talk about that camp. Only recently she recounted one event. One day, her period came back suddenly. She was standing by her machine in the factory hall and there was blood on the floor. The young women were dressed in rags; they had no underwear, not to mention sanitary napkins. The SS women guarding the prisoners saw the blood. First they burst into laughter and started pointing at Mom in such a way that everybody looked at her. And then one of them beat her up. Women? Animals. One of the prisoners, an Italian, helped her. He brought her some clothes, a bit of cotton wool. Italians lived in slightly better conditions in camps and were treated better than Jews. Pepi took a liking to your mom and helped her as much as he could.

In Czechoslovakia we visited Theresienstadt, another camp where Mom had been taken at the end of the war, literally at the last moment. She and the remainder of the surviving Jews there were saved from an inevitable death by the Russian army.

All was going well at work after my return from the States. One of the publications from that period—not too bad, but, when I think of it now, not remarkable—was discussed and commented on in one of the most respected magazines in my field, the British *Nature*. People from my profession read attentively and greatly valued these anonymous assessments (nowadays such remarks are usually signed). This comment proved very beneficial later, allowing me to

---

[43] Tr: Ordnung muss sein (German): there must be order.

"skip" one rung on the tenured professor ladder at NYU medical school; not too bad. Soon after my return to Warsaw, I received news from the US that I had been given a grant for which I had applied before the trip. A foundation, one of many supporting scientific research, was asking which bank they should use to deposit the money. And so it started, a hassle that lasted almost a year, since who ever heard of such a thing, and where does it say that a private person, not even a professor but some modest docent,[44] would have dollars in his account and would be getting money from America? I was asked to prove that the foundation was not a CIA (spy) cover. All the correspondence was done by the president of the institute, Professor Józef Heller, one of IBB's[45] founders, a biochemist known already before the war, a man of great integrity, by now rather elderly. As a young man he had served in Piłsudski's Legions and I saw the Marshal's photo on his desk; this was unusual in Warsaw in 1964. After several exchanges of letters, it became clear that the whole thing was hopeless and that I would not be allowed to get the money. Heller told me then very sensibly: "Mr. Włodzimierz, it's really too bad, but our heads are not for knocking against a brick wall." And that would have been the end, except that Poland was (and still is?) a country of buddy systems (and thank God for that). It so happened that a friend's wife knew someone who had a relative or a friend who was highly placed in the communist party, and that luminary kindly agreed to see me. I convinced him and he sent me to some state department, finance, I think. The department's deputy secretary talked with me (this is not a mistake, I needed a bigwig to open a foreign currency account!) and again I had to explain, to coax, and to thank. It all ended well, but I was furious because I had received that grant thanks to my hard work (the amount was several times higher than the entire Institute's yearly allowance) but my reward was to grovel before these dimwits. What to do, that was Poland, there was no other. I brought some equipment from Western Europe, including an ultracentrifuge, then widely used and very expensive (today a tool no longer as important as it used to be). The final chapter happened much later. In 1977, I finally was granted a much-coveted Polish visa to attend a conference. I found myself in Warsaw for the first time in ten years, and a friend showed me around the Institute. We entered the equipment room, where two young women who didn't know me where arguing loudly who

---

[44] Tr: Docent: an academic who possesses the habilitation degree, similar to the rank of an associate professor on the tenure track in the US.
[45] Tr: IBB: Instytut Biochemii i Biofizyki (Institute of Biochemistry and Biophysics).

booked "Szer's centrifuge" first. Another time I was refused a visa to attend a conference for the twenty-fifth anniversary of the Institute; the mighty are finicky. In the consulate, a jackass carefully examined our passports and declared that "People's Republic of Poland doesn't desire" our visit; he knew it. Our passport numbers most probably indicated that we were "unwanted elements."

There was no indication that the coming year, 1967, would prove to be so full of events for us, that it would be the year of immigration. A new war broke out in Israel in April, the Six-Day War. Contrary to the predictions of Arab countries' leaders, the Jews were not slaughtered and "thrown into the sea," with their throats slit. They had superior leaders, better equipment, their soldiers had better training and motivation, and, what's most important, they had to win, since a defeat would signify the end of their existence. The Arabs could afford to lose; this was not a threat to their survival. It's horrible but true. Our Polish "leader" Gomułka gave a great, that is, extremely long speech on that subject (that man was not able to speak proper Polish). It so happened that I had been suffering from a headache that day. I came home from the lab early, laid down on the sofa and . . . I turned the TV on. Leaving work so early, watching television—that's not my style, so was it fate? No, just a coincidence. Gomułka was giving a speech at some meeting of "their" fake unions. Normally I wouldn't dream of either listening to it or to reading about it in a newspaper. The camera was filming the audience and I could see sleepy eyes. Suddenly the image changed, the listeners woke up at the very moment when Gomułka began to talk about the "Zionists," that is, about Jews. Lying on the couch I learned that we should not rejoice in Israel's victory because we, Polish Jews, should have only one motherland, and that we were the "Fifth Column" (which was, before World War II, the definition of the German minority living in neighboring countries and acting as spies and a sort of outpost for German troops entering Czechoslovakia, Poland, and other countries.) All this, with the exception of the Fifth Column, got published in the press the next day. With this speech Gomułka achieved two goals. As long as he was maligning Israel, he was keeping up with the official Soviet line. Zionists, that is, Israelis, were disgusting imperialists in the service of the Americans. Arabs were, of course, the embodiment of progress: after a short wait they would begin to build "socialism." The Russians were well aware of what they were doing. To reach the Mediterranean through the narrow straights, to take over Arab harbors—this has been, for centuries, the dream of the tsars, for this they fought the Crimean War of 1855. But where did the true interest of Poland lie? On the opposite side of Israel, since Poland had no use for an even stronger Soviet Union. Also, by slandering us, Gomułka started, on his own initiative, a "creative development of Marxism-Leninism": he used Jewish party members for the communist party infighting and was counting on awakening widespread anti-Semitic feelings. This was exceptionally mean and significant: Jews as scapegoats—a tactic known to us for centuries. But the popular tendency in Warsaw was to support little David rather than the enormous Goliath. Sometimes one phobia (hatred for the USSR) would obliterate the other (anti-Semitism): "Our kikes are clobbering Russian Arabs," or "this Moshe, this one-eyed Dayan won because he had graduated, before the war, from the Polish military school in Modlin." General Dayan, born in Palestine, had never been to Poland. And one more joke from this period: "Together with Soviet weapons, Egypt had accepted the Soviet military doctrine: retreat far into the country and wait for cold weather." The poet Antoni Słonimski,[46] known for his sharp tongue, was credited for having said what became a popular joke in Warsaw: "I am not opposed to having just one motherland, but why does it have to be Egypt or Syria?"

Now things were happening fast. In August we received the permit to immigrate, followed by a nomination from Ochoa to join his department at NYU medical school. We left Warsaw for Gdynia on October 2, 1967, and continued through the Atlantic on the ship *Batory*. This entire period was very difficult for all four of us. Karusia was against leaving because she had a boyfriend. We convinced her by promising that, if she didn't like the States, she could go back a year later. She did not. Among my three women, Dzidzia objected the least; at almost sixteen, she was still very young. Felusia was worried, afraid to go to an unknown place. Here—she argued—we have our rhythm, our friends, an apartment, a car, perhaps in couple of years you will go again to the US and replenish our assets, we have signed Karusia up for an apartment co-op and have been paying the dues (getting an apartment, if at all possible, was to happen, in the best case scenario, in many years), we are not young—she had many arguments and all of them were, frankly, sensible. Finally I persuaded her; she was an accommodating person. At that point, excited by the upcoming departure, she decided to make preparations similar to those undertaken years ago for a young bride: bed linens, sheets, etc. It wasn't easy to convince her otherwise.

Saying goodbye to friends and co-workers was touching and, frankly, emotionally draining. My doctoral students gave me Krzysztof Penderecki's *Threnody for the Victims of Hiroshima* and I have learned that, because I had

---

[46] Tr: Antoni Słonimski (1895–1976): Polish poet, playwright, and prose writer of Jewish origin, known for his devotion to social justice.

to leave, they were ashamed of being Poles. I heard similar statements at the going-away party after a session of my Institute's Scientific Council (of which I was a member). Back at home I got literally ill: for the first and only time in my life, I suffered from an acute migraine attack. My friends from the Institute presented me with a beautifully done album of our photos—a very precious gift indeed.

This was "my" Poland: beautiful and noble. But there was another one. Customs officials recognized us at once: Zionists, that is, kikes, looked down at by the authorities, what an opportunity to have fun! Getting through customs turned into a nightmare. First we had to make a detailed list of everything we were taking with us, and then all was checked and rechecked in our presence and yet again without us. They were looking for Jewish treasures and destroyed whatever was possible. This was particularly nasty. At one point I got angry and started to shout at them. Dzidzia, aged fifteen, was standing near me and calmed me down. While unpacking in the States, we realized that some things had been stolen. Sad, but they didn't take much. In Gdynia, where the customs officers checked our hand luggage, all went well, without any unpleasant incidents; clearly, there were no rules.

And then: America, with a normal, ordinary life of an ordinary professor, and you were big girls, and if you wish you may continue, in the future, perhaps when you retire, this Szer family saga.

I often wondered why there is so much hatred directed against us and why we, Jews, from time immemorial have been and still are today burdened with collective responsibility. Volumes have been written on this subject. Pogroms date back to ancient eras, like the one in the Jewish part of Alexandria in the times of Ptolemy. Riffraff, the ordinary populace, believed that too many Jews were holding important government positions, that too many were wealthy. Jealousy? Certainly. Otherness? No doubt. The reason, or perhaps pretext, for pogroms in ancient Egypt (and later the reason for the Jewish War of 66–72 AD), was the refusal to worship emperor Augustus as a god (the title Augustus means divine, equal to gods), since this was contrary to the basic tenets of monotheism. A pretext is easy to find. To deal with this, Jews sent to Rome a delegation headed by Philo of Alexandria (20 BC–50 AD), the greatest Jewish thinker of the Hellenic era. He did not accomplish much. Philo's family was one of the most influential in Alexandria. Among its members were important government officials and notable diplomats, and his nephew Tiberius Julius Alexander abandoned Judaism for paganism and became Egypt's governor. Holding this post, Alexander was able to control the export of Egyptian wheat to Rome, essential to the empire's economy, and his endorsement greatly helped Vespasian (70 AD), the founder of the Flavian dynasty, to gain the throne. Alexander participated actively on the Roman side in the Jewish War. He acted as the deputy of the Roman army's main commander, Titus (Vespasian's son and future emperor), during the siege of Jerusalem and the destruction of the Temple. His uncle wouldn't have been very proud. The uncle had been somewhat lucky: he was no longer alive to be able to observe his nephew's stunning rise. Our history is full of such careers. Some, so familiar to us, don't bring us much glory. Since our arrival in the US over forty years ago, we have witnessed numerous Wall Street scandals in which Jews played the main parts (and Jews are very good at this). There is a chronicle that tells how the Amsterdam stock exchange was controlled, at the end of the seventeenth century, by several Jews: Isaac Pinto, Tereira, and baron Jouasso. By receiving information inaccessible to others, they were able to amass a great deal of money; a primitive and to this day common fraud. Greed has no moderation or limits, it conquers honesty and *noblesse oblige.*[47] The Amsterdam stock exchange was less crowded on Saturdays than on weekdays, because Jews were not doing business. And here's what the *New York Times* (10.2. 2006) says about the New York stock exchange: "Volume was light as some market players were out for Yom Kippur holiday." I see the same thing every year on Yom Kippur; *nihil novi sub sole.*[48] Now, the other side of the problem demands not to be forgotten. For years I have been observing a paradox: there are many Jews among the most astute and effective federal prosecutors and investigating judges who fight against Wall Street's financial crooks. And what about the eminent Jews: scientists (about 30 percent of Nobel Prize winners in physics, as well as in chemistry, medicine, yet we constitute less than 0.3 percent of world population), writers, musicians, artists? Well, these are known facts, but our entire history shows that the latter ones do not counterbalance the former, that they don't eliminate them from people's consciousness. (Too bad that a coin doesn't have three sides: in the course of my long life I have met so many dense and stupid Jews.) But what do I, an ordinary Polish Jew, have in common with all this? There are so many such as me. I neither want any part of these great ones' fame and glory nor do I wish to carry the responsibility for the deeds of crooks, scoundrels, and criminals, only because, as the poetess says: "unexplained quirk of fate, Phenomenon for the depth of cosmos"[49] caused

---

[47] Tr: Noblesse oblige (French): here: good, proper conduct.
[48] Tr: Nihil novi sub sole (Latin): There is nothing new under the sun.
[49] Au: S. Kurylo, Wyspa Wspomnień, Format-AB (Warszawa, 1997), 100.

me to be born and walk through life as a Jew. All I want is to be responsible for myself. Clear? Crystal clear. Possible? Not in our times, perhaps in the future. I would like to believe that. It has been two centuries since this greatest of the great made an old Jew the hero of a Polish national poem and sent Zosia, the embodiment of female charm, to stroke his beard; it didn't take long to persuade Jankel to start his concert.[50] Let's be hopeful that his books finally will be widely read and will solve our problem.

And one more thing. Since my early childhood, at home and as a member of children and youth organizations, I was brought up in the Bund tradition, that is, in the spirit of humanism, and, without any doubt, of Marxism mixed with social-democratic ideals. Marx enjoyed a special adoration and all kinds of Bolsheviks and communists were considered bad. Since I was little I had been given, at home, various bio(hagio)graphies of Marx.[51] It's impossible to remove it, to wipe this away, but the experience of a long life has changed "my" Marx greatly. That man, who sat for years on end at the British Museum's library (while neglecting his family living in poverty), had invented, described, and wanted to make real a system which would render all humanity happy. Perhaps it's utopia, but it makes no sense for us, sinners, expelled from paradise. There has been no theory of changing society "from above" on such a scale. Socioeconomic mechanisms emerged, developed spontaneously, and little by little have been changing for generations and centuries. And Leszek Kołakowski[52] argues—and he was an expert—that "every attempt to introduce basic ideas of Marxist socialism would most probably result in creating a political organization closely resembling the Stalinist system."[53]

---

[50] This is a reference to the epic poem "Pan Tadeusz" by Adam Mickiewicz, the great Polish romantic poet, published in 1834. Both Zosia, a young girl, and Jankiel, an old Jew, are characters in that poem. This is perhaps the first time in Polish literature that a Jew is portrayed as a great Polish patriot. Zosia treats him in a friendly manner and asks him to play his dulcimer. The author suggests here that, following Mickiewicz's (the "greatest of the great") example, Poles should accept that Jews are true Polish patriots and should be treated as friends and equals.

[51] Au: I especially liked a large book by Franz Mehring (1846–1919), a German Social democrat, *Karl Marx: The Story of His Life*. In a post-war edition that I lugged with me from Warsaw via New York to San Diego, the communist editor published a preface by a certain Roman Werfel, who "interprets" Mehring and corrects his "mistakes."

[52] Tr: Leszek Kołakowski (1927–2009): Polish philosopher and historian of ideas, known for his critical analyses of Marxist thought.

[53] Au: *Czy diabeł może być zbawiony i 27 innych kazań* (*Can the devil be saved and 27 other sermons*) (London: Aneks, 1982), 245 (all the "sermons" are very wise).

Figure 21 With Felusia, celebrating our fortieth wedding anniversary, 1986.

Felusia and I visited London again in the 1990s, where we spent an entire day at the British Museum. Felusia became very tired from running around the museum and sat down to rest, while I continued and suddenly had the idea to see the reading room where, according to Mehring, Marx used to sit and write. I didn't know that the library had been separated from the museum long ago and was now housed in a detached building. Several museum employees encountered on the way looked at me suspiciously when asked where Marx used to work, as if I were a bit crazy. They gave me unclear answers and disappeared as fast as they could. Suddenly a door opened. I would have never noticed it, because it was of the same color as the wall, which made it invisible, and a short, elderly, unremarkable man in a librarian's shirt came out, carrying a pile of books. I like librarians and thought that he may be my soul mate. I approached him and explained what I had been looking for. He looked at me in an incredulous but friendly manner from above his glasses and disappeared behind the door. He came back a minute later without the books and explained that he knew where the public reading room had been located in the nineteenth

Figure 22 Felusia's eighty-fifth birthday celebration, San Diego, 2008. Two daughters, two sons-in-law, five grandchildren, and one great-grandchild (there are six now).

century, and that most probably Marx had worked there. It was a big, round room, more like a hall, crowned with a beautiful, tall dome, and with many old, possibly mahogany desks fastened to the floor. I thanked my guide and looked around. There were old maps in glass cabinets on the desks. I liked that place. It was here that Marx sweated writing *The Capital*. Before the war, my dad told me that *The Capital* would be too difficult for me, but that I could read Kautsky. When I placed rather well—second or third—in a local chess tournament in Rembertów at the beginning of the 1950s, I received *The Capital* as the prize. I have it to this day.[54] I looked around one more time and went back to Felusia.

---

[54] Au: I have almost all the classics of Polish literature at home, books I kept buying in the early 1950s, and I have noticed a particular definition of value: mine and my Grandma Helenka's beloved Żeromski's volumes had been printed on paper of the worst, newspaper quality and have become completely yellow. The same has happened to Prus and Orzeszkowa. Sienkiewicz has fared better: his books got yellow but not as much. Marx has remained snow white, Mickiewicz as well. After October 1956, I noticed, at my friend's houses, those "worse" yellow authors on better paper. Each edition had an awful introduction which was supposed to teach the reader what and where was ideologically improper. Only Maria Dąbrowska's introduction to Prus' works did well, but even she had to compromise from time to time.

I have said goodbye to Marx. What's left? Perhaps a bit of altruism—and a dislike for all the "isms"—and a belief, but not a certainty, that history of the *Homo sapiens*—we are not called this for nothing!—is changing for the better, no matter how slowly, even if not in a straight line ("once to the left, once to the right, a bit forward, a bit back")[55] from barbarians through blue blood and privilege of wealth to equal opportunity and meritocracy. Amen.

---

[55] Tr: This is a reference to a Russian song. The correct lyrics are: "Two steps to the left, two steps to the right, one step forward and two steps back."

Afterword

We met Włodek Szer for the first time in 1959, when he began to come in to Prof. Shugar's laboratory in the afternoons in order to synthesize modified dinucleotides, which constituted substrates for enzymatic polymerization of model oligo- and polynucleotides. His abilities as a chemist combined with close conceptual collaboration with Prof. Shugar allowed for the synthesis of numerous model polyribonucleotides. Conformational studies on the latter, for example those containing methylated pyrimidine bases and their complementary polyribonucleotides, confirmed the Watson-Crick model of stabilization of double-stranded helical structure by hydrogen bonding and hydrophobic interaction between the methylated thymine and 5'-hydroxycytosine.

These and similar published findings on the complex properties of model polynucleotides constituted Włodek's doctoral thesis and brought him the postdoctoral fellowship with Nobel Prize winner Prof. Severo Ochoa at the biochemistry department of New York University medical school. There, he used the synthetic polynucleotides in studies of their properties as messenger RNAs in in-vitro protein synthesis. Upon returning to Poland in 1964, he earned the degree of doctor habilitatus and continued these studies with several graduate students.

Włodek's expertise in organic synthesis led other members of the laboratory to undertake synthesis of novel compounds applicable, for example, in histochemical localization of nucleolytic enzymes. Although these projects resulted in several publications, Włodek, who literally guided us in those initial studies, refused to co-author our publications because they were not conceptually his own. This is worth mentioning given the contemporary culture of collective publications, where every minute contribution is acknowledged by co-authorship, declining this right is a sign of high moral standards and altruistic camaraderie.

In 1967, Włodek immigrated with his family to the US, where he was offered a tenured position in the biochemistry department of New York University medical school, subsequently succeeding Prof. Ochoa as its acting chairman and then chair. He resigned from the chairmanship after one term, preferring to devote his full energy to research and teaching of medical students. He was repeatedly voted by students as the best lecturer within the department, until his voluntary retirement, when he, though no one else, decided that his performance might be declining.

At NYU he continued his previous studies on the binding of model and viral messenger RNAs to bacterial ribosomes and showed that their binding to the 30S subunit occurred only in a single-stranded form. He discovered in ribosomes the double-stranded mRNA unwinding protein S1 that initiates protein biosynthesis in E. coli and other organisms; this discovery he rightly considered to be his major achievement.

In the 1980s, Włodek became interested in eukaryotic heterogeneous nuclear proteins (hnRNPs), forming nucleosomes during transcription of pre-mRNA. He isolated and characterized several of these proteins, establishing their conserved structure in the course of evolution. By binding polyclonal antibodies to the hnRNP proteins in in-vitro maturation of b-globin pre-mRNA, he showed that hnRNPs are an essential component of the complex responsible for the maturation of mRNA. He characterized the domain structure of the major core hnRNPs in HeLa cells (A1, A2 and C3) and showed that proteins A1 and A2 preferentially bind to native mRNA via their N-terminal domains, resembling an analogous domain in single-stranded DNA-binding proteins. Protein C3, on the other hand, was found to destabilize residual secondary structures in native mRNA and in model double-stranded polynucleotides, preferentially recognizing G- and U-rich sequences, which was indicative of its binding to the 3'-end of introns in pre-mRNA splicing.

In 1991, he began his last collaboration, this time with his daughter Ilona Szer, now a pediatric rheumatologist, interested in finding a marker for uveitis, a devastating complication of juvenile rheumatoid arthritis. Nuclear proteins were known to constitute autoantigens, causing an autoimmune response in patients with rheumatic diseases. This collaboration, between a bench scientist and a clinician, led to isolation of the 45–DEK protein, which turned out to be the product of an oncogene occurring in a mutated form in leukemic cells. Further studies showed that autoantibodies to the DEK protein are most prevalent in sera of children with Oligoarthritis, strongly associated with uveitis in young girls. Six publications ensued with Ilona Szer, MD and Włodzimierz Szer, PhD as co-authors.

Dr. Szer authored 170 publications in leading international journals. He lectured extensively, happily reviewed grants and abstracts, chaired many scientific sessions, and educated several generations of physicians, including his daughter and son in law.

While in the US, Włodek maintained close contact with us at the Institute of Biochemistry and Biophysics PAN in Warsaw. He showed selfless devotion to friends and colleagues, opening his home in Manhattan (within walking distance to his laboratory on the second floor of NYU medical school) to us and offering help in finding useful collaborations, necessary reagents, know-how, and occasionally, even medical consultations from his previous medical students, who had become his devoted physicians. Among his American, Indian, Pakistani, Lithuanian, and other postdoctoral fellows and collaborators, there was almost always someone from Poland working in his laboratory. He visited us often and was one of the most conscientious members of the Institute's Advisory Committee. His wide knowledge and understanding of major trends in molecular biology helped in critical evaluation of our research presented at the biennial symposia. These visits allowed him to walk the streets of his beloved Warsaw, go to the theater, and spend time with old friends.

Włodek was a man of many interests, a lover and an ardent consumer of culture. He was deeply interested in history and profoundly knowledgeable in biographical details. He read much and widely. In his later years he limited himself to non-fiction, mainly science, history, and politics. He subscribed to the Parisian Polish language *Kultura*, Yiddish New York daily *Unsere Kayt'*, the *New York Times*, and anything he could find about Poland on the Internet. He loved classical music and art, the latter in a much wider range than the former.

Włodek and his beloved Felusia spent their vacations tirelessly trekking through museums and monuments of Europe, following itineraries he carefully planned many months in advance. He wrote detailed notes on the back of postcards. He saved them all, along with his childrens' and grandchildrens' letters and cards.

He was an excellent and a passionate chess player, whenever possible beginning every day with a game of chess from the *New York Times* chess column, and later the Internet. He liked good company and he was good company, enjoying all types of food and drink. Conversations with him were always interesting, full of colorful anecdotes and stories, while his analysis of current political and social state of affairs was keen and highly competent; in retrospect, of great prognostic value.

Włodzimierz Szer died in San Diego on August 31, 2013, surrounded by his family. Despite the many years of separation, we feel that he was one of us and we miss him dearly. His scientific achievements, however, survive as part of the history of molecular biology.

Kazimierz L. Wierzchowski, PhD
Institute of Biochemistry and Biophysics
Polish Academy of Sciences
Halina Sierakowska, PhD
Long time friend and collaborator in both Poland and the United States

Index

www.ingramcontent.com/pod-product-compliance
Lightning Source LLC
Chambersburg PA
CBHW070411100426
42812CB00005B/1708